BRINGING SCHOOL
REFORM TO SCALE

BRINGING SCHOOL REFORM TO SCALE

Five Award-Winning Urban Districts

Heather Zavadsky

HARVARD EDUCATION PRESS

CAMBRIDGE, MASSACHUSETTS

Library of Congress Control Number 2009931672

Paperback ISBN 978-1-934742-40-2
Library Edition ISBN 978-1-934742-41-9

Published by Harvard Education Press,
an imprint of the Harvard Education Publishing Group

Harvard Education Press
8 Story Street
Cambridge, MA 02138

Cover Design: Schwadesign, Inc.

The typefaces used in this book are Minion for text and Eurostile and ITC Stone Sans for display.

THE EDUCATIONAL INNOVATIONS SERIES

The *Educational Innovations* series explores a wide range of current school reform efforts. Individual volumes examine entrepreneurial efforts and unorthodox approaches, highlighting reforms that have met with success and strategies that have attracted widespread attention. The series aims to disrupt the status quo and inject new ideas into contemporary education debates.

Series edited by Frederick M. Hess

CONTENTS

ACKNOWLEDGMENTS

First and foremost, I would like to acknowledge the work of the teachers, principals, central office leaders, parents, and other internal and external supporters associated with these five exemplary districts. Behind their extraordinary accomplishments are dedicated, thoughtful, hard-working people that have united for the sake of providing a high quality education to every child in their system.

I have met many exceptional educators in other districts honored by The Broad Prize for their ability to move student achievement to higher levels. The work of leaders and teachers in Bridgeport Public Schools, Charlotte-Mecklenburg Schools, Jersey City Public Schools, Miami-Dade County Public Schools, Houston Independent School District, Jefferson County Public Schools, New York City Department of Education, and San Francisco Unified School District all provide examples of districts improving education to scale. If my selection of repeat finalists and winners had been after 2005, this book would have included the New York City Department of Education, the 2007 Prize winner, as an example of a very large system led by a steadfast visionary, Joel Klein, and team that made observable improvements at all levels from one year to the next.

This work was made possible by the commitment of Eli and Edythe Broad to support and shine a spotlight on successful urban systems that are making marked improvements in achievement for all students. The $2 million dollar Broad Prize for Urban Education, funded by The Eli and Edythe

Broad Foundation, is an annual award honoring urban school districts that demonstrate the greatest overall performance and improvement in student achievement while reducing achievement gaps among poor and minority students. Since its inception in 2002, the Prize has raised public awareness and faith in urban education, and provided valuable lessons from districts that have lead the way to taking reform to scale.

The National Center for Educational Achievement (NCEA), one of the first partners with The Broad Foundation on The Broad Prize, provided much of the structure still used today for the Prize process. The Best Practice Framework, used as an organizational guide for this book and for site visits prior to 2007, was developed by Dr. Jean Rutherford from NCEA, an experienced practitioner who well understands the importance of connecting the right practices and levels within a district to truly impact education systems. Dr. Chrys Dougherty and his programming team provided much of the preliminary work forming the Prize methodology used to represent student performance among the eligible districts. MPR Associates, one of the nation's leading education research firms, and SchoolWorks continued the Prize process after 2006. Their work on the Prize report cards and fact sheets on past winners also provided me invaluable information on the current performance of these five featured districts. Both organizations continue to add impressive value to the Prize process.

There are a number of people that provided expertise and guidance for this book. I want to specifically thank Dr. Fredrick Hess and Juliet Squire for encouraging me to put all of this research on paper, and for their ongoing assistance. Additionally, I would like to thank Marina Walne, Celeste Alexander, and Lee Holcombe for their willingness to critique and support this work. I also would be remiss for not acknowledging the hours of editing assistance provided by Amy Dolejs who is always there when I need her. Any mistakes made in this manuscript are completely my own. Finally, I want to specifically thank the district superintendents, Laura Schwalm, Chris Steinhauser, John Simpson, Nadine Kujawa, Wanda Bamberg (Nadine's replacement), and particularly Tom Payzant, for their generosity with their time and for their candidness.

I would also like to acknowledge Harvard Education Press for their thoughtful insight on this book, and particularly for the personalized assistance from the publisher, Douglas Clayton and his staff.

Last but certainly not least, I wish to thank my family. My husband Vlad has always been my strongest advocate and sounding board. To my sons Alexander and Benjamin, thank you for waiting for what must have seemed an eternity for mommy to have more time to play Candy Land.

FOREWORD

There are many compelling reasons to invest in and be hopeful about raising student achievement in urban education. Difficult challenges should not become excuses for inaction. Public education must be improved in every community in America.

Suburban communities, and the increasingly urbanized rings outside cities, will not survive unless the cities they surround are successful. It is in everybody's interest to provide the resources necessary to support all of the children in our public schools. These schools were created to serve the common good. It requires a commitment to ensure that every child in every classroom, every classroom in every school, every school in every school district and every school district in America embraces the opportunity to learn so that all students achieve and graduate from high school ready for postsecondary education and the workplace.

The challenges facing public education in the United States changed dramatically as standards-based reform gained traction in the 1980s. The standards framework included elements that were not unknown to some educators. After all, clear expectations about what students should know and be able to do was not a new idea. Curricula that provided teachers and students access to rigorous content sounded familiar except for one word—*rigorous*. Professional development designed to support the improvement of instruction also appeared to be a benign idea, perhaps ignored by many whose experience with professional development had been negative. However, the fourth element, assessments, did not escape notice. In retrospect, the focus was on *summative assessments*—end-of-year tests that would generate data to be used for accountability purposes. *Formative assessments*, which produced data for teachers to use to reflect on the appropriateness of the curriculum and the effectiveness of their teaching, took more time to gain acceptance.

What was different about the standards-based framework? The intent was to align the elements and to create coherence among them so that the whole would be greater than the sum of its parts. This challenged conventional thinking and practice about what to teach, how to teach and how to measure student learning outcomes.

The radical idea was a clear and dramatic shift in expectations. The goal of standards-based reform is to educate all students to reach the same high standards traditionally designed for select groups of students.

During the 1980s and early 1990s, the teacher organizations focused on national curriculum and provided leadership for creating voluntary standards in the core subjects: English language arts, mathematics, science, and social studies. Many educators in those subject areas were proponents of national standards, but they quickly discovered how strong the opposition to this idea would become and that potential involvement of the federal government would derail the movement.

The 1994 reauthorization of the Elementary and Secondary Education Act (ESEA) set the policy focus for standards-based reform by requiring the states to develop standards for what students should know and be able to do and assessments which would generate data for assessing learning outcomes. What evolved was significant variation in the quality and rigor of the standards and assessments developed by the fifty states. Thus, the focus on accountability for improving student achievement and holding school districts and schools accountable for student achievement was delayed until the next reauthorization of ESEA, the No Child Left Behind Act (NCLB), enacted by a bipartisan coalition in the House and Senate in 2001 and signed by President George W. Bush early in 2002.

This legislation continued the policies requiring state standards and assessments embedded in the 1994 reauthorization of ESEA (the Improving

American Schools Act). However, NCLB made dramatic changes in the annual improvement targets states, school districts, and schools were required to meet. The targets were set for all students, regardless of gender, language, disability, race, and income level. Sanctions were prescribed for school districts and schools failing to meet targets. Data were disaggregated by each subgroup and a bright light exposed those who had been satisfied in the past with reports containing aggregated data that masked the differences in performance between subgroups of students.

Controversy surrounding NCLB, particularly its accountability provisions, became a dominant factor as candidates discussed education policy during the 2008 presidential campaign as well as state and local election campaigns.

It is not yet clear what will happen with the reauthorization of NCLB and the direction federal education policy will take during the Obama administration. However, it is likely that standards-based reform will not fade away anytime soon. There is renewed interest in developing common standards in the core subjects as long as the federal government does not take the lead in creating them. The states, with leadership from governors and chief state school officers, will have a key role in steering efforts toward collaboration in developing common standards that will eliminate the existing wide discrepancies in the rigor of standards and assessments among the fifty states as demonstrated by the gaps between the proficiency standard set by the National Assessment of Educational Progress (NAEP) and the proficiency standards for each of the fifty state tests. And at this juncture, there is increasing demand for the United States to embrace more rigorous international benchmarks for standards and assessments as a necessity for the country to remain competitive internationally and to be able to prepare its high school students to acquire the twenty-first-century skills essential for gaining access to postsecondary education, challenging jobs and a good life. Now standards-based reform raises the bar with the expectation that the goal for all urban, suburban, and rural school districts is to graduate every student from high school, to be ready without remediation for postsecondary education.

What will it take to reach this goal? Some believe that the change and improvement required to meet this goal will happen only one school at a time. With ninety-five thousand public schools in the United States, it appears to be an unreasonable, if not impossible, stretch assignment to take this strategy to scale. However, the charter school movement has shown that this strategy works with evidence of impressive improvements in student achievement. Private schools continue to provide an alternative to public schools for those families who can afford them or for students who receive scholarships. Private nonprofit as well as for-profit providers have created charter management organizations, such as the Kipp Schools, which have carved out a small but important piece of the market share that is demonstrating that it is possible to educate low-income students and prepare them to achieve rigorous standards and continue on to post-secondary education.

Policy in some states authorizes in-district charter schools that are approved by local school boards who hold them accountable for meeting student achievement goals set forth in their applications and contracts. This in-district strategy also serves as a means to keep families in public school districts who otherwise might leave urban school districts for the suburbs or, if they can afford it, to enroll their children in private schools. One challenge to these strategies for change and improvement is the fear that they will harm traditional school systems and schools by taking some of their students and funding away, making it more difficult for traditional school districts to survive.

Urban and rural systems of schools have a greater challenge than suburban systems to set high standards and to educate all students to meet them so that they graduate from high school ready for postsecondary education. This is because the urban and rural systems often have not had the resources or the belief that it is possible to reach this goal.

Well-documented examples that demonstrate what it will take to transform systems of schools are essential. The Broad Prize shines a spotlight on urban school districts that have demonstrated that it is possible to beat the odds and make substantial progress toward improving a whole system of schools. Each year a hundred eligible urban school districts in America are reviewed with a focus on their improvement compared with similar districts in their own states. Five finalists are selected by a review panel and site visits are scheduled by teams that observe and interview stakeholders in the community, district and schools. It is not just quantitative data that are examined. The qualitative variables of successful teaching, district and school leadership, district governance, and community engagement are assessed as well.

Each of the school districts highlighted in this volume clearly understands the key levers necessary for change and improvement, and the ongoing rhythm of determining what should be sustained and what needs to be changed and improved. Each is committed to improving a whole system of schools and is not satisfied with having just a few more good schools. These districts know that data are essential to assess what is and is not working for students, and that they must execute a few strategies well rather than many strategies superficially. They are not afraid to argue that less sometimes is more, and their results confirm it. They have a laser-like focus on teaching and learning, knowing that the two most important variables the schools control are the quality of teaching in the classroom and leadership in the schools.

The challenge for each of the school districts is to take instructional improvement to scale. It is not a short-term target. It requires intentional steps over multiple years where the goals remain the same and strategies are refined based on careful in-depth study of both qualitative and quantitative information. Key essentials shape the frameworks for strategic plans. They typically include instruction, data for decision making, training and development for all staff, distributive leadership both in districts and schools, budgets that serve as financial plans for allocating resources to support the district's educational plan, family and community engagement, and operational support from the central office.

These districts keep striving to become learning organizations. They know that there must be alignment between the strategies in the strategic plan, that coherence in organizations is essential to achieve clarity of purpose, clear goals, measures of improvement, appropriate allocation of resources, and accountability for results. Continuity of leadership in their governance structures has led to continuity of leadership for their superintendents.

Above all, The Broad Prize finalists and winning districts provide hope for the future of urban education in America and challenge all who accept the responsibility for improving them to learn about what it takes to improve a whole system of schools and to stay the course to ensure that it happens.

Thomas W. Payzant
Former Superintendent of Boston Public Schools

INTRODUCTION

This book provides a unique opportunity to learn about five exemplary urban public school districts that have demonstrated higher performance and/or greater improvement than similar districts in their states. Despite facing the extreme challenges often found in urban districts, the districts discussed in this book stood out among one hundred other eligible urban districts for national recognition in student achievement and improvement scores. Each of the districts—Aldine Independent School District (Texas); Boston Public Schools (Massachusetts); Garden Grove Unified School District (California); Long Beach Unified School District (California); and Norfolk Public Schools (Virginia)—is a winner of the prestigious Broad Prize for Urban Education.[1]

These five urban districts have demonstrated exceptional persistence in developing tightly integrated practices across their entire systems with the aim of raising student achievement and closing ethnic and income achievement gaps. The successes highlighted in this book do not represent one-year positive performance blips; these districts have shown evidence of sustainability over time. Aldine has been widely recognized and cited frequently by organizations such as The Education Trust for its high levels of performance since 2000—well over nine years; and the district was selected as a winner in 2009. Boston, a five-time finalist and a winner, provides a rare opportunity to learn about a successful decade-long reform path led by one of the nation's most respected urban superintendents. Garden

Grove shows strong performance in many areas compared with the state, particularly in building an entire K–12 pipeline that is addressing college readiness, despite its large English language learner (ELL) population and the sixty-eight languages spoken in the district. Long Beach caught the eye of many major newspapers and education journals for rising back to the top as a Prize finalist again after its win, and for the honor of having two high schools in the coveted *Newsweek* list of top-performing high schools in the nation. Norfolk, a predominantly African American urban district, improved its performance to the extent that families moved back from wealthy neighboring districts to enroll their children there.

Even those only vaguely familiar with The Broad Prize should appreciate the difficultly and rigor of the process. Every type of available data and every analysis that can be performed are presented to a sizeable, hand-picked selection jury of well-known educational and civic leaders, which scrutinizes eligible districts closely to select five finalist districts from among one hundred districts. The data include an analysis of math and reading proficiencies at the elementary, middle, and high school levels, both in comparison to the state and demographically similar districts; numerous ethnic and income gap analyses; three different graduation analyses using different methods; and numerous college-readiness measures such as SAT and ACT scores and success on AP exams, The five finalists undergo a thorough and rigorous three- to four-day site visit, during which additional documents are collected and interviews conducted at all system levels to detail district and school practices. The end result is a set of finalists and a winner that prove their success empirically, anecdotally (from their stakeholders), and over time.

The cases in this book are developed from years of Prize data and interviews and additional post-Prize interviews. Much of the information derives from firsthand observation, as I served as the Austin-based project director of The Broad Prize from 2003–2006. The cases are designed to guide practitioners and policymakers through the process of understanding how the districts changed each piece of their system to move from unacceptable to exceptional performance. This book does not provide a list of best practice silver bullets that sound effective but cannot be applied outside a unique context. Rather, the book describes the paths these districts took over years of intentional, sustained, patient focus on improving teaching and learning that fully aligns instructional practices across all organizational levels of a school system—something that can be done in any district given the right knowledge and tools.

The importance of focus cannot be overstated; these districts all adopted a long-term view and resisted any temptation to veer off course or get pulled in too many directions. The end result is five districts that have clearly defined what students are to know and be able to do; teachers who feel supported and respected; and students who progress through seamless K–12 educational programs. Those three points may seem obvious, since we tend to assume that all schools operate with such clarity at all levels. However, the reality is that the educational program a given student experiences is often fragmented, usually as a result of undesirable district and school practices such as implementing too many separate reading programs, providing one-shot professional development that is unrelated to what teachers do in the classroom, or failing to review the K–12 curriculum holistically to ensure that each subject's scope and sequence does not include skips or unnecessary repeats.

Although many case studies highlight schools that are beating the odds and doing great work within challenging circumstances, those cases are sporadic, and the schools are individual standouts rather than parts of well-aligned districts that serve all students well regardless of which school they attend. The districts featured in this book represent successes on a larger scale. They face the challenges typically found in urban districts—60 to 85 percent of their students are on the free- or reduced-price lunch program, and 54 to 80 percent are minorities. Yet their student achievement and improvement scores stood out among the hundred districts eligible for The Broad Prize.

Some education commentators voice skepticism about the ability of educational reforms to actually affect student achievement on a scalable level, as few large-scale reforms have had significant measurable effect on student learning.[2] One theory posed by Richard Elmore for this lack of progress is failure to change the "instructional core" or "how teachers understand the nature of knowledge and the student's role in learning" and how that understanding affects actual teaching practices.[3] Elmore also refers to the importance of "organizational practices" that support student/teacher relationships, such as the physical layout of classrooms, student grouping practices, stakeholder communications, and processes for assessing student learning. Using Elmore's example, a high school can change its class schedule from traditional sixty-minute periods to ninety-minute instructional blocks. However, if teachers do not change their views on the construction of knowledge, they will still teach and interact with students in the same manner. The solution, Elmore says, is to understand (and create) the conditions in which teachers "seek new knowledge and actively use it to change fundamental processes of schooling."[4]

Elmore posits that changing the instructional core to scale is difficult and seldom occurs beyond a few classrooms—much less in entire schools. Yet progress in changing the instructional core on a larger scale has been made, and we are learning more and more about how to effect such change across districts. The process has been slow and difficult, but the performance increases in these districts show that scalable reforms are possible.

One could say that the standards-based movement and the availability of more and better data created the need for new knowledge about school processes. Despite widespread opposition to the No Child Left Behind (NCLB) Act of 2002, many of us in education research have found that the availability of disaggregated student performance data and the heightened focus on curriculum standards and instructional alignment prompted by the act sparked a change in instructional approaches.[5] With this additional data, educators began minutely unpacking their curricula to uncover unnecessary repeats and skips in their instructional sequences, gaining new knowledge that they had not realized was there to be gained. As a result, teachers became more aware of what was required of students, not only in their own grade assignments, but also in the grades preceding and following their own. When I asked principals and teachers in 2003 about some of these changes—such as why teacher collaboration suddenly became a common practice—several explained that the standards resulting from NCLB provided a common language for teachers to use to discuss teaching and learning. From that year forward, I found in my fieldwork increasing evidence of opened classroom doors, with teachers sharing ideas and lessons and even reviewing data together to brainstorm instructional solutions.[6]

In addition to an increase in teacher collaboration, researchers have found instruction affected through improved use of data and data systems; more sophisticated teacher hiring, development, and retention practices; better program selection methods; and more structured interventions for students, teachers, and schools.[7] By 2006, the term "data-based decision making" had become commonplace among educators.[8] Also post-NCLB, my colleagues and I saw an increased focus on clearly defining educational goals and aligning the appropriate resources to support those goals.

While all those changes are positive, districts still find large-scale improvement to be difficult. One urban district leader recently put it well in a conversation with me: "We know what areas we need to focus on and that systemic alignment is important; we just don't have the specifics on how to pull the pieces together to take reform to scale." In other words, we know teacher collaboration is a good thing, but how does a district institutionalize it as a practice? Does it need to be mandated? How often should teachers meet? How can teacher meetings actually affect instruction and curriculum alignment? What other tools can a district and schools provide to enhance teacher collaboration?

Such details are important for making a scalable impact on student achievement. For this book, I used several years of Broad Prize interview data and documents to describe how five unique systems moved from having an overall dissatisfaction about their students' performance to demonstrating higher performance and/or greater improvement than similar districts; the voices quoted throughout this book are from these studies and follow-up interviews. An additional "retro study" conducted in 2005 of past Broad Prize winners—Aldine, Garden Grove, Long Beach, and Norfolk— adds additional depth to these cases. The retro study provided important information on how each system sustained performance after its win, what practices changed, and what practices remained the same. Finally, I conducted several follow-up interviews with leaders in the districts to gain perspective on their current performance and practices. It is important to keep in mind that while these practices formed much of their work, several of the districts have since made changes based on current system needs.

To make the large-scale changes necessary to markedly improve teaching and learning, the districts figured out how to operationalize a new vision of high expectations for students through clear goals, aligned curriculum, powerful instructional techniques, and accessible supports across the entire system. Their stories illustrate how they approached reform to scale to gain systemic alignment and improve student achievement districtwide.

1

Escaping the Forty-Year Road to Nowhere

Bringing School Reform to Scale

REFORMING REFORM

We have been engaged in a fragmented, vacillating reform frenzy for years.[1] Our keen interest in improving student achievement dates back over forty years, when the groundbreaking 1966 Coleman report cited wide gaps between African American and white student achievement.[2] Concern increased to an almost panicky urgency with the publication of *A Nation at Risk* in 1983, which claimed that only one-third of seventeen-year-olds could solve a math problem requiring several steps; only one-fifth could write a decent persuasive essay; millions of adults were illiterate; and SAT scores were dropping.[3]

In the past forty years of focus on educational reform, research by hundreds of the nation's most brilliant educators and researchers has resulted in thousands of reform strategies implemented in schools; yet those efforts have shown little scalable impact on student achievement.[4] Lack of progress is often blamed on haphazard reform stops and starts that focus on the newest program or instructional technique. Another commonly identified culprit is reforms that are implemented in isolation without consideration of context or systemic effects. For example, breaking large, comprehensive high schools into smaller communities improves instruction for some students but has limited results for students who are significantly behind academically. Creating a longer instructional day (a solution proposed in *A Nation at Risk*) is not helpful without a clear understanding on how to best invest that additional time. Along the same lines, pushing algebra down to earlier grades should not be done without first considering how to obtain well-trained teachers, appropriate professional development, and the right textbooks. The end result with these examples has been a hard lesson: piecemeal reform seldom works.[5]

Besides being ineffective, the constant churning of reforms may be dangerous for other reasons. While one district is leaping off the bandwagon it jumped on the previous year, its neighbors are optimistically clambering aboard with fervent hopes that *this* will be the one to solve their problems. This stopping-and-starting regimen results not only in program fragmentation for both educators and students, but it also leads to school systems that are patched-together pieces rather than intentional, well-thought-out educational programs. All of this results in a pervasive culture of "this, too, shall pass" that permeates the ranks of teachers and administrators. Many of the teachers I have interviewed and known have been frustrated with their districts' continuous cycles of training, implementing, and discarding programs and reforms.

Urban systems are fertile ground for reform, as they are typically large, diverse systems with significant numbers of underperforming students.[6] The pressure for addressing those problems falls on the superintendent, who often is hired to address one specific issue (e.g., reduce the number of students dropping out, serve as a data guru, improve leadership at the district and school levels) and serves a tenure (sometimes by individual or board choice) of three years or less.[7] The best way for a new superintendent to garner support and confidence is to initiate a new reform that will make visible changes in the system—until the next new leader arrives three years later. This preoccupation with short-term gains in one area rather than a long-term focus on the whole system contributes to the policy churn and endless cycling described above.

Since a large number of our nation's children are educated in urban districts, many of which experience frequently publicized poor performance, urban systems have been a topic of interest to researchers for several years. Commonly cited solutions to urban school reform include strengthening school leadership, creating competitive markets, hiring "effective" teachers, and establishing small schools.[8] Yet so far, these movements have resulted, at best, in small successes in individual schools, failing to spark "excellence on a grand scale."

Systemic Reform

Responding to concern over piecemeal reform, the U.S. Department of Education provided funds to state agencies in the early 1990s for competitive grants to schools adopting reform approaches targeted to strengthening the entire school program. This model focused on developing a coherent school vision and aligning research-based educational strategies to every aspect of operations, including governance, curriculum, professional development, and assessment.[9] Additionally, the model attempted to strike a balance between the traditional extremes of driving reform with a centralized top-down method or with a bottom-up grass-roots effort.

In the top-down method, a district might hire an outside consultant to develop curriculum and mandate that all teachers use it. The risk with this approach is that teachers may not buy in to the curriculum if they had no involvement in the process, and the district would be overlooking their most reliable resources on instruction and student learning. In a bottom-up grassroots effort, teachers might develop curricula themselves, but they might spend too much time out of the classroom, at the expense of instructional time, to complete the work; and if small groups of teachers in various schools developed their own curricula, there would be no alignment districtwide. The Department of Education's model proposed a balance in which a district's central office would drive supports to schools, while schools would communicate their needs up to central office.[10] A well-balanced approach using the curriculum example would use central office to facilitate the curriculum-development process by convening an appropriate group of teachers and central office curriculum experts to structure and complete curriculum design and alignment. Within that process, people at all levels of the system have equally important roles and work together to make decisions.

These key vision and alignment strategies have remained consistent in literature on school reform. Since at least 2000, researchers from the Education Trust have closely studied high-poverty/high-minority schools to highlight schools that beat the odds. Commonalities held by these exemplar schools follow a model for setting a coherent vision that focuses on raising expectations for students and aligning the appropriate pieces of the system. The Education Trust proposes that educators learn from successful high-performing schools by following a similar systemic approach rather than focusing on isolated issues or practices.[11] Along similar lines, Frechtling asserts that practitioners must align "all of the components of the educational system—curriculum, instructional materials, student assessment, educational policies, professional development, and evaluation."[12] Relating educational systems to business, Green and Etheridge believe that schools fail because teachers are not supported by a well-coordinated system.[13] They discuss school reform in terms of districts' facilitating systemic change by establishing a common vision, promoting from within, using collaborative decision making, and focusing on students.

One important commonality shared by the five districts featured in this book is their understanding that affecting student achievement to scale requires aligning the parts of the system around core elements directly linking to teaching and learning. Elmore credits this new understanding and demand for specialized knowledge of curriculum, pedagogy, and organizational improvement in schools and school systems to the performance-based accountability movement that reached a crescendo after NCLB was passed. He asserts that while we have seen some improvements in instructional practice, those improvements occur far too infrequently and do not connect to typical school practices. This disconnection, he posits, is what keeps isolated successes from replicating to scale.[14]

Pulling the Pieces Together—Bringing School Reform to Scale

Raising achievement for all student groups beyond one great classroom or school requires changing the way we think about education reform. Rather than a single program or short-term fix, we must consider what outcomes we want and build the system accordingly, with an understanding of who the drivers should be, what pieces need to be aligned and in place, how to communicate and provide supports across the system, and how to monitor and evaluate implementation and progress.

As you read the five cases presented in this book, you will see living examples of systemic reform that affects the instructional core by aligning the appropriate elements that support instruction across all organizational levels of the district. The end result is a large-scale change in teaching and learning that produces a seamless educational program for students, regardless of their location within the district.

The district serves as a key force or driver for pulling the pieces together. This concept is a departure from research in the 1990s that characterized districts as overbureaucratized organizations that impeded more than helped schools and teachers.[15] Perhaps resulting from accountability pressures from NCLB, district leaders realized that improving achievement meant, as Togneri and Anderson put it, fundamentally changing "both instructional support and instructional practice." Togneri and Anderson cite evidence that districts were making a shift from a fragmented operational focus to building a common base or vision and then building the infrastructure to support the vision.[16] Agreeing, Muller points out that the central office is a logical centralized catalyst for building commitment and alignment across district levels, as it frequently sets personnel, instructional, and resource policies and serves as an important element in providing necessary resources to schools.[17]

Detailing how a district's central office can move from setting a vision to affecting actual practice, the small body of research on the role of districts in school reform identifies "effective" districts as those that focus on student improvement and raising standards (by setting the vision), continually reviewing and redefining instruction, emphasizing the use of data, and aligning operations and supports around common goals. Thus, districts set a clear purpose and goals, assist with alignment and setting priorities, and then focus on supporting their "customers"—the schools. These basic elements are found in all five case study districts.

The Importance of Using a Model

Many case studies, like Chenoweth's *It's Being Done*, provide vivid details about the practices, culture, and even student opinions of particular schools.[18] A few similar case studies focus on district-level details. While these studies provide an inspirational view and ideas from schools that are creating innovative and powerful programs, it is difficult to identify a tangible way the practices fit together to affect the instructional core that Hess and Elmore reference as the key element to meaningful reform.[19] Business leaders assert that using a clear theory of change supported by a visual model makes a program easier to communicate, sustain, bring to scale, and evaluate, since the pieces are clearly defined and displayed within a logical model.[20] Similarly, Elmore asserts that change cannot occur on a large scale without "some deliberate theory of improvement."[21] The cases in this book outline each district's reform story or "theory of improvement" through the use of a graphic organizer both to collect the data on each system and to organize the systemic practices for the reader.

THE NCEA BEST PRACTICE FRAMEWORK

The National Center for Educational Achievement's (NCEA's) Best Practice Framework ("the Framework"), provides a visual organizer of the essential components of an educational system and the levels at which the work must take place.[22] The essential components are delineated by five themes essential to supporting the instructional core.

The five themes include:

- *Curriculum and Academic Goals:* Clearly delineating what we expect all students to know and be able to do by grade and subject.

- *Staff Selection, Leadership, and Capacity Building:* Selecting and developing the leaders and teachers to ensure that every learner in the system achieves the district/school goals.
- *Instructional Programs, Practices, and Arrangements:* Utilizing the right resources (programs, materials, time, technology, etc.) to deliver the curriculum.
- *Monitoring, Analysis, and Use of Data:* Monitoring and assessing instructional progress.
- *Recognition, Intervention, and Adjustment:* Providing researched-based responses to support student learning.

In addition to five themes, the three levels of every school system—the district (central office), school (school leadership), and classroom (teachers)—provide a second organizational dimension to the Framework. Each organizational level within the five themes plays a particular role in the various practices. Different levels of the school system must be involved to differing degrees in order to reach maximum effectiveness in the specific theme area. The assignment of practices to a specific school level may be as important as the practices themselves.[23] This ensures that the people with appropriate expertise are involved in a process like curriculum development, that the work is manageable (rather than resting solely on the backs of teachers, for instance), and that the shared process creates alignment across the system. Thus, NCEA's theory of action is that "districts create a [systemwide] environment for powerful learning; schools set individualized goals based on the particular needs of their students; and teachers receive the resources and support to deliver high-impact learning." This theory is similar to the balance discussed above—using the central office to coordinate the vision and resources across a system driven by student/teacher/school needs.

It is important to clarify that the Framework focuses on management principles that support instructional decisions rather than on actual programs and pedagogical techniques. For example, rather than saying all districts, despite their unique context, should use "X" math program, the Instructional Program and Practices theme addresses a district's specific process for selecting, monitoring, and evaluating programs. In high-performing districts, that process often includes assessing needs through data review, selecting research-based programs that demonstrate a proven record with similar populations, implementing small-scale pilots, continuously monitoring for evidence of desired results, and having an action plan for treating programs that fail to yield appropriate results.

This point about context is crucial; if there were one answer that would work everywhere, we would have already found it. When people ask me, in the course of the years I have spent conducting Broad Prize site visits, "What's the best math program?" my response is "That depends on your unique needs." The Framework provides a useful visual organizer and serves to collect data on unique systems, but it does not prescribe how to do all things in all places. For that reason, we used the Framework for all The Broad Prize visits from 2002 to 2006.

To capture more of the political and social context of each district, the cases discussed in this book contain an additional section called "Influencing Factors." These factors are an important part of capturing each district's reform process, since the practices falling within the five Framework themes do not exist in a vacuum. Rather, they are influenced by a host of controllable and uncontrollable factors that are well documented as having impact on the success and eventual scalability of most reforms, large or small. The importance of these factors is to connect the pieces of the system, support the system's stakeholders, and help mitigate things out of the system's control, such as high numbers of students on free or reduced-price lunch, high student mobility, and budget constraints for example.

In addition to following NCEA's inclusion of stakeholders as one of these factors, these cases discuss governance and decision making, resource allocation, and climate/culture. While these cases will describe the power structures behind each district's key internal and external stakeholders, these three additional factors are crucial reform elements that detail who is involved at the decision-making table and how authority is distributed across the system; how fiscal resources are allocated and how those allocations relate to the district's goals; and how the overall climate supports these reforms.

STUDY DETAILS

Apart from site selection, the methodology used in this project is primarily qualitative. From a theoretical perspective, the research uses qualitative data analysis with a case-study format utilizing the NCEA Best Practice Framework.

The five districts discussed in this book were identified through The Broad Prize for Urban Education selection process. NCEA managed the data analysis and site visit process for The Broad Prize from 2002 to 2006. From 2003 to 2006, I was NCEA's project manager for the overall selection process. The review board chose five finalists each year. There were thirteen Broad Prize finalists between its first year in 2002 up to and including 2006 (several were repeat finalists). For this book, I chose to feature five districts that were repeat finalists before 2006 and that demonstrated strong, integrated systems. Although the base year for student performance measurement differs among the five districts, all finalists were selected using statistical measures for modeling performance and improvement through a four-year longitudinal view. Finalist selection involves a multidimensional process that spans over a year's time.

Each year, using publicly available performance data from state-mandated tests for eligible urban districts, NCEA researchers compared the districts' performance with the performance of districts with similar poverty levels in their states. Researchers also gathered data on graduation and SAT/ACT performance. Eligibility was determined by size, student demographics, and urbanicity (having a Locale Code of 1, 2, or 3 in the U.S. Department of Education's Common Core of Data). A separate review board consisting of prominent researchers and education leaders closely examined data to review achievement and performance in each district. Achievement measures included performance on state-mandated criteria-referenced tests and relationships between poverty levels and performance. Improvement measures included achievement growth over a four-year span.

Data Collection and Analysis

The main source of data for this study was interviews and documents collected during Broad Prize finalist site visits. For the site visits, teams of five members consisting of superintendents, principals, professors, and researchers were selected and trained to conduct site visits at each finalist district. During each visit, the teams spent one day at the district office to investigate district practices, one day divided among one district-selected elementary, middle, and high schools to investigate school and classroom practices, and one day conducting four separate focus groups of randomly selected new and experienced principals and teachers to gain a broader perspective on district/school relationships. In addition to interviews, the research team gathered district and school documents to further describe and support the practices being studied. Finally, at least one team member attended a teacher team meeting at each selected school to observe the structure and content of collaborative meetings.

At each district visit, a total of nine sixty- to ninety-minute interviews were held with the superintendent, assistant superintendent for curriculum and instruction, school board president, union president, business and parent leadership representatives, and other senior district staff. Nine interviews were also conducted at one district-selected elementary, middle, and high school in each district. School interviews were held with the principals, the school site–based management team, and teams of teachers. The four separate focus group interviews with randomly selected new and experienced principals and teachers provided a broader sample of perceptions across the district's schools.

All interviews were taped and completed under signed consent. Detailed interview protocols based on the NCEA Framework were used in the district and school interviews. To confirm that the Framework model did not drive the interview results, each interview began with a number of open-ended questions. At the completion of each site visit, the interviews were transcribed and analyzed using Atlas.ti qualitative software that organizes coded data. A code list was developed and interviews were coded and analyzed by two site visit team members to create inter-rater reliability. Site visit summaries were written to report the results, which were confirmed for accuracy by each district.

District and classroom documents were collected at each site visit. These documents included district planning documents, recruitment advertisements, and details on professional development programs. Documents were not coded, but were used to triangulate the results.

In addition to interviews and documents, observations of teacher team meetings were conducted at each district-selected school to discern the structure and content of collaborative meetings. Field notes recorded the number of participates, the purpose of the meeting, the meeting activities, and the frequency and typical structure of meetings. Team meeting observation notes were not coded, but were used to triangulate the results.

A Note About the Data

Those who are only vaguely familiar with The Broad Prize are unaware of the huge volume of data that is collected and analyzed by the review board and jury to determine eligibility, the finalists, and the winners. When reading reviews of books identifying "successful" schools or districts, I have noted that many critics focus on picking apart the methodology that identified the successful schools or districts or on querying the definition of success itself. However, I believe these districts represent powerful systems that are moving in the right direction, despite the limitations outlined briefly below.

Analyzing student performance across state lines is extremely difficult, as many variables within each system are left to state discretion, such as the level of rigor of the state exam, or where cut points are set. Thus, for The Broad Prize, numerous researchers worked together for years on producing a fair and reasonable analysis. The site visit process serves as an important resource for determining whether the finalist districts really represent strong, well-aligned systems that are working hard to serve all students. Not only have these districts shown noteworthy performance for at least two consecutive years, but several of them have won other honors and awards and are frequently cited by other resources for their successes.

There are also some limitations to using qualitative data in case studies. These cases represent what the interviewees said about their systems and thus do not represent the entire system. It is also at least remotely possible that the interviews have been tainted by the fact that they occurred during a site visit attached to a prize that would result in student scholarship money and an excellent reputation for the finalist and winning districts. It is possible that, under those circumstances, the interviewees, whether selected by the district or randomly, were prepped to put their best foot forward. However, if a district can coordinate a scripted message across more than fifteen central office interviewees, principal and teacher focus groups, and large groups of parents, board members, and community members, then they truly are operating in alignment! Additionally, we found the same practices and approaches in subsequent years when districts were repeat finalists, though the interviewees changed from year to year.

Designing these cases involved some difficult decisions regarding how to represent the whole and yet explain the parts. I could have parsed each theme out by level, detailing the work between the district, school, and classroom; yet that would have taken away from the whole picture and falsely represented distinctions that weren't always that clear. I could have also divided the themes between elementary, middle, and high school, which would be interesting but difficult, as the level of detail in the interview data varied depending on the interviewer and the interviewees. In the end, I decided to begin with a holistic view of the reform goals and theory of action for each district, then detail the work by Framework themes to explain how the pieces fit together, and end with a consideration of the influencing factors. Thus, some practices will appear to repeat as themes overlap, as they should in a systemic approach.

The Broad Prize process provides not only great lessons learned from these five successful repeat finalists and winners, but also a great amount of data that can support the claims that each has made great strides in raising and improving achievement for its students. Because The Broad Foundation has made this data publicly available, these cases provide the reader with a fairly comprehensive picture of how these districts performed, given the availability of their data, before, during, and after they became finalists. It is important to note while you review this data that comparing the districts' performance can be problematic owing to variations in state and local policy and practices. The fact that Aldine often performs similar to or above the state standards and Boston does not is not an indication that Aldine did better with its students. As the cases mention, the standards in each state have differing levels of rigor, and thus the reader should focus on how well the districts performed over time, and the areas in which they showed the greatest improvements.

CONCLUSION

We celebrated the forty-year anniversary of the Coleman report in 2006 and the twenty-year anniversary of *A Nation at Risk* in 2003. These two landmark reports raised the alarm about the state of our educational system and sparked years of reform churn in our nation's schools and classrooms. We have seen a lot of changes come and go and have learned some lessons that are starting to take hold. There is recognition that reform should affect the instructional core, and we have some ideas about the pieces that need to be aligned. We also have better tools for monitoring student progress and responding to problems before they become unmanageable. Yet we still seem to get stuck in understanding how to manage such changes on a larger scale, particularly in the complex systems within which urban districts operate.

The case studies in this book attempt to capture how five exemplary urban districts pulled the pieces together to change the business of teaching and learning on a scalable level. Using multiple years of student achievement data and interviews at all levels of the system during Broad Prize site visits and through an additional retro study of past winners, each case provides performance highlights from The Broad Prize analysis, a brief background of the district, insight on the district's improvement approach, and then details of its system through NCEA's Best Practice Framework and of additional influencing factors.

These case studies are unique in that they use an organizational schema to describe how each system started from a point at which the district felt student performance was unacceptable and then pulled together the necessary instructional and operational pieces to improve the instructional core. Interviewees were careful to say that although they are pleased with their progress, they still have a lot of work ahead of them and still have problem areas to tackle. However, they believe they are moving in the right direction and feel that the changes will continue to move student achievement forward and will sustain over time.

Chapters 2 through 6 provide details on how Aldine, Boston, Garden Grove, Long Beach, and Norfolk redefined their vision for students and aligned their systems to improve teaching and learning to become award-winning urban districts. Chapter 7 provides a systematic comparison of the five districts through the NCEA Best Practice Framework themes, interviews with key stakeholders, information about governance and decision making, information about resource allocation practices, open-ended reform questions, and finally, highlights from the different reform paths taken by each district.

2

Aldine Independent School District

Located just north of Houston, Texas, Aldine Independent School District (ISD) is the seventy-third-largest school district in the nation and is the tenth-largest school district in Texas. In 2004, its first year as a Prize finalist—Aldine won in 2009—the district had 66 schools, 3,616 teachers, and 56,292 students. At that time Aldine ISD's student population was 33 percent African American, 58 percent Hispanic, and 7 percent white, with 76 percent of students eligible for free and reduced-price lunch and 25 percent designated as English Language Learners.[1] These demographics have remained similar proportionally through 2007, although the enrollment increased somewhat in 2009 (the year they won the Prize).

Aldine ISD is located in an unincorporated area in Harris County near Bush Intercontinental Airport and serves a population with numerous challenges. The median household income is approximately $32,437, according to the 2000 census, and about $35,518 for a family.[2] The area is densely populated, and only 28 percent of the relatively young population has a high school diploma and 8 percent a post–high school degree. Aldine has seen some demographic shifts over the past thirty years, owing partly to the development of the Bush Intercontinental Airport. In 2000, the predominant ethnic group, at 56 percent, was Hispanic, representing a 20 percent drop in the white population since 1980.

Aldine has gained attention in Texas as a district that embraced the accountability movement early and showed success with a challenging population before the implementation of the No Child Left Behind (NCLB) Act. Aldine was nominated three times as a Broad Prize finalist between 2002 and 2008, and won in 2009. Highlights of the performance contributing to the district's pre-2006 nominations show that Aldine has:

- Met Adequate Yearly Progress (AYP) targets in 2004 for 100 percent of its schools.
- Consistently outperformed demographically similar districts between 2001 and 2004.
- Narrowed the external gap (the district's disadvantaged group versus the state's advantaged group) for all groups in reading and for low-income and Hispanic students in math.

DISTRICT DEMOGRAPHICS AND ACHIEVEMENT LEVELS

Data from The Broad Prize report cards provide specific details that illustrate why Aldine stood out among approximately sixteen other eligible districts in the state to be selected three times as a finalist and then a winner. Since The Broad Prize report cards provide longitudinal data on all other eligible districts, these charts are able to represent Aldine's performance before, during, and after its first two finalist nominations in 2004 and 2005. When considering Aldine's proficiency rates compared with the entire state, the reader should keep in mind that while in 2004 Texas had 52.8 percent of students on the free and reduced-price lunch program (FRSL) and 58 percent were minority students, Aldine had 76 percent of students on FRSL and 89 percent minority students.[3]

Overall, the district performs relatively well compared with the state both in reading and math, and it has made some impressive gains in narrowing ethnic and income achievement gaps compared to the state. Figure 2.1 illustrates that the percentage of Aldine's students scoring at or above proficient in elementary (grades 3–5 for all Aldine data) reading increased steadily

FIGURE 2.1

District and state elementary reading proficiencies: All students

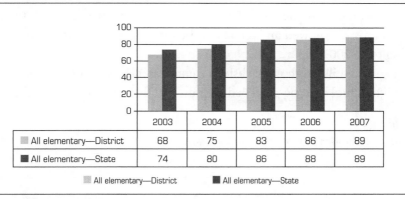

	2003	2004	2005	2006	2007
All elementary—District	68	75	83	86	89
All elementary—State	74	80	86	88	89

All elementary—District   All elementary—State

from 2003 to 2005, and remained only 3 percentage points behind the state's average students scoring at or above proficient of 86 percent in 2005.

Although the elementary math proficiency rates in 2003 began slightly lower than the state, the scores accelerated past the state in 2006 and 2007 (figure 2.2).

FIGURE 2.2

District and state elementary math proficiencies: All students

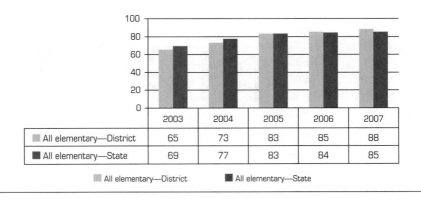

	2003	2004	2005	2006	2007
All elementary—District	65	73	83	85	88
All elementary—State	69	77	83	84	85

All elementary—District   All elementary—State

In middle school (grades 6–8 for all Aldine data), reading proficiency also improved steadily, and remained just 2 percentage points below the state's scores from 2003 to 2004, and 1 point below in 2005. Both the district and state showed an increase and equal performance in reading proficiency in 2007 (figure 2.3).

Figure 2.4 illustrates that district trends essentially followed state trends in high school reading proficiency rates, with increases in 2004 and 2006.

FIGURE 2.3
District and state middle school reading proficiencies: All students

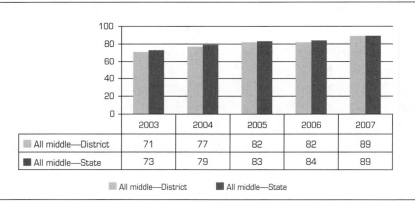

	2003	2004	2005	2006	2007
All middle—District	71	77	82	82	89
All middle—State	73	79	83	84	89

All middle—District   All middle—State

FIGURE 2.4
District and state high school reading proficiencies: All students

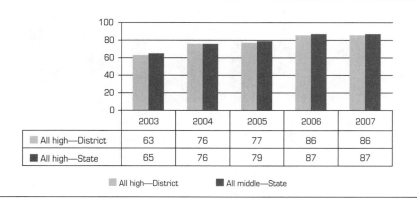

	2003	2004	2005	2006	2007
All high—District	63	76	77	86	86
All high—State	65	76	79	87	87

All high—District   All middle—State

Typically, school districts will show an inverse relationship between grade levels and achievement scores, with higher performance in the lower grades and lower performance in the upper grades. Figure 2.5 illustrates that theory holding true for district reading proficiencies only in 2003, when high school reading proficiency was lower than middle school proficiency. All three levels were very similar in 2004, and in the years following, high school performance only occasionally slipped very slightly below that of middle and elementary schools. It is surprising to see such consistent performance in reading between the elementary and middle school, since middle school achievement remains a difficult challenge in many urban districts. Overall, all three levels show a relatively steady increase in performance over time.

The grade-level comparison for math, however, is quite different, and is consistent with expectations. While middle school also shows steady increases, particularly between 2005 and 2007, the middle school proficiencies remained about 8 points behind elementary in 2007 (figure 2.6).

Aldine has done well relative to the state in narrowing its ethnic and income achievement gaps. Figure 2.7 illustrates that the achievement gap between the district's African American and white students in high school

FIGURE 2.5
District reading proficiencies: All levels

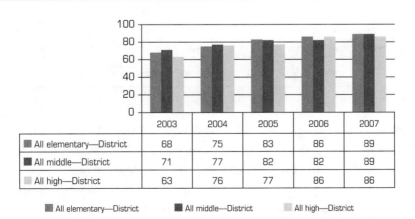

	2003	2004	2005	2006	2007
■ All elementary—District	68	75	83	86	89
■ All middle—District	71	77	82	82	89
▨ All high—District	63	76	77	86	86

■ All elementary—District　　■ All middle—District　　▨ All high—District

FIGURE 2.6

District math proficiencies: All levels

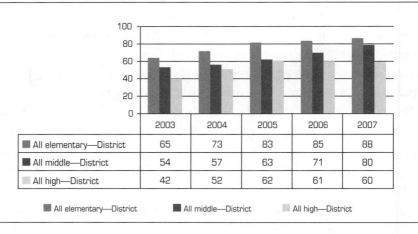

	2003	2004	2005	2006	2007
■ All elementary—District	65	73	83	85	88
■ All middle—District	54	57	63	71	80
▨ All high—District	42	52	62	61	60

■ All elementary—District   ■ All middle—District   ▨ All high—District

FIGURE 2.7

District high school reading achievement gap between African American and white students

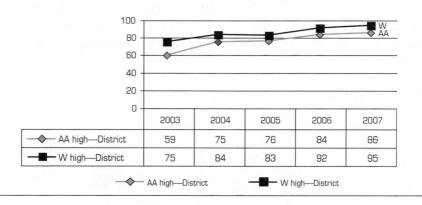

	2003	2004	2005	2006	2007
◆ AA high—District	59	75	76	84	86
■ W high—District	75	84	83	92	95

◆ AA high—District   ■ W high—District

reading starts at –16 in 2003, narrows to –6 in 2005, and then widens again slightly to –9 in 2007. During the same period, the achievement gap between the state's African American and white students in high school reading (figure 2.8) begins somewhat wider at 23 in 2003, and while it narrows steadily to –13 in 2007, it remains wider than the district's similar gap.

FIGURE 2.8

State high school reading achievement gap between African American and white students

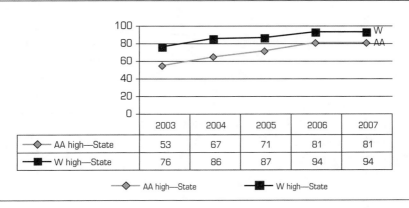

	2003	2004	2005	2006	2007
AA high—State	53	67	71	81	81
W high—State	76	86	87	94	94

The district is near success in eliminating the achievement gap between Hispanic and white students, particularly in middle school reading. Figure 2.9 illustrates that the district began with a Hispanic/white gap in middle school reading of –12 in 2003. In 2007 it reopened slightly to –6, partially due to a sharp increase in white student scores. In contrast, figure 2.10 shows

FIGURE 2.9

District middle school reading achievement gap between Hispanic and white students

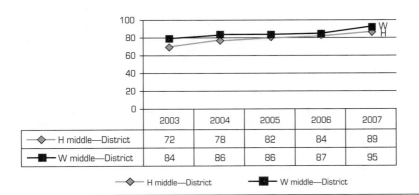

	2003	2004	2005	2006	2007
H middle—District	72	78	82	84	89
W middle—District	84	86	86	87	95

FIGURE 2.10

State middle school reading achievement gap between Hispanic and white students

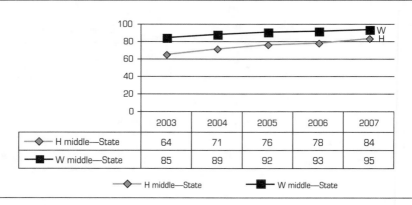

	2003	2004	2005	2006	2007
H middle—State	64	71	76	78	84
W middle—State	85	89	92	93	95

that the state's Hispanic/white gap began much wider at –21 and gradually narrowed over time, ending at –11 in 2007, nearly the same gap size that marked the district's starting point in 2003.

Figures 2.11 and 2.12 compare the district and state's achievement gaps between African American and white students for elementary school math over time. While there is still a significant gap between African American

FIGURE 2.11

District elementary math achievement gap between Hispanic and white students

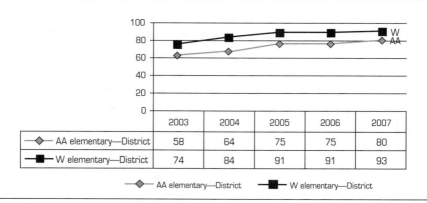

	2003	2004	2005	2006	2007
AA elementary—District	58	64	75	75	80
W elementary—District	74	84	91	91	93

FIGURE 2.12

State elementary math achievement gap between African American and white students

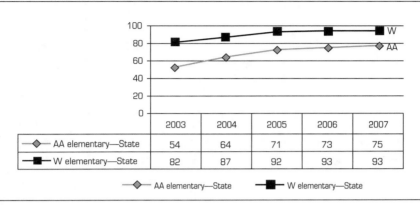

	2003	2004	2005	2006	2007
◆ AA elementary—State	54	64	71	73	75
■ W elementary—State	82	87	92	93	93

◆ AA elementary—State   ■ W elementary—State

and white students in the district, that gap is narrowing at a slightly faster rate than the state's, without white performance decreasing in order to narrow the gap.

Figures 2.13 and 2.14 present an interesting comparison of proficiency gaps by income in high school math between the district and the state. Figure 2.13 shows that low-income and non-low-income students in the

FIGURE 2.13

District achievement gap between low-income and non-low-income high school math students

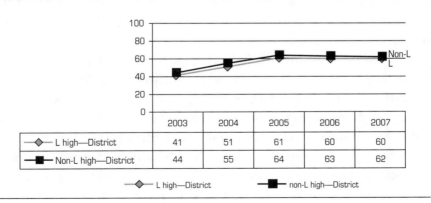

	2003	2004	2005	2006	2007
◆ L high—District	41	51	61	60	60
■ Non-L high—District	44	55	64	63	62

◆ L high—District   ■ non-L high—District

FIGURE 2.14

State achievement gap between low-income and non-low-income high school math students

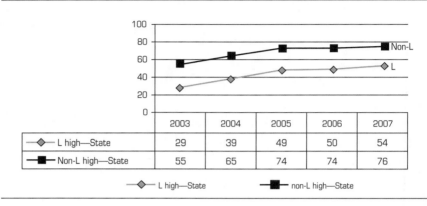

	2003	2004	2005	2006	2007
L high—State	29	39	49	50	54
Non-L high—State	55	65	74	74	76

◆ L high—State   ■ non-L high—State

district perform along a similar and tight trajectory and maintain a low-income/non-low-income gap of between –4 and –2.[4] The second chart, depicting the state's performance in the same subject and grade, shows substantially wider gaps of –26 (2002) and –22 (2007) between low-income and non-low-income students. However, regarding overall achievement, the district's performance decreased after 2005 while the state's slowly increased, showing higher achievement levels for all students and for non-low-income students.

Analyzing how well a district is doing compared with a state encompassing such differing overall demographic trends as Texas poses a number of challenges. Thus, NCEA developed a type of analysis that enables Prize reviewers to compare each district's performance against similar districts across the same state.[5] For each district, the expected or predicted proficiency level based on the regression was calculated. The difference between the district's *actual* percentage of students who tested at or above proficiency and the *predicted* or *expected* value is the residual. A positive residual indicates that the district is performing better than expected on the state test, while a negative residual indicates lower-than-expected performance. The analysis takes into account the district's relative (not actual) performance. Figures 2.15 and 2.16 show that the reading and math residuals,

FIGURE 2.15
District reading residual analysis: All levels

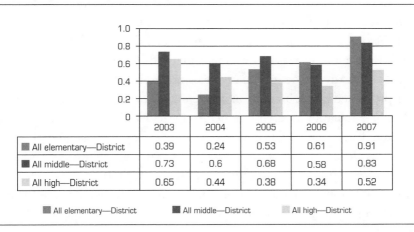

	2003	2004	2005	2006	2007
■ All elementary—District	0.39	0.24	0.53	0.61	0.91
■ All middle—District	0.73	0.6	0.68	0.58	0.83
■ All high—District	0.65	0.44	0.38	0.34	0.52

■ All elementary—District   ■ All middle—District   ■ All high—District

FIGURE 2.16
District math residual analysis: All levels

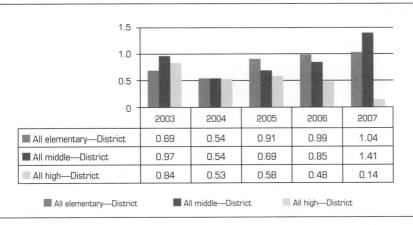

	2003	2004	2005	2006	2007
■ All elementary—District	0.69	0.54	0.91	0.99	1.04
■ All middle—District	0.97	0.54	0.69	0.85	1.41
■ All high—District	0.84	0.53	0.58	0.48	0.14

■ All elementary—District   ■ All middle—District   ■ All high—District

respectively, in all grade levels are positive, with several quite large residuals appearing in math. Noteworthy residuals include .73 in middle school reading, .97 in middle school math, and .84 in high school math in 2003; and .91 in elementary school reading and 1.04 and 1.41 in elementary and middle school math in 2007.

High School Graduation Rates

Depending on which graduation rate calculation is used, Aldine's graduation rate is slightly below the national average graduation rate of 75 percent.[6] Around 2004, the National Center for Educational Accountability (NCEA) began to use several different methods for estimating graduation rates to take advantage of the advances made in graduation rate calculation, prompted by the increase in data available through NCLB. Thus, three different calculations were presented to Prize decision makers for reviewing each district's graduation rate. The district's disaggregated graduation rates look different in each of the methods, particularly in the Manhattan Institute method. Aldine's graduation rate from 2001 to 2004 remained somewhat below the national averaged freshman graduation rate (AFRG) of 70 percent.[7] The highest graduation rate found for Aldine in 2004 was under the AFRG method at 62 percent for all students, and under the Manhattan Institute method in 2003 and 2004 at 79 percent and 73 percent, respectively, for white students.[9] Increasing the graduation rate is one area that now-retired Aldine superintendent Nadine Kujawa cited in interviews as a remaining issue of focus and concern for the district.

DISTRICT PRACTICES BY THEME

Although some areas still need improvement, the data included in this case illustrates increases in student performance in areas where many districts struggle. Even when compared with the state, Aldine has shown areas of excellence that suggest the district is moving in the right direction with its educational practices.

Interviews with Aldine staff from central office down to the classroom revealed a tightly knit community of people who are vigilant in their commitment to their students. Unlike many districts that cite their challenging demographics early and frequently as an obstacle to success, Aldine educators mention their students' hardships only as a reason for urgency in improving instruction and for raising expectations and creating opportunities for success. Central office interviewees primarily focused on what the adults in the system needed to do to raise student achievement. In the schools, principals and teachers often discussed their work passionately, frequently in their descriptions of their students. One principal referred to students in his school as, "Kids who are fearful but have great potential." A teacher's comment represents a sentiment captured in numerous teacher interviews:

A lot of our kids are raised by themselves or a stranger. A lot of the teachers take the place of the parents, so we involve ourselves a lot more than other people. Many students come to class sleepy; maybe they don't have a place to stay. It's not an excuse; we still expect them to learn. For many of them, their only dream is what goes on here. We try to teach them there is more to life than just survival.

Aldine's work is based on the core belief that all students can learn. This is not an uncommon belief statement; I have heard it in many districts. Yet central office leaders, principals, teachers, and even parents in Aldine can explain exactly what that means. In 2004, Superintendent Kujawa stated:

We have to believe we can make a difference in the learning of each child. A lot of things have to come into play to support that belief. Teachers have to know what the child has to master. We need to give the teacher the tools. As [educators], we are guilty of saying, "If you just teach, they will learn." We've got to come back in with new tools that give that teacher the strategy and tools to help that child learn. Professional development also fits in, and you have to monitor. All those things add up, but there has to be the belief, first of all, that we can make a difference.

When asked where their "reform story" began, central office leaders responded that it began with the state accountability system and the knowledge that students "felt good" but that the data showed that students could not all read or write. Meanwhile, colleagues from area colleges and businesses also pointed out the need for Aldine students to improve, with several stating that Aldine students "cannot even read technical journals." Deciding that below-grade-level performance for any student was unacceptable, the district embarked on "a top-down to grassroots reform," focusing on a change in philosophy involving the entire district.

Superintendent Kujawa explained that Aldine's reform path was difficult and required an "aggressive stand." The main point of resistance came from a handful of high school teachers, who were told, "Low student performance in not acceptable. You have to deliver or change." The important next step, according to Kujawa, was ensuring the actors in the system had the tools and support for change. To ensure that teachers and students truly understood what had to be taught and learned, Aldine began its reform work by clearly defining what all students must know and be able to do at all grade levels, and focusing consistently on the same goals and priorities over time, making changes only to further refine its current work.

Once teaching and learning expectations were defined, the district worked to fully align and coordinate all practices through consistently communicating clear curriculum standards and outcomes to all stakeholders; providing tools to all system levels to achieve desired outcomes; carefully and frequently monitoring implementation and outcomes; and providing effective interventions at the first sign of trouble. When asked to identify the practice area they began with to create their well-aligned system, Aldine administrators pointed to the first theme of NCEA's Best Practice Framework: Curriculum and Academic Goals. Although it did significant work within the other Framework themes, the district worked initially and most extensively on its curriculum.

Curriculum and Academic Goals

Aldine developed its curriculum by starting with the state standards, which district and school staff felt lacked the clarity needed for teachers to know exactly what to teach and when to teach it. The components of Aldine's curriculum now include benchmark goals based on six-week units, instructional calendars (pacing guides), model lessons, and assessments. The benchmarks clearly articulate the objectives of each state standard to provide greater specificity, and include examples for teachers. The district has mandated benchmark assessments to measure the successes of benchmark goals. The curriculum and its components were created by vertical teams of teachers led by program directors in every academic subject. These teams use data to drive curriculum development, sequencing, and revision. Regular meetings of pre-K through grade 12 "bridge builder" teams closely monitor grade-level transitions to ensure there are no sequential gaps between grades.

The process that got Aldine to its current system of curriculum development and review took several years. Aldine's first large-scale curriculum articulation process was completed in the summer of 1997. During that first part of the process, the district's curriculum-development teams collected feedback from every teacher in the district on what should be taught and at what time of year. The curriculum director stressed the importance of teachers' involvement in the curriculum-development process because "they will be the ones to use it every day." They wanted the final product to create complete understanding by teachers of exactly what was to be covered within each grade level, and to ensure that no essential skills would be missed or unnecessarily duplicated. A second important step in 1997 was to mandate that everybody teach the curriculum, because, as district leaders stressed, "We knew some people were skipping things or staying too long on something." They monitored adherence to the curriculum by using data. Teachers who did not follow the curriculum received "terrible results," as one principal said, on their benchmark assessments. Another principal mentioned a situation with a science teacher who focused most of her time on her favorite topic: genetics. Most of the students in her class missed numerous quarterly exam items that were not covered during that quarter, providing "a real wake-up call" for that teacher.

Looking at data was an important part of the entire curriculum revision process and helped uncover some early gaps in instructional sequencing. For example, teachers found a gap in the curriculum in addressing rounding numbers, so the team added an instructional strand to address that gap. Additionally, the curriculum developers found that the state standards were not rigorous enough to prepare students adequately for graduation and college readiness, so they aimed to extend the standards beyond the minimum state requirements for each grade level. Changes made through the review process created a more seamless "spiraled," or continuous, scope and sequence focused on higher academic levels. When we visited Aldine schools in 2004 and 2005, we saw many lessons that extended instruction to higher cognitive levels through the application of Bloom's Taxonomy.[9] During one team meeting, we observed elementary teachers identifying the cognitive level of their lesson questions based on Bloom's model. Teachers explained that they identified each cognitive level for all their lessons to ensure that their instruction moved beyond basic knowledge and comprehension to higher-level skills, such as application and evaluation.

Further aligning instruction across classrooms, schools coordinate instructional timelines and activities during collaborative planning times so that daily warm-ups, lesson plans, practice and review exercises, and homework assignments are consistent across classrooms. As explained by one teacher, "The curriculum alignment throughout the district works well for our highly mobile population. With our alignment, whatever kids do on one side of the district feeds over to all of the vertical teams." This proved to be true. During two separate visits to Aldine, site visit team members reported seeing similar math warm-ups in different schools and locations. They also saw posted academic objectives of each lesson and a "word wall" in every elementary classroom.

In addition to coordinating instruction across classrooms, the school leadership takes the lead on monitoring implementation of the curriculum and providing supports where they are needed. Implementation is monitored by principals, assistant principals, and core subject "skills specialists," who work together to monitor instruction frequently as well as participate in regular teacher team meetings. Concerns are addressed from a service-oriented perspective, with questions like, "What do you think about that lesson?" or "What might you do differently next time?"

Our classroom visits and focus groups with teachers yielded many positive comments about the curriculum, its components, and the development process. Teachers appreciated having a role in curriculum development and felt that the alignment between grades had a positive impact on their students. One teacher commented

> I think the biggest strength is that our district provides an aligned curriculum for all of our teachers. It addresses the curriculum for every six weeks. It puts the bulk of defining teaching and learning at the district level so that new teachers are not stressed with what they should be teaching. The curriculum addresses each objective and the prior knowledge that should be there. When I started teaching, there was just a guideline, but now there is no question about what you should be teaching.

The teachers interviewed did not seem to feel stifled by having instruction outlined in specific six-week increments. They felt they could easily strike a balance between covering the designated objectives in each six weeks and having freedom to decide exactly how to teach. New teachers in particular thought that having clear guidelines for instruction and pacing was helpful. One teacher said, "Our curriculum is a strength, as I know where I am going day to day. It has helped me prepare for future planning."

When asked how their intense curricular focus affected student achievement, district interviewees stated that the link between benchmarks, pacing guides, and common assessments moved the district from Academically Acceptable to Recognized status in a year's time.[10] Interviewees asserted that this performance jump was not owing to a tighter focus on test scores, but rather to a focus on exactly what teachers should teach and when. One district leader said, "We can't close the door and just teach dinosaurs in a vacuum just because we always did that unit. If you teach the curriculum, the test takes care of itself."

In addition to curriculum, goal planning is an aligned activity in Aldine. In the elementary school we visited, teachers said that they all sit down together at the beginning of the year and review data from the previous year to identify target goals. Goals are set to address academics, attendance, and interventions for students. School goals are based on each school's unique needs, and then summarized into vertical goals (school feeder pattern), which roll up into the overall district goals.

Staff Selection, Leadership, and Capacity Building

One way to ensure consistency across a district is to have a stable workforce. Aldine's leadership and teaching force is marked by longevity at both the district and school level. Numerous teachers and administrators remarked that they had been with the district for over twenty years. The district is vigilant in getting the right people into place, training them well, and providing easily accessible support. One method of ensuring strong principals is a multistep interview process involving a district screening by an area superintendent, a panel review with other principals addressing numerous operational and instructional topics, a written document prepared by the prospective candidate to be reviewed by the panel, and an interview with a panel of school staff members where the vacant position resides.

The details of this multistep process demonstrate the effort Aldine puts into selecting appropriate leaders for its schools. The initial district screening interview, done at the area superintendent level, focuses primarily on the needs of the building associated with the position opening. The district human resources (HR) director asserted that this tailored process is working well to match candidates to schools. After the initial screening, several candidates are selected to interview with a panel of current staff members within the vertical team that the new principal would work with. The same instrument is used during these panel interviews; it addresses instructional management, student management, hiring processes, facilities, community, and stakeholder engagement. There is also a curriculum and instruction component that drills down to the specific needs for that school. For example, a candidate interviewing for a school that is struggling with the performance of English language learners (ELL) would need to show knowledge and experience in teaching ELL students. The candidate also is expected to provide a written narrative on how he or she will take the prospective school to higher levels of performance.

New principals are often recruited from within the district in order to maintain the district's culture and processes. District culture is bolstered by two internal preparation programs—one for new assistant principals and the other for more experienced assistant principals who have three or more years of experience and are ready to become principals. This internal recruitment process was executed with extreme care and forethought to address a gap in the principal pool created by attrition due to a large number of retiring principals and the simultaneous opening of two campuses. To provide an ample supply of principals, particularly at the secondary level, the district trains elementary principals to become leaders at middle or high schools. While the regular internal program prepares them for the instructional aspect, this secondary-focused approach requires more training on managing buildings where the scale of operations and practices is much larger. Moving elementary principals to secondary schools has also resulted in the interesting side effect of bringing useful elementary concepts to higher grade levels, such as the use of proven reading remediation practices.

When asked about retaining principals, the HR director first mentioned the importance of correctly matching principals to schools. Second, he pointed to the importance of providing quality support to new leaders, because, "Everyone has to have a first year, whether they are a principal or a teacher." These supports are extremely important for new principals, because, as the HR director said, "You can't afford to lose a year with eight hundred children." Thus, new principals have a mentor (often a retired principal), and area superintendents bring in people to assist new principals with budgets and instructional issues and to conduct leadership-related book studies. To provide systemwide connectivity and additional support, all principals receive assistance from their area superintendent and the district superintendent through monthly principals' meetings and trainings, opportunities to meet with school-level peers once a week, and vertical team meetings of principals twice a week. In addition to its support efforts, the district attributed its positive principal retention rate to its ability to offer some of the highest salaries in Texas.

Aldine leaders work equally hard to put high-quality teachers in its classrooms. Given that Aldine ISD might be less well-known and perceived as less appealing than its larger metropolitan neighbor, Houston ISD, the district works very hard and applies a "global marketing strategy" to lure talented educators to its district. To recruit teachers, Aldine uses a plethora of methods, such as maintaining close partnerships with universities; recruiting from job fairs; placing ads on billboards, in newspapers, and on the radio; and engaging a consultant who identifies where specific teachers can be found. Additionally, the district hosts a large number of student teachers, who often become candidates for permanent positions. As one way to obtain more bilingual teachers, the district created a "grow your own" program to encourage bilingual aides to become teachers by paying their full salary, tuition, and books. In return, the aides work twenty hours per week and must earn a C+ or greater in their coursework. Another recruiting method is to offer annual stipends ranging from $1,500 for regular teachers to $3,500 for teachers in hard-to-staff areas such as special education, bilingual education, math, science, and reading.

Teachers are selected through an initial screen at central office and then through intensive school-based interviews. At the school level, teacher selection in Aldine is often more dynamic than the traditional question-driven interview. At the elementary school we visited in 2005, the principal described how interviews are tailored to the specific position and require the candidates to respond to various instructional scenarios. Candidates are asked to teach a model lesson or to bring in a sample lesson plan. One high school principal told us that she intentionally hires a small number of elementary teachers to infuse early-grade approaches in her high school, such as creating print-rich classrooms. She felt the addition of teachers who "are not wedded to their subject" helped transform the overall philosophy of her staff.

As it does with principals, Aldine retains teachers through above-average salaries, attractive compensation packages, numerous professional development opportunities, and timely instructional supports. In addition to the typical supports, such as mentors and principals who are well-trained instructional leaders, Aldine provides continuous and accessible assistance to teachers through campus-based instructional specialists who work with teachers directly in their classrooms. Many schools choose to use Title I dollars to fund positions for additional specialists; for example, it gives some elementary schools as many as five core-subject specialists who plan instruction, observe and coach, and team-teach with classroom teachers. Teachers meet with the specialists at least weekly on an individual basis and also attend weekly grade-level meetings.

Another key resource for teachers in Aldine is other teachers. Collaboration was frequently mentioned by interviewees, who said that it is "not mandated" but is "strongly encouraged." District and school schedules allow for regular collaboration among same-grade-level (horizontal) and across-grade-level (vertical) teachers. In elementary schools, structured collaboration time is easier to implement because the elementary school schedule typically provides common planning time for teachers in the same grade and subject. In high school, due to block scheduling, teachers are not able to maintain common planning time as easily, but many were able to work around the schedule. In a 2005 interview, Superintendent Kujawa noted that high school teachers were given an additional period off to meet and plan together. During team meetings, teachers work together to plan calendars and activities, review student progress, and share classroom lessons and materials. When asked about their main source of support, teachers often cited their fellow teachers as an invaluable resource for ideas, materials, and encouragement. One new teacher pointed out how different the collegial astrosphere was in Aldine compared to her old district:

Teamwork is the one thing I was not accustomed to. I came from a state where there was no team aspect and I was on my own. Here, there are three other teachers in my grade, and we help each other plan for the next week by dividing the work . . . which is great, because knowing what I'm going to be doing for the next couple of weeks allows me to come to work with a smile on my face and not be stressed. That has been great.

During one teacher team meeting observed by the site team, a group of third-grade teachers followed a preformed agenda and discussed math lessons for the week. The meeting was led by a math-skills specialist who ensured that everyone had a chance to talk. During the meeting, teachers shared ideas on how they taught place value, and several teachers brought their own materials to share with their colleagues. The teachers' animation and willingness to share ideas and materials confirmed the value they placed on each other's expertise while they worked to further align their classroom instruction.

When asked which districtwide reform had the greatest effect on improving student achievement, the superintendent cited "the simple act of getting teachers to plan together, to talk together, and support each other for the benefit of the youngsters." Teacher collaboration, according to Kujawa, was crucial for changing the culture in the district from being teacher-centered to student-centered. In Aldine, that meant moving from an "I deliver the information and it's your [the student's] job to get it; and if you don't, I did my part" mind-set to "I take full responsibility for my students' learning, and if they don't learn, it's up to me to figure out how to do it differently."

Professional development is selected based on student needs identified in school plans and by teacher and principal requests. When describing professional development, interviewees at all system levels mentioned that the process starts with reviewing data to target problem areas and ends with reviewing data to evaluate the effectiveness of various training offerings. There is a balance between district-mandated uniform training and school-selected training. Schools create their own professional development plans based on their student performance and classroom walkthrough data. Principals take the professional development training before teachers do, so they know what to look for when monitoring lessons to support implementation and instruction. To help make training more concrete, the district makes videos of model lessons for principals and teachers to view and discuss.

To bridge the gap between training and actual implementation of new instructional strategies or programs, the district- and school-based skills specialists provide training follow-up for teachers. This follow-up is an important element that is often missing from professional development programs. Rather than expecting a teacher to be able to confidently implement a new instructional strategy after one afternoon training session, the district and schools provide teachers guidance—allowing co-teaching with a skills specialist, providing observation feedback, or giving teachers the opportunity to observe other teachers with more experience in that particular instructional strategy.

In the high school we visited in 2005, a principal told us that professional development and collaborative planning time was carved out in the schedule during weekly forty-five-minute sessions (half of their weekly ninety-minute planning time). During that time, teachers reviewed data reports and discussed student needs. The department head who also attended the interview said that she emphasized having teachers themselves model training to make the meetings more hands-on and interactive. Explaining how it worked, the teachers referenced a session they had developed on teaching reading, which is a difficult challenge at the high school level. They trained numerous teachers on their selected method, including a science teacher who then applied what she learned in her science classes. Convinced that her students were doing better because of the increased focus on reading, she advocated for every department to replicate the training across the school. She also asserted that she would not have felt as comfortable teaching reading concepts had the training not been as interactive and practice-based.

Teachers who participated in interviews made many positive remarks about the numerous training opportunities offered by the district and their schools. One told us that the district tended to focus on "refining" staff development rather than "just jumping on a bandwagon." She mentioned that she had had six consecutive years of training in higher-order thinking (Bloom's Taxonomy) that allowed her to continually drill down to understand and implement the model well. The well-structured design of the district and school professional development was a pleasant departure from the typical 150-page book I receive in many districts when I ask about teacher training. In Aldine, teachers pointed out how specific training topics helped them improve classroom instruction and that their training opportunities were seen as a valued benefit provided to them. Regarding structure, teachers and principals described how training offers were based on areas of need indicated by student performance data. Teachers often stated that the training they received in their district and school was relevant and directly tied to their needs and instructional goals.

New teachers also felt their induction experiences were helpful. They particularly appreciated the opportunities provided by their schools to observe various experienced teachers to understand different instructional and management styles. In our focus group with eight randomly selected new teachers, there was not one teacher who did not have a story about how a particular principal, teacher, or team of teachers helped him or her through what is well known to be a very difficult time. One new teacher told how she took over a position midyear and was impressed that she was immediately given a mentor, a substitute teacher to free up time for her to observe other teachers, and the opportunity to meet with a team of teachers who shared their materials and helped her plan lessons. She felt the support provided to her was above and beyond what typical new teachers receive. To her surprise, "They didn't just throw me in; it was an easy adjustment for me." Another new teacher described how the skills specialists were extremely helpful during her first year, assisting her to "get through all the paperwork, the teaching aspect, and all the information like the cumulative folders [student records]." From receiving daily e-mails with lesson plans to having someone in the classroom modeling instructional techniques, the new teachers felt they were provided with the best possible resources to succeed.

To this day, I remember how enthusiastic some teachers were when asked what motivated them to teach in their particular district and school. During one school-based interview in 2005, one teacher praised the high-level of support she received at her school: "I'm sold! I'm here! I'm telling you, whatever I need, they make sure I have, so I stay here. I'm very impressed with how the district supports you with what you need." When I asked another teacher, "What keeps you here at Aldine?" she responded:

I feel respect. When I first started teaching [in another district], I didn't feel respect, and I feel it now, and it makes a difference. I love teaching. I always wanted to be a teacher and to work with low-income kids. Nobody could pay me enough money to leave; it's nice. But it's not about the money, it's about the kids.

Instructional Programs, Practices, and Arrangements

Although Aldine mandates the use of the curriculum and certain practices such as participating in regularly scheduled teacher team meetings, the district does not mandate that its schools use particular programs. Therefore, principals and school staff have the autonomy to select programs suited to their needs as determined by student achievement scores, benchmark results, and teacher input. Consequently, Aldine has adopted the philosophy that "results, not programs, are mandated." Though program selection is a school decision, district program directors review program implementation at schools, model instructional approaches, and provide feedback to the district on the progress of each program. When the data reveals a weakness, they provide schools with extra funding and/or support for programs or other initiatives (i.e., professional development, extended time for instruction or planning, etc.) to support improvement. One very important practice that the district remains vigilant about is replacing programs that do not work rather than continuing to use them and hoping for better results. Principals are also encouraged to conduct a cost analysis and review research prior to program selection to ensure programs yield maximum results while being cost-effective.

In our 2005 focus group with principals, we decided to get a sense of how decisions were distributed between schools and the central office. When asked if principals liked that central office selected instructional programs, one principal responded,

Central office people have time to review different programs and find out what research says, and they share that with us. It's great for me to allow them that freedom. I don't have to deal with finding time for research—I have enough on my plate. Central office supports us and involves us to the extent we want to be involved.

Another commented, "It takes some pressure off of us and allows us to stay focused as instructional leaders and not managers.

The site visit team heard about a newly developed ninth-grade academy during our 2005 visit to a high school. The principal said that the academy was based on the "small learning community" concept. The academy would tie ninth-grade students to a career connection, and those students would stay in that academy until they graduated. Core teachers would have the same students three days a week and meet in teams with other teachers who shared their students to coordinate the students' entire instructional program. The program was designed to provide more individualized attention to the school's growing number of struggling ninth-graders.

To ensure proper implementation of selected programs, classroom instruction is continually monitored by district and school administrators looking for evidence of high-quality teaching and learning. Principals review lesson plans regularly to determine if the plans appropriately address standards and reach high cognitive levels, and principals follow up their reviews with frequent classroom observations. When asked what "high-quality" teaching looks like, one principal responded that it is evidenced by higher-level thinking skills, which means products instead of worksheets. She continued, "We want lots of hands-on activities so kids can see connections and understand [that] what is taught is important and relevant."

Because instruction appears to be based on student need instead of on the state standards, school interviewees often mentioned that they created materials rather than relying solely on textbooks. One teacher said, "Textbooks are seen as supplemental resources rather than what drives instruction. It is the timeline and curriculum that drive instruction." After we heard this message at several schools, teachers clarified for us that they created lessons based on their district curriculum rather than following textbook pages from the first to the last page. One skills specialist noted that her school tended to use funds to hire additional support staff and purchase manipulatives rather than buying expensive print materials.

One of the reasons why The Broad Prize process includes an extensive site visit is to observe system connectivity and to witness teacher meetings and classroom instruction. We want to know if a district's performance success results from rigorous test-prep drilling or if there is something it is doing that truly points to high-quality instruction. In Aldine, there are many references to formative and summative assessment results, but only as a means of focusing the system on student needs, supports, and resources. As far as instruction goes, the goal is to extend the minimum state standards to ensure students are prepared for graduation and the next steps. Interviews throughout the district, even with the chief finance officer, emphasized that "the test doesn't matter; good instruction will yield good results." At the elementary school, the principal described her instructional philosophy as "Teach the content, not the test, and teach the kids." However, she did admit that the new Texas Assessment of Knowledge and Skills (TAKS) (first implemented in 2003) was more difficult and that the campus had to "kick instruction up a notch." Thus, she worked with the district's initiative to raise instruction to higher cognitive levels, and with teachers on helping students apply their learning to real-life situations. She gave estimation as an example: "First you teach them the actual skill, and then have them apply it to real-world situations, like estimating prices when they go to the grocery store with their parents."

The district has also shown a lot of creativity in solving programmatic or instructional problems that it could not solve internally. In our 2005 interviews, central office administrators described a partnership they formed with Rice University to help them retool the math curriculum to address issues with number sense. Personnel from both organizations sat down and discussed which concepts should be taught and in what grade to teach them. The end result was an improved math curriculum. Aldine administrators believe it is important to provide teachers with the necessary research, support, and training to be successful in raising achievement for their students.

Monitoring, Analysis, and Use of Data

The previous three themes allude to the importance Aldine places on data to inform its decision-making processes and practices. Central office administrators asserted that data provides the road map to (1) identify strengths and weaknesses of curriculum and instruction; (2) monitor alignment of written curriculum, classroom instruction, and student assessment; and (3) monitor progress from the district, campus, teacher, and student levels. Bolstered by the philosophy of leaving nothing to chance, Aldine has a rich data and monitoring system that includes formative and summative assessments, a multilevel scorecard, a structured walkthrough process, and a powerful data management system that ties all the pieces together.

One of Aldine's most impressive features is the frequency with which the district monitors student progress on an ongoing basis. District-mandated and -developed benchmark assessments are given every nine weeks in all core areas. In addition to district-level assessments, schools have developed common assessments that are given as frequently as every two to three weeks in all grades and core subjects.[11] Frequent feedback from these assessments helps teachers and principals identify weak instructional objectives early and are often used in teacher team meetings to plan future instruction.

Aldine tracks common and benchmark assessments using the Triand data management system.[12] Serving as a "one-stop data shop," Triand allows teachers to access student scores on summative and formative assessments; student profiles, records, and transcripts; as well as curriculum scope and sequence, lesson plans, and resource materials. It also allows them to query state and local assessments immediately with a powerful disaggregation and item analysis tool. To maximize effectiveness, Aldine mandates that every teacher upload classroom data into this system with the help of Scantron machines that eliminate the need to enter data by hand.

In addition to analyzing performance data, Aldine frequently monitors classroom activities through observations and walkthroughs. Teachers are routinely observed by principals, department chairs, and their peers who have been trained to use a structured rubric to record their walkthrough observations and conduct follow-up conferences. Area superintendents and program chairs also spend time in schools and classrooms monitoring instruction.

The common assessments, student performance data, and walkthroughs are used to develop district, department, campus, and subject- or grade-level action plans. Each action plan delineates goals and objectives, specific tasks, people responsible, measures of success, monetary resources, and timelines. The action plans are monitored by scorecards that are tied to each level of an action plan. Based on the Baldrige model, the scorecards measure the success levels within the action plans.[13]

Superintendent Kujawa illustrated how well the pieces tie together to the scorecards: the scorecards monitor progress toward district and school goals, and the goals "go right back to the improvement plan and show how well we met the goals." Once the scorecards are compiled, a vertical plan goes to the district, and campuses can compare their results with each other and compare their data. The data is also distributed to department chairs and teachers. Kujawa describes the philosophy of their approach as:

> Monitoring as you go, and doing more frequent monitoring at the lowest level. A scorecard comes up [from classroom to district] the system; it doesn't start with the district and go down. It is a very systemic structured way of knowing immediately that forty out of one hundred of my kids didn't master that concept. Then we move to root causes to solve it.

Principals and teachers in Aldine stressed that the district's close scrutiny at every level is seen as an important tool for instruction rather than a "gotcha." Teachers and administrators alike highlighted the importance of having information early to focus on prevention rather than intervention. Illustrating this theory of action, one principal stated, "We're a very focused and proactive district. We are looking ahead and are not reactionary. We anticipate trends and make adjustments as needed." An appreciation for information was prevalent at all levels of the district and was a prominent topic of discussion throughout the site visits.

One principal in a 2005 focus group acknowledged that any change, such as when the district first introduced the benchmark process, "can be frightening, as it [puts] a lot more accountability on teachers for what they [are] covering in the classroom." However, he felt that the biggest tension was not in the benchmarks as much as in "getting all the revisions and everything done." Although he felt the new benchmark system was "rough in the beginning," he also felt that teachers were grateful for "having an organization of what they need to do and are expected to teach." Another elementary principal told us that she was not yet implementing scorecards on the teacher level because she did not feel her teachers were comfortable or ready for it yet. Acknowledging a similar challenge, a high school principal said that he had had teacher-level scorecards for the past two years, and that it had taken those two years to get teachers comfortable enough that "they could have open dialogue and talk about constructive suggestions and understand they aren't personal." He said the process "cannot be done overnight"; that it is a sensitive issue that has taken a lot of reading and discussing about how to build learning communities and break the common high school model of "content-driven academies." Now his teachers are so comfortable with data that they post their assessment results where all staff members can look and see where gaps need to be filled. This principal felt the scorecards prompted collaboration and ownership of "what the whole school is doing."

Teachers at all grade levels referenced efforts to help students monitor their own progress by keeping track of their mastery of objectives in portfolios. Students are made aware of how missing homework affects their grades, and they know overall how they are doing. One teacher described how she addresses this issue with her students:

> I show each student their grades in my electronic grade book. Then I replace a few of their grades with zeros and say, "See what happens with a few zeros? Or, see how much these three 70s can pull down your grade?" Then they understand the importance of each assignment.

One high school teacher described the process she uses with her students as using "checkpoints" to track their instructional objectives for the year: "The students know what their objectives are and know where their weaknesses are. We can pull out their portfolios and show them, 'This is where you were, and this is where you are now.'"

Recognition, Intervention, and Adjustment

The many data systems in Aldine help identify strengths and weaknesses at all levels of the system. When weaknesses are found, district initiatives and interventions are selected through a systematic "root cause analysis." Stakeholders from all levels of the system are involved in this process and work together by backward mapping through the data to pinpoint deficiencies. Some recent initiatives resulting from this process include extended reading time mandated across the district and the disbursement of class-size-reduction grants targeted for second- through fifth-grade classes.

Interventions for struggling schools are addressed through an intervention team of program directors and area superintendents whose task is to help build and implement specific improvement plans. Typically, schools receive assistance as soon as scores begin to drop so that support comes before problems become extensive. The interventions may include additional staff development and planning time for teachers, extended-day programs for students, or additional resources like materials or subject-specific skills specialists. Interventions for struggling teachers begin with classroom visits and walkthroughs by school administrators and/or core subject department chairs at the high school level. Areas of concern are addressed first informally through additional supports, such as assistance from skills specialists, or through training.

One department chair described how he supports several teachers at once through impromptu one-hour training sessions held before school. Department chairs and school leaders also match struggling teachers to mentors or "buddies" who are available for teachers to ask for advice. Principals may decide to develop a more formal plan to address specific teacher needs. Plans may include additional support from program directors, one-on-one time with skills specialists, or opportunities to attend targeted professional development. If further intervention is needed, the school or district may mandate corrective activities or seek intervention by the human resources department. At the high school level, departments often work together to support teachers. One math department chair described how the department supported its teachers by having them conduct walkthroughs to learn different instructional strategies, identifying areas that need work, and then working with the teachers to develop a plan of action to address the issue. The entire process is supported by reviewing data, particularly by item analysis, to ensure the instructional interventions are working with the teacher.

Struggling students are supported through the creation of individual plans designed to address specific needs or objectives missed on assessments. The plans may include specific interventions such as extended-day, -week, or -year instruction, night and virtual schools, tutoring, double-block scheduling, remediation courses, learning labs, and assistance by skills specialists.

Teachers at Aldine feel that they have many tools and supports available to address the individual needs of their students. One teacher commented,

> Students are looked at as individuals rather than a group. For example, we had 30 seniors who failed the TAKS test, and we pulled them into a focus group where an experienced teacher who had prior success with those kinds of students worked with them to help them succeed. I like that we have that kind of flexibility to help students.

The site team witnessed the philosophy of collective accountability for all students in action, observing the flexible movement of students from one teacher to another. One elementary principal explained that teachers use data from common assessments to pair student weaknesses with teacher strengths to allow flexible movement from classroom to classroom for the benefit of students. Sure enough, we saw third-grade students moving from one classroom to another to work with a small group of students and a teacher. It appeared to be a common comfortable practice within that school.

INFLUENCING FACTORS

Many of the themes delineated above contain factors under the control of most educational systems. However, we know that schools and districts do not exist in a vacuum; they are located in neighborhoods and communities, and can serve as either key supports or barriers for improvement efforts. Aldine is a district that exists within a tight, supportive community that appears to all have the same goals for the district and subsequently the community. Both internal and external relationships are characterized by much support and pride in the district's accomplishments.

School Board

Stability, trust, and support are all characteristics found within the district's relationships with other key stakeholders. In the 2004 and 2005 Aldine interviews, both the superintendent and school board president described their relationship as one of respect, trust, and open communication. Aldine has an elected board with seven seats and long-term stability evidenced by board tenures ranging from two to twenty years. The board member I interviewed in 2005 said she had served for thirteen years, and many of the other members fell between fifteen to twenty years of service. The newest member had been elected the previous May. In addition to longevity, the board shared a lot of team-building activities. Superintendent Kujawa observed that her long tenure in the district holding various positions also helped garner the board's respect for her leadership. Her approach to the board was always "honest, upfront communication." She explained further, "If something is going on, we get knowledge to them before anything hits the TV." Kujawa also mentioned that she respected the board's role in setting the vision and expectations for the district, as well as its governance and monitoring authority. This approach seems to work well; Kujawa told us that there were few noteworthy policy disagreements during the previous year or at the time of our 2004 interview. She attributed that fact to their relationship and ability to "hammer things out" through discussions and by reaching consensus.

The board president confirmed Kujawa's statements, saying that the board relied on her expertise and experience and felt that Kujawa would "do what is best for the students and employees." They liked that she communicated frequently with them and worked hard at team building. The board president also mentioned the importance of the district having a set vision and data to measure progress toward that vision. She also felt the tools put in place by the district provided a clear-cut action plan with measurable goals and objectives that could be assessed and used to communicate progress to various stakeholders.

Union/Association

Although Texas is a right-to-work-state, there is still a union (often referred to as "association") presence in the districts. Like the school board president, the association presidents in both 2004 and 2005 were well aware of the district's goals and plans and cited student achievement and success as the district's number-one focus. The association president interviewed in 2005 felt that the district hired qualified teachers, and that the teachers were well supported. When asked about the role of the association, she stated that it was to "make sure all teachers and students are treated fairly." She felt the district did a good job working jointly on the same goals, and that they worked together to "give students and teachers the best and safest place to come to." This leader also noted that the movement of professional development to a more local school-based model was an important mutually agreed-on change with the district, and mentioned no particular issues of contention. Regarding educational issues, she stated that the association "doesn't come into it very much in an official capacity." However, she did observe that the superintendent was always willing to listen to input from the association, and she characterized Kujawa as "always having an open door." This association leader, like the board president, felt that Kujawa was "very student centered" and would do "whatever it takes to make sure that learning takes place."

Community

Interviews with a focus group of various community and business leaders also confirmed their awareness of the district's goals of "producing the nation's best." One business leader said, "The board and district believe that setting high expectations for the kids, providing encouragement, and allocating the proper resources to support instruction will help [the students] live up to those expectations."

In addition to having a thorough knowledge about what was happening in the district and schools, community members often quoted Nadine Kujawa or other district leaders and teachers. They frequently mentioned the district's consistency and focus, using a favorite quote of Kujawa's: "Keep the main thing the main thing." Another stated, "Let's not be bashful when we need to be bold." The community members emphasized the importance of the district as an integral part of the community, and they appreciated the district's efforts to solicit their input as partners in education. The power of that partnership is illustrated through an example involving a poor district neighborhood near an airport, which had 454 apartment units that had become dilapidated. When the owner was sent to prison on unrelated issues, the redevelopment authority and district jointly contributed $2 million to buy the property and build a new elementary school.

Almost every member in the community focus group described the district as being very "child-centered" and focused on the individual student. One interviewee who represented the local YMCA gave a particularly poignant description of the culture and climate of the district, stating:

> This district has a number of kids who would fall through the cracks and end up being a burden on society as opposed to an asset without the district's individual attention. Their intent is to break a cycle of people that are growing up in areas that might not be conducive to achievement. A lot of these kids are walking around thinking no one cares about them, but then they come to the classroom and see that teacher and administrator that knows them

by name and really shows a personal interest in them. That helps that child to start believing in themselves. Some of them are not getting that positive reinforcement at home, and they are getting it here.

Parents

The parent group also immediately cited "all children can learn" as the district belief during their focus group interview in 2004. Parents recognized that the district and schools worked hard to communicate with parents and include them through a "teamlike" atmosphere. The parents also liked the district's "open-door policy," which meant they were welcome to come anytime to observe classroom instruction. Others mentioned the many resources provided to parents by the district, including workshops to help with parenting skills and teaching methods, and subject-specific nights like reading and science night.

As with many urban districts, parent involvement was a common topic of concern that came up in the district, school, teacher, and even parent interviews. The parent focus group members mentioned that the district tried to accommodate parents by offering to pick them up for meetings and encouraging other parents to become involved with the schools. High school parent involvement, the eternal tough nut to crack, was also a concern at Aldine. Some of the parents thought that the high school students did not want their parents involved because they feared they would be stigmatized by their peers. Many parents cited obstacles to parent involvement such as language issues, fear of the school in general, and long work hours.

The parents mentioned looking forward to a new student information system being developed that year, a "parent portal" that would allow them to see their children's homework and ongoing progress through an online system. When asked what reforms they believed were the most effective for student achievement, they cited the district's focus on the early grades such as pre-K and kindergarten and their "child-centered" approach.

Governance, Organization, and Decision Making

In addition to the board and superintendent clearly understanding their roles, central office and school leaders also understood the areas in which they had authority and which practices were more centralized or decentralized. We paid particular attention to this issue during our 2004 interviews, as there was much research percolating at that time about which practices were best centralized and which were best decentralized. We wanted to know what budget authority principals had, and how staffing, program selection, and other instructional decisions were made between central office and school leaders.

When asked how decision-making authority was distributed, Superintendent Kujawa said, "It is the principal's responsibility to see that children in their school learn, and that is nonnegotiable. Other than that, they have flexibility within reason." She further elaborated that flexibility depended on what the request was and the particular principal's record. If the issue is curriculum, she noted, the principal would have to go through the "proper channels." Additionally, Kujawa mentioned that she always ensures principals are "kept in the loop" through the area superintendents, and that was a priority for her. Regarding outsourcing functions from central office, Kujawa listed the development of the data system and some HR marketing materials, and that the Regional Service Center outsourced electrical resources.

Principals in both individual and focus group interviews all seemed to agree that they had the authority to make appropriate decisions to support student needs in their schools. While they listed a few nonnegotiable areas such as the district benchmarks and assessments, they felt they were provided an appropriate amount of freedom to make their own decisions about delivering instruction. One principal observed, "There are some guidelines the district passes on to us, but the delivery of that is left to the campus." Regarding budget discretion, principals also felt they had authority over their budgets. A principal in one focus group remarked:

> I have discretion over the use of my funds. I can plan my programs how I would like. It is very straight forward—we have to serve our students. We

have control over how our schools are run and over the things we need. We are trusted to do the best thing for our students, teachers, and our schools. Daily operations are left to us.

Teachers also felt their input and expertise was well utilized by both central office and school leaders. Several teachers mentioned having the opportunity to meet with the superintendent and that they had weekly access to area superintendents. Teachers voiced appreciation at having "a place at the table" at their schools in decision-making processes, and they enjoyed sharing their expertise in areas such as curriculum development and lesson planning. Illustrating the "open climate" and ability to provide input, one teacher asserted:

> We can attend stakeholder vertical team meetings and have access to area superintendents almost weekly. If people are upset and not taking these opportunities, it is their own fault. You don't always get your way in a large district, but there are tons of things we are voting on. We have input if we give it.

Resource Allocation

Aldine is one of the districts in Texas that receives what is called "recapture" funds under Chapter 41 of the Texas Education Code, known as the "Robin Hood" plan.[14] As Aldine relies heavily on these funds, it is important to understand a little bit about Chapter 41 and how changes in Texas school finance legislation can affect this district.

In Texas, most school district operations are financed through state funding or local property tax revenues. As local tax bases increase, state contributions to school districts decrease.[15] Because the value of properties varies widely across the state, the Texas Legislature enacted Chapter 41 in 1993 as a means of equalizing wealth for educational spending. Under Chapter 41, a school district is considered wealthy when its property value exceeds a threshold of $305,000.[16]

According to the superintendent and CFO in 2004, Aldine receives approximately $16 million in recapture funds, which helps them "make their budget whole." Thus, as the Legislature discussed revamping the Texas finance system in 2005 (which ended up not happening), Aldine was struggling unsuccessfully to figure out how to replace that potential loss of funds. At the time of the 2005 interview, the district was still unsure if the funding formulas would change and how they would change. During that time, Nadine Kujawa stated:

> If we lose these funds, it will be the first time in our history and mine here that we will not send salary statements with an increase in pay and we do not know what our pot is. It is very risky if the taxing authority moves to the state and we lose control of setting local tax. We have been fiscally sound for the last four years and had a balanced budget by spending within our means—and still we educate our students.

Aldine's funding during the 2004 and 2005 site visits was 58 percent from the state (including recapture funds); 36 percent from local sources; and 6 percent from federal funds. Outlining their financial struggles over the past few years, the CFO mentioned that they had cut $34 million from the budget the previous year, which helped them finish that year with a balanced budget. When asked how they were dealing with the cuts, the superintendent responded, "On a district level, we do not have luxuries." (I can testify to that with the fact that all visitors must pay for coffee out of a machine.) She also mentioned that the district raised teacher–student ratios and focused on streamlining work to be more efficient and effective to offset budget cuts.

The district's overall approach to budgeting is outlined by a very thoughtful, aligned process. The CFO, who has been in his position for over ten years, mentioned that the district bases many of its fiscal decisions on data and student need, rather than on simple formulaic processes. If a school has students with more needs, the CFO ensures they have the resources necessary to meet their educational goals. An additional testimonial to the systemic alignment behind resource allocation in Aldine is the fact that the CFO has intimate knowledge of student performance and the educational programs across the entire district.

The budgeting process at the school level is relatively similar across the district. One high school principal explained that his campus budget is set by a committee comprising of school leaders and teachers. During budgeting, the school receives a lump sum that has some specific earmarks for various federal programs. The committee assesses teacher needs through subject-level department chairs and then builds the budget according to where the data shows attention is needed. The budget is cleared through the area superintendents, CFO, and superintendent.

A middle school principal also described how his committee reviewed data to determine how to target goals and subsequently funds for the upcoming year:

> We sit in our committee and decide, looking at the data, what our needs are. We will direct our spending toward what the data indicates. Last year, the data indicated we fell down in math, so we allocated a little more of our resources for math instruction. With that money, we brought in additional teachers to reduce the student teacher ratio. Also our teachers were sent to workshops to help reform our methods of teaching mathematics.

Agreeing that additional instructional support is a worthwhile investment, an elementary principal described how his school used its large pot of Title I funds mainly for skills specialists to work with teachers. This principal felt putting people directly in classrooms to support teachers provided the best "bang for the buck." "We invest in people, not in things," stated the principal, who hired "six talented teachers whose only duty is to support teachers and work with students."

When asked how the budget cuts affected them, the superintendent and CFO asserted that they work very hard to avoid cutting instructional programs. Superintendent Kujawa recognized that many of the special programs were in "jeopardy," but that the district would hold on to their extra curriculum programs to the "bitter end" because she felt those programs were integral for keeping students tied to their school. School leaders also agreed that the budget reductions affected them, but several asserted that they did their best to invest their funds wisely and to raise whatever they could through grants and creative business and community partnerships.

When asked about challenges, every one of these stakeholder groups mentioned their concern about budget cuts due to the school finance issues that were being addressed at that time. Under the reemerging threat that the equalization legislation would be overturned and concerns over rising costs of fuel and health care, the district continually addresses the challenge of cutting its budget while leaving its instructional program as intact as possible.

Although the district continues to operate with fiscal challenges, it is still managing to be successful, winning The Broad Prize in 2009.

Climate/Culture

District leaders characterize the climate at Aldine as being one of trust and mutual respect. Nadine Kujawa named longevity of staff members and investment in building relationships across the district as major factors in achieving their positive climate. Leaders and teachers at the high school described their school as a place where staff and students want to come. The principal asserted that the school had intentionally focused on climate in the past few years, which included making cosmetic enhancements to make the building look appealing and having staff members study books on poverty and education. Clearly this endeavor must have been successful, as many teachers appeared to be happy in their positions, with one stating that it was a "pleasure" to work at the high school. In fact, her presence in the high school focus group is forever etched in my brain because she suddenly jumped up and told us:

> There is a support system for students, teachers, everyone. It's not easy, there are times that are hard, but we are team members and are there for each other. I can't tell you enough! If I could talk to Broad [Eli Broad, of The

Broad Foundation] himself, I would tell him what I'm doing here and that it is something that I was destined to do! I'm molding minds and futures; it's powerful!

The principal at that high school told us that one of the most important things she learned was how to build a warm climate. Citing an astonishingly low turnover rate of 2 percent (due to retirement), she said it was important to make sure teachers are happy and that they are the emphasis of her focus, a "look from the bottom up." She thus made sure that her teachers felt validated and their opinions were heard. This principal even went up to the school occasionally on Sundays to put a personalized note in every teacher's box. Teachers at all levels across the district described their schools as being very team-oriented, with some of them referring to their colleagues as "family."

The personalized support extended from the teachers down to the students, exemplified by numerous stories told by sometimes-tearful teachers and principals about their students and the importance of their happiness and well-being. Teachers from both elementary and secondary schools were adamant that they did whatever was necessary to help their students succeed in school, whether it meant giving them soap, time to air their fears about events at home, or access to free health-care services. One teacher at an elementary school recounted how she had found a free clinic for one of her students who repeatedly came back to school with pink-eye because his mother could not afford to take him to a doctor. Another teacher told us about a girl whose hair she used to brush every day because "it was a mess, and she was sort of a discipline problem." The student responded well to the personal attention; she continued to visit this teacher throughout her school career and eventually graduated from Xavier University. The teacher was extremely proud of her success, especially because this particular student had had had a traumatic childhood: she had witnessed the murders of both her father and sister when she was in elementary school. As this teacher put it, "We are like their haven. This is probably the only safe structure and environment they have."

Although it is impossible to capture scientifically, most people can describe the way a district or school feels when they first walk in and then see if that "feeling" holds through extended conversations and observations. I can attest to Aldine's positive climate through my own observations, and my opinion has been supported by comments made by various site visit team members and even the project's transcriptionists. Debriefs about the Aldine site visits (even the vicarious ones from the transcriptionists) showed that everyone was happy to be working there. The district's staff members seemed genuinely fond of each other, passionate about their students and work, and proud of their accomplishments in raising student achievement. District and school leaders always discussed their work using the word "we" instead of "I" and often characterized their discussions with others around data and problem solving as supporting one another.

REFORM AND STUDENT ACHIEVEMENT—BRINGING IT TO SCALE

It is always interesting to study a system that has made measurable changes to see what practices or decisions sparked those changes; whether those changes were intentionally designed and connected, what challenges occurred along the way; and how well the changes were actually acculturated throughout the system and sustained. The previous sections highlight the importance Aldine placed on each of the five themes in the Framework and on building positive relationships with internal and external stakeholders. In reviewing where Aldine's reform story began, it appeared the catalyst was the extensive curriculum alignment and revision process that began in the late 1990s. From there, the rest of the pieces were strategically put into place with strong data monitoring systems, effective instructional supports, and a trusting and child-centered culture—all resulting in a well-aligned, connected system.

When asked in the 2004 and 2005 site visits to identify the main reforms that influenced student achievement over the past three years, Superintendent Kujawa mentioned (1) the districtwide change in beliefs that students could achieve at higher levels and that poor student performance was unacceptable; and (2) the importance of teacher collaboration. Additionally, she and many other site visit interviewees also referenced as key the district's curriculum alignment process; use of frequent assessment and monitoring systems; and solving problems collaboratively using the root cause analysis.

Kujawa described the changes in their district as being, "from top down to grass roots, a focus on district and school leadership and setting clear expectations." To bolster the explicit expectations set across the district, Kujawa said, the district led the way by putting strong staff development in place and ensuring that teachers had the right tools and strategies to meet their instructional goals. Once the data showed improved student achievement, stakeholders at all levels of the district were more receptive to the ongoing changes being implemented across the district. Kujawa emphasized the importance of leading off with areas of potential success because, "Success is the biggest motivator of change." To anyone in the system that resisted change, Kujawa would ask, "How important is that child's diploma to you?" Bringing the entire system into their reform strategy took "a lot of collaboration, high expectations, and a lot of assistance from area superintendents, program directors, and curriculum staff to support the change process."

When asked about specific challenges encountered in implementing new practices and structures across the district, Kujawa observed that high schools seemed to be "the most difficult to change." She was referring to the work the district had done to help high school teachers become more "child-centered," rather than teacher-centered, in "a higher education style." The district achieved this shift gradually over a three-year period by having teachers develop lessons collaboratively and share ideas. She felt the change was just beginning to "take root" and show some positive impact on student achievement.

In addition to tackling challenges at the high school, district leaders mentioned the need to focus future efforts at the middle school level. One strategy Aldine plans to implement in the middle school is finding more ways to engage students in their own school work by soliciting ideas from a student advisory group. One such previous group told Kujawa that they could tell when teachers invested more time in lessons and that they appreciated feeling more of a personal connection to their teachers.

When principals were asked about reform challenges, they often mentioned the adoption of the benchmark tests, which teachers were skeptical of at first, but eventually decided were worth the effort. Eventually, principals saw that the frequent instructional feedback gained from the benchmarks helped teachers become more strategic and systematic by anchoring their lessons to a well-paced and aligned curriculum. One principal stated that the resulting communication between teachers both across grades and vertically from lower to higher grades "excited him." He felt the common language developed through the benchmarks allowed teachers to "really talk about instruction and help each other make education better for kids." The benchmarks were also very useful for helping principals and teachers offset the high levels of student mobility they experienced in the district by creating instructional uniformity. One principal said, "No matter where [students] go, east or west, they learn the same thing for the same six weeks."

Although some principals admitted there was "a lot to keep up with" regarding their management and monitoring systems, they did not cite the district's approach to accountability as an issue. In fact, many of them described the district's accountability system as a means of focusing on individual student achievement and identifying and providing support where it was needed. This data-driven strategic approach was much appreciated by the leaders of the schools, as illustrated by one principal who said that the district's performance expectations were:

> . . . very clearly driven to us in a positive way—not beating up the principals. Some districts do that, especially after the scores come in, but I never had that feeling. When I was new two years ago, I knew exactly what my goals were, and I knew looking at all the scores was related to the vision. It was very motivating—not a "gotcha."

Additionally, school leaders voiced appreciation that the district's vision remained focused and unchanged over time. When things got overwhelming and issues became clouded, various stakeholders in the district asked each other, "Stop—what's best for the kids?" From business leaders to custodians, everyone knew the district mantra: "Keep the main thing the main thing."

Teachers typically cited the district's well-aligned curriculum as one of the main reasons their district has been successful. They felt the curriculum focus and communication not only helped them keep well informed about the expected outcomes from each grade level, but also helped them better respond to the needs of business and community members regarding student outcomes. When discussing challenges, teachers mentioned their students' lack of wealth more as a reference for understanding why their students might need more background information than as an excuse for low expectations. When asked how they addressed the challenges their students posed, many said that they respected their students and expected them to succeed. One teacher further explained, "These kids are not used to succeeding. Once they do it, their attitudes change."

Typically, when we are conducting interviews in a district (or any organization, for that matter), it is not difficult to find at least one or two disgruntled teachers, even when conducting interviews for a prize. That was not the case at Aldine. Whether selected by their principal or randomly, teachers made comments about changes in the district and their schools over time that closely mirrored what we heard from central office leaders and principals. For instance, one teacher offered:

> We are never upset with central office. They don't say things we disagree with. It is a process that starts top-down sometimes, and then it becomes a bottom-up process. We work collaboratively. Sometimes we initially squirm, but once implemented, we see how it works.

Another teacher in the focus group agreed, stating, "It seems we are always pushed a little out of our comfort zone, but that is how progress happens. You become willing to take more risks and that is how your comfort zone gets bigger."

Overall, when any stakeholder group in the district was asked about challenges, the most frequently cited concern was the school finance issues and the ability to continually trim their budget without sacrificing their instructional program. A second challenge mentioned by both internal and external stakeholders was raising parent involvement, particularly at the high school level.

Current Performance and Practices

In almost every subject and grade, Aldine's student performance has continued to improve after 2005, as illustrated in the charts provided earlier in this chapter. Additionally, the district exceeded the state in both elementary and middle school math proficiencies, and was almost even with the state in reading in all three aggregated grade levels. Numerous achievement gaps were narrowing at a faster rate than the state in 2007, including the gap between African American and white students in high school reading, between Hispanic and white students in middle school reading, between African American and white students in elementary math, between all minority students and white students in middle school math, and between low-income and non-low-income students in high school math. Figures 2.17 and 2.18 illustrate that Aldine's African American, Hispanic, and low-income students have higher proficiencies rates than their state counterparts in reading and math at every grade level category in 2007.

Additionally, SAT scores for African American and Hispanic students rose between 2004 and 2007; average SAT scores for African American students increased by 23 points and for Hispanic students by 18 points over this period.[17]

Follow-up interviews and discussions with district leadership revealed that the district changed the requirement for administering common assessments every three weeks to being optional every three weeks but required every six weeks, to comply with a recent state policy limiting the number of days a district can test students. However, according to one administrator, some teachers still continue to administer those assessments

FIGURE 2.17

District and state reading proficiencies for 2007 by student group

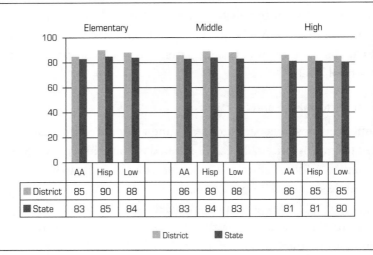

FIGURE 2.18

District and state math proficiencies for 2007 by student group

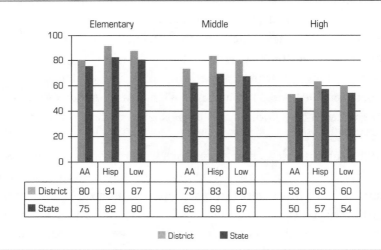

every three weeks, while others feel they are receiving adequate instructional feedback by following the six-week guidelines.

Another interesting change in the district is an addition made to the district's data management system called Desktop Analyst.[18] According to the new superintendent, Dr. Wanda Bamberg, this system helps the district look at operational practices and compare them by student and by schools. In 2008, the district purchased a similar product called Classroom Analyst, which helps leaders examine the growth of students by individual teachers through value-added modeling. District leaders feel this system has helped provide more detailed information on teachers to better match students and/ or classrooms to teachers. According to Dr. Bamberg, these additional pieces have provided even more in-depth information about their school and district practices. Last year, district leaders were able to identify a dropout problem they might not have otherwise found. A second follow-up interview with a district central office leader in 2008 highlighted the district's current focus on math and science, particularly for African American students.

CONCLUSION

Aldine is a relatively large urban district with a number of challenges. Yet the district has been getting attention for its performance successes for almost ten years. During our site visits, we found that Aldine had one of the most integrated, aligned, and data-driven systems of all the finalists. Its scorecard system keeps relationships between the district, school, and classroom levels well coordinated. Additionally, it has managed to keep the same focused goals since 2002; stakeholders just improve upon them and "keep the main thing the main thing." The curriculum is very much aligned, moves beyond the minimum state requirements, and is frequently requested by other districts.

Aldine's climate is one of trust and customer service, which was confirmed by various stakeholders, including representatives from the board, union, community, and parents. Data is used to understand performance and identify where supports might be needed. Conversations about performance are often collaborative and center on brainstorming solutions rather than on finding blame. Teachers' comments about their schools and students are full of optimism, determination, and high standards. As one teacher said, "Children are our main focus. That's what this building and district are about. That is the whole focus—their success."

After years of recognition as a finalist, Aldine finally won The Broad Prize in 2009. What is most interesting about this district is its continued success with a difficult set of circumstances and its ability to create a well-aligned system that fully supports the adults and students in the system. Prior to NCLB, Aldine was working on aligning its system and refining its work. While other districts in the state are just beginning to catch up to Aldine's early successes, regarding student performance, Aldine still remains one of the most talked about and celebrated districts in Texas.

3

Boston Public Schools

Boston Public Schools (BPS), one of the few high-poverty, high-minority school districts in Massachusetts, is the sixty-seventh-largest school district in the nation. In 2005, it had 144 schools, 3,926 teachers, and 60,150 students. BPS has approximately 46 percent African American students, 30 percent Hispanic students, and 14 percent white students, with 73 percent of its students eligible for free and reduced-price lunch and 19 percent designated as English Language Learners.[1] Because Boston has attracted many immigrants, there is much diversity within each of the larger ethnic groups, including sizeable subgroups of Dominican, Cape Verdean, Haitian, Chinese, Vietnamese, and South and Central American immigrants.[2]

By 2005, seventeen of the schools were designated as "Pilot Schools" under an agreement with the Boston Teachers Union to create a group of innovative schools that could operate with more freedoms in scheduling, hiring, budgeting, and curriculum. In addition to the pilots, three of the high schools were called "Exam Schools"—admitting only the district's top-performing students, as determined by a required entrance test.[3]

Established in 1647, BPS is the oldest public school system in the country. Given its size and its history of racial tension and political difficulties—within the culture of the city, in various pockets within the district, and with their teachers union—BPS has many challenges. Throughout its history, the district has experienced involvement from different external stakeholders, including the courts, the business community, and the mayor. The courts became involved during the 1960s and 1970s over racial segregation issues that resulted in a mandatory busing plan and the creation of community-based monitoring and support structures to monitor school compliance with the desegregation orders.[4]

Assisted by the court-mandated partnerships forged between area colleges, public schools, and business schools to support BPS, Boston was primed to provide grassroots community-based support to the district through the creation of the Boston Compact in 1982. The Boston Compact comprised business partnerships with the district, along with higher education institutions and the Boston building and trades unions, to improve learning outcomes to support the overall community. A second compact was signed in 1989, emphasizing parental control over student assignment (i.e., school choice) and an increase in site-based management for schools. These changes were prompted by growing community frustration over how the schools were run. An economic downturn during the late 1980s reduced the Compact's ability to focus on the district, leading to significant fiscal cutbacks. One important note about the Compact is the perception by some Bostonians that it was a top-down reform from the elites that left out many of the city's other groups.[5]

In 1991, Mayor Raymond Flynn called for education reform and an end to a decade-long, tumultuous governance battle between the city and the primarily elected thirteen-member Boston School Committee.[6] With the support of the mayor and various business and community leaders, the decision to dissolve the elected board was supported by a 53 percent public referendum vote. Thus, a new Boston School Committee was formed with seven appointed members. Around the same time, the Boston Teachers Union (BTU) asserted its intention to play a more prominent role in BPS reforms.

The powerful external actors involved with the district provided much-needed support to BPS; however, they also added a measure of political strife. Amidst all the social and political dissention, BPS was also undergoing frequent leadership turnover, which is not uncommon in many urban districts. When Tom Payzant was hired to lead the district in 1995, he became the third superintendent to serve in five years. However, his entrance into the district brought focus and stability to the system and marked one of the longest tenures in urban district superintendency in the history of American education. Payzant' s experience and clear vision, along with the backing of the School Committee and mayor, helped Boston pull its system together to raise student achievement and improve opportunities afforded to all its student groups. The successes created through the synergy of these forces illustrate why Boston stood out among similar districts in the state and was selected as a Broad Prize Finalist for four consecutive years and finally won in 2006. Highlights of their performance leading to its 2006 win show that Boston has:

- Consistently outperformed other Massachusetts districts with similar low-income populations in six out of six areas (reading and math at the elementary, middle, and high school levels) measured by The Broad Prize methodology from 2002 to 2005
- Demonstrated greater improvement by African American students than similar districts in the state in five out of six areas (math at the elementary, middle, and high school levels, and reading at the middle and high school levels)
- Improved fourth- and eighth-grade students' reading and math scores at a faster rate than other large American cities, on average, on the 2005 National Assessment of Educational Progress (NAEP) Trial Urban District Assessment (TUDA).

DISTRICT DEMOGRAPHICS AND ACHIEVEMENT LEVELS

Data pulled from The Broad Prize report cards show that, in spite of many challenges, BPS has performed as well as the state in some areas, but the data also shows some pockets of poorer performance in that comparison. This may be due to the stark contrast in Boston's demographics of 74 percent low-income students and 76 percent minority students, as compared with the state's overall education demographics of 29 percent low-income students and 24 percent minority students.[7] Additionally, Massachusetts has been recognized for years as having some of the toughest standards in the nation, providing partial explanation why some of the performance proficiencies appear to be lower than one would expect.[8]

Figures 3.1 and 3.2 illustrate that BPS had the most success in increasing proficiency rates over time at the high school level (defined as grade 10

FIGURE 3.1

District and high school reading proficiencies: All students

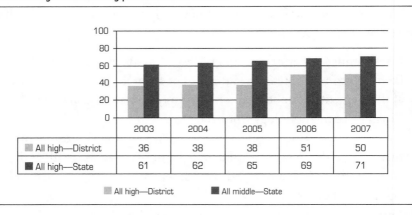

	2003	2004	2005	2006	2007
All high—District	36	38	38	51	50
All high—State	61	62	65	69	71

■ All high—District   ■ All middle—State

FIGURE 3.2

District and high school math proficiencies: All students

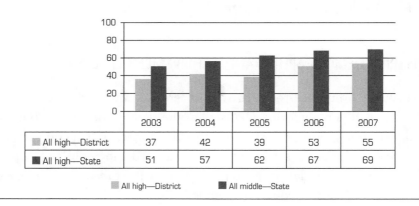

	2003	2004	2005	2006	2007
All high—District	37	42	39	53	55
All high—State	51	57	62	67	69

■ All high—District   ■ All middle—State

in the Broad analysis) in both reading and math, which is a bit surprising, considering that typical trends show districts with stronger performance in lower rather than upper grades. In high school reading, the district increased the number of proficient students from 36 percent in 2003 to 50 percent in 2007, showing an increase of 14 percentage points. The state performed relatively higher during the same time period, moving from 61 percent to 71 percent, an increase of 10 percentage points.

The district's high school math proficiency scores increased between 2003 and 2007 by 18 percentage points, which is still lower than the state but shows a marked improvement rate and an upward trajectory after 2006.

Figures 3.3 and 3.4 compare reading and math proficiency rates, respectively, across elementary (defined as grades 3 and 4 in the Broad analysis), middle (defined as grade 7 in the Broad analysis), and high schools. In reading, middle school performance surpasses elementary and high school until 2006, when high school passes both the elementary and middle levels. In 2007, high school performance lowers by one point, and middle school catches up to high school (figure 3.3).

FIGURE 3.3
District reading proficiencies: All levels

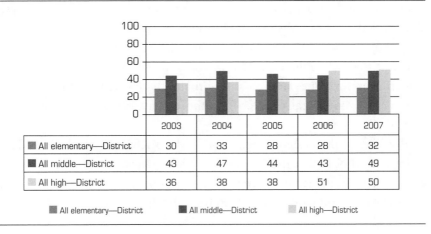

	2003	2004	2005	2006	2007
■ All elementary—District	30	33	28	28	32
■ All middle—District	43	47	44	43	49
▨ All high—District	36	38	38	51	50

■ All elementary—District   ■ All middle—District   ▨ All high—District

FIGURE 3.4
District math proficiencies: All levels

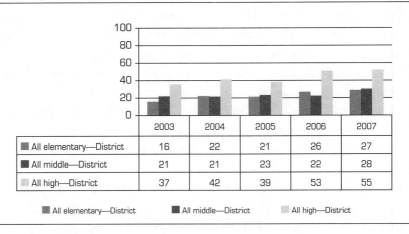

	2003	2004	2005	2006	2007
▓ All elementary—District	16	22	21	26	27
▓ All middle—District	21	21	23	22	28
░ All high—District	37	42	39	53	55

▓ All elementary—District   ▓ All middle—District   ░ All high—District

In math, high school performance is significantly higher than the other two levels from 2003 to 2007, almost to a surprising degree (figure 3.4). This result warrants more investigation into the cause, particularly since 2007 marked a point at which the district had a few years under its belt in implementing its smaller high school model.

Case details reveal the district's concern and intense focus on its wide ethnic and income acheivement gaps. Data from The Broad Prize analyses show that the district was making headway in narrowing gaps with certain subpopulations, particularly with its Hispanic students. Figures 3.5 and 3.6 illustrate that, while there exists a sizeable gap between Hispanic and white students' performance in high school math, the Hispanic students in BPS were performing slightly better than those across the state between 2003 and 2007.

However, as illustrated in figures 3.7 and 3.8, African American students in middle school math in BPS perform slightly lower than African American students in the state. There remains a significant gap between all African American and white students in both the district and state.

FIGURE 3.5

District high school math achievement gap between Hispanic and white students

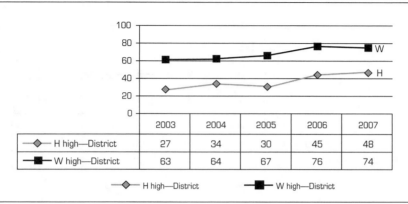

	2003	2004	2005	2006	2007
H high—District	27	34	30	45	48
W high—District	63	64	67	76	74

FIGURE 3.6

State high school math achievement gap between Hispanic and white students

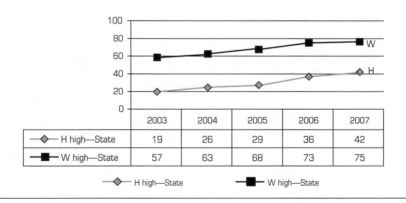

	2003	2004	2005	2006	2007
H high—State	19	26	29	36	42
W high—State	57	63	68	73	75

Regarding gaps between non-low-income and low-income students, there are a few subjects and grades where BPS has narrower income gaps than the state. Figures 3.9 and 3.10 illustrate that, in most years (except for a slight drop in 2005), the district's low-income students performed higher in high school math than the state's similar population, making a narrower

FIGURE 3.7
District middle school math achievement gap between African American and white students

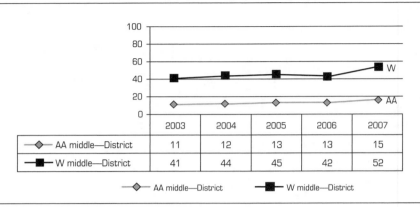

	2003	2004	2005	2006	2007
AA middle—District	11	12	13	13	15
W middle—District	41	44	45	42	52

◆ AA middle—District   ■ W middle—District

FIGURE 3.8
State middle school math achievement gap between African American and white students

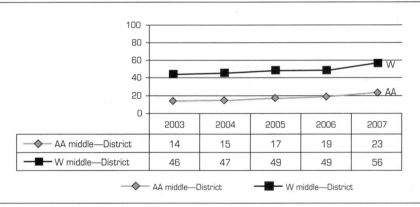

	2003	2004	2005	2006	2007
AA middle—District	14	15	17	19	23
W middle—District	46	47	49	49	56

◆ AA middle—District   ■ W middle—District

gap for that subpopulation. However, the state's non-low-income students performed significantly higher between 2004 and 2007 than both the district's income groups.

In the residual analysis, in which performance is compared with expected performance in similar districts in the state, BPS has all positive residuals in each aggregated grade level in reading from 2003 to 2007, with

FIGURE 3.9

District achievement gap between low-income and non-low-income high school math students

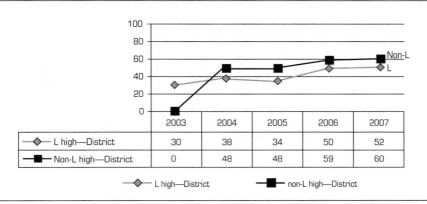

	2003	2004	2005	2006	2007
L high—District	30	38	34	50	52
Non-L high—District	0	48	48	59	60

FIGURE 3.10

State achievement gap between low-income and non-low-income high school math students

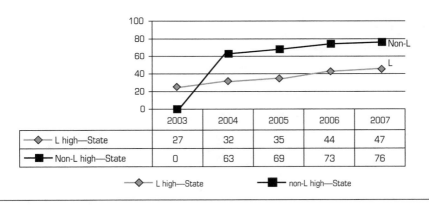

	2003	2004	2005	2006	2007
L high—State	27	32	35	44	47
Non-L high—State	0	63	69	73	76

the exception of elementary reading in 2003, 2006, and 2007 (figure 3.11). Some of the residuals in middle and high school reading were above 1.0, particularly in 2004 and 2005, and in high school in 2006.

The math residual analysis appears stronger and more consistent than in reading, showing all positive residuals, except for elementary math in 2003 (figure 3.12). Many of the math residuals are at 1.0 or above, except

FIGURE 3.11
District reading residual analysis: All levels

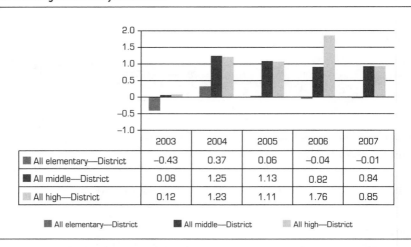

	2003	2004	2005	2006	2007
All elementary—District	−0.43	0.37	0.06	−0.04	−0.01
All middle—District	0.08	1.25	1.13	0.82	0.84
All high—District	0.12	1.23	1.11	1.76	0.85

All elementary—District　　All middle—District　　All high—District

FIGURE 3.12
District math residual analysis: All levels

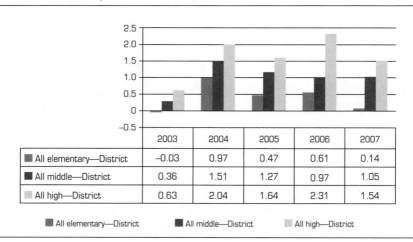

	2003	2004	2005	2006	2007
All elementary—District	−0.03	0.97	0.47	0.61	0.14
All middle—District	0.36	1.51	1.27	0.97	1.05
All high—District	0.63	2.04	1.64	2.31	1.54

All elementary—District　　All middle—District　　All high—District

in elementary reading in all five years and high school reading in 2005. The residuals remain around 2.0 in several years in high school math, which is considered to be a high residual data point in the Broad analysis.

In the 2005 Trial Urban District Assessment (TUDA) conducted by the National Assessment of Educational Progress (NAEP), fourth-graders and eighth-graders in BPS performed as well or better than their counterparts in other large central cities in both reading and math.[9] Additionally, average scale scores in reading and math for African American eighth-graders were significantly higher in Boston than for African American students in other large central cities.[10]

High School Graduation Rates

When comparing different graduation formulas, graduation rates look higher using the averaged freshmen graduation rate (AFGR), which shows a steady increase between 2002 to 2004 to 72 percent, and then a decrease to 62 percent in 2005. Disaggregated graduation rates under the AFGR method show that white and Asian American students' graduation rates were consistently 8 to 10 percentage points higher than those for all minority students, and African American students' graduation rates were approximately 6 to 10 percentage points above those for Hispanic students, illustrating a trend similar to that for national graduation data.[11] The aggregated numbers look somewhat lower with the other methods, hovering around the upper 50s.

DISTRICT PRACTICES BY THEME

Leaders and teachers in Boston attribute the district's successes to a long, steady process of pulling many disparate pieces into one stable, aligned system. Performance sustainability over time is challenging for any district, but it is particularly so for an urban district that faces numerous barriers to stability, marked by lingering conflict over school choice and school assignment, ongoing racial tension, high student mobility, union opposition, and budgetary challenges. Tom Payzant, who served the district for eleven years before retiring in June 2006, discussed his long-term priority for Boston as "improving a system of schools beyond more than just a few good ones." He characterized that process as a "K–12 issue" involving a whole-school improvement strategy, where "the whole is greater than the sum of its parts."

Boston's reform story begins with aligning governance and leadership forces to allow the visionary Payzant to indoctrinate a very clear, long-term process for setting goals and expectations for instruction and instructional support across the district. The long-term focus is a particularly important point, since typical urban reform efforts contain more churn and changes than were seen in Boston's ten-year reform effort. In my last interview with Payzant in 2006, he reflected on his long-term tenure, reiterating that the work in Boston "is about [being] systemic and focusing on sustaining; improving the whole system." Payzant attributed his ability to help champion that long-term focus by having "continuity of leadership on a government side," and his ability to stay long enough to "go deep rather than be superficial in a lot of different areas." The fact that this point has been emphasized in over five interviews with Payzant is a testament to the importance he puts on governance and leadership in urban reform. Summing up in our final interview, he referred to the mayor's support and that of the appointed Boston School Committee as being "a huge factor, given the history of Boston, that has really made a difference."

With the right governance structures in place, Payzant was able to move forward with a clear strategy to improve student achievement. Dr. Payzant's key focuses for the district were strong leadership and instruction that would function within a standards-based framework; the provision of clear expectations and curriculum; support systems for teachers connected to learning standards; and strong accountability measures. The visual he provides to illustrate the guiding principles behind his strategy, originating from Dr. Ron Ferguson from the Harvard Kennedy School, is a triangle with "relationships at the pinnacle, curriculum at one corner, and instruction at the other." According to Payzant, the beliefs and attitudes are critical to these relationships because they drive "how adults work with each other and with kids." Having a rigorous curriculum is important for helping move students up to all standards, and instruction has to be of a high enough quality to ensure students are well prepared for the next level they envision for themselves beyond their K–12 experience.

When we visited with school leaders and teachers in BPS, we found an appreciation for the focus in the district and the "sense of direction" school personnel felt within their work. Reflecting back on the days prior to Payzant's leadership, a principal in a focus group stated:

> We used to laugh that there was no real firm direction. You were told, "Now we're doing this in English," and we had these little booklets. Remember those days? The curriculum was a piece of paper. You were supposed to read it and disseminate it to your staff. Now there's a very clear message and expectations. The term *teaching and learning* is embedded in every individual, from students to parents. The expectations for administrators, teachers, and even parents and students is clearly delineated. Everyone understands the direction the school system is going. That's a powerful message.

Another principal recalled seeing school leadership change from being "operational" to "instructional." While teachers tended to discuss their work from their own classroom perspective, their comments often referenced the same priorities addressed by the district and school leaders, such as raising student achievement, improving instruction through data analysis, collaborating with others to connect the work, and having difficult conversations with colleagues on ways to address the district's ethnic and income gaps.

Similar to Aldine, the reform pieces in Boston were first pulled together within the first theme in the National Center for Educational Achievement's Best Practice Framework, Curriculum and Academic Goals.[12] The goal-planning process provided targets for the district to work backwards from to better align, clarify, and refine their curriculum and instructional practices.

Curriculum and Academic Goals

Boston Public Schools began building its curriculum by clariying the state's educational standards (Massachusetts Curriculum Framework), which resulted in clearly articulated grade-level expectations well before the implementation of NCLB. When asked about the quality of the state standards, most interviewees at all levels agreed that they were good, citing the Framework's high national ranking as a testament to their rigor. Principals and teachers agreed that the district was focusing on "pushing high standards" and increasing rigor in classroom instruction. They also felt that the district's focus on literacy and mathematics throughout the curriculum was important, and that the next step would be to refine other topics, such as social studies and, particularly, science. While many teachers felt the English language arts curriculum was relatively well aligned, some dissension remained around the district's math curriculum, which emphasized problem solving rather than basic skills. However, interviews in 2006 showed that the district and schools were working to adjust the math curriculum to address those concerns. Overall, teachers felt it was important and useful that the district mandated the curriculum to create instructional alignment across schools, while allowing enough freedom to add to the curriculum based on issues revealed by their formative and summative assessments.

Since the start of the curriculum revision process in the mid-1990s, Boston has modified and expanded its curriculum to meet changes in state standards and, more importantly, to continue to improve alignment between grades and enhance the instructional program. In addition to clarifying the Massachusetts Framework, Boston added "graduation portfolios" for grades 5, 8, and 12 and core reading lists for each grade.[13] The curriculum revision process is now initiated by the central office and involves "inquiry groups" of instructional leaders and teachers. These groups review the curriculum and identify gaps and instructional issues made visible by data and teacher input. Sample outcomes from that process include moving algebra instruction to lower grade levels and adding a structured writing program.

Between 2002 and 2006, the site visit teams saw Boston continue to refine and align its curriculum and the supporting curriculum guides to meet students' instructional needs. In the first two years, several interviewees voiced appreciation for the increased quality of instruction across all grades, but they felt that the improvement was somewhat stalled in the early grades and was somewhat lacking in the upper grades. However, we did not find any similar comments within secondary-level interviews during 2005 or 2006.

Overall, principals and particularly teachers felt that their schools had some autonomy to respond to their data and adjust their curriculum as needed, and that the central office provided help and support when they had a curricular question or concern. For instance, several teachers discovered an instructional gap in the fifth-grade math curriculum, which sparked further investigation that uncovered the same problem in the sixth-grade math curriculum. The teachers got together and developed a unit that addressed the issue. Teachers from another school described how they developed a unit on money for kindergarten, because they believed it needed to be addressed earlier than prescribed by the district's scope and sequence. Teachers asserted that, while the district mandates that the curriculum be followed, teachers are able to supplement instruction when they find problems that surface through their formative assessments.

The curriculum revision process is also informed by schools through instructional coaches. One middle school math coach described how she covered various classrooms, taking notes to bring information back to the curriculum committees on any concerns she found. She felt this process was important for getting a broader perspective across classrooms to "find the hiccups in our scope and sequence." She mentioned that there were times when several coaches found the same issues across several schools, which was important information for informing the district's overall curriculum revision process. In that particular year, 2005, the district changed the order of math units based on information the coaches brought from the classrooms.

Boston also uses resources around them to address curricular needs and concerns. When the district decided it needed to target skills for students entering their system underprepared, it collaborated with SUNY Buffalo College of Education professors to build a robust pre-K curriculum.

The curriculum is available both on paper and online, along with supporting materials that include pacing guides, course descriptions, instructional activities, and sample formative assessments. Additionally, the state provides a document with supplements to the standards, which outlines the entire K–12 curriculum. One principal remarked that the supplements were useful in helping her school look at "where sixth grade is supposed to be and exactly where you are trying to get them by the eighth grade." District specialists work with schools to build a curriculum calendar with benchmarks throughout the year. All teachers receive curriculum standards and pacing guides at the beginning of the year. The district expanded its assessment program in 2006 to include more districtwide year-end, midyear, and end-of-chapter tests. Teachers felt that the assessments, pacing guides, and units of study were very useful for helping them plan and "keep instructional staff on track." From these documents, they built yearly instructional plans and felt they had a good system of "checks and balances."

The district conducts curriculum-implementation reviews of the middle and high schools that resemble "mini accreditation visits." Deputy superintendents observe individual departments to give feedback to every teacher on their classroom instruction. These visits also review how well campus administrators support and monitor instruction. One high school principal noted that the principals really liked the visits for both the feedback they and their teachers received on the quality of instruction and the administrative supports provided to teachers.

In addition to the formal reviews, many schools in Boston take proactive steps to ensure instruction is kept on track. Instructional coaches and subject-specific department heads conduct regular weekly walkthroughs, meeting with teachers to find out whether they are on pace with their instruction and whether they are experiencing any challenges. One middle school math department leader described those conversations: "[The visitor will, ask] 'Where are you? What page? You might want to cut this piece out.' The teachers tell him 'This is what I have planned, but this is where I am having trouble right now.'"

The district and school curriculum and implementation reviews helped create uniformity across schools throughout the district, with the 2006 site visit harvesting numerous testimonials as evidence of increased alignment. As compared with prior years, more administrators and teachers commented on the importance of coordinating instruction across the district. One teacher said,

> The advantage I see is that we are all using the same curriculum this year, so the students coming into the sixth grade are actually prepared to be writers or readers. It brings consistency throughout the district. No matter if a child comes from a different school, that child is familiar with the content we are using.

Teachers and principals alike agreed that it was important that a student "moving from school A to school D" have the same curriculum and instruction.

The process of identifying and tracking academic goals in Boston is very structured and is aligned between the district and each of its individual schools. The unifying academic goal is to "accelerate the continuous improvement of teaching and learning to enable all students to meet high standards." The five-year plan to monitor the district goals and reform efforts is called "Focus on Children II" and is the 2001–2006 sequel to the original "Focus on Children I," which spanned 1996 to 2001. Each year, the superintendent and the School Committee set four to six goals to set expectations and establish benchmarks for the entire district and schools. The district provides the schools with a template called the Whole School Improvement Plan (WSIP) to create and manage their goal-setting process through extensive data analysis. One principal noted in 2005 that the WSIP had been streamlined and put online, allowing the deputy superintendents to easily review it to make comments or suggest revisions for the principals.

Schools based their goals on student achievement results, as well as on the Six Essentials (outlined in the following section), which delineate expectations for instructional practices. The goals are developed through multistakeholder school site council clusters and must be SMART—strategic, measurable, attainable, results-oriented, and time-bound. In a 2003 interview, Superintendent Payzant emphasized that one of the biggest challenges is that maintaining a clear, deep focus on a limited number of things becomes challenging as different constituents blur the focus through the natural temptation to try to do too many things at once. One way Boston tackles the issue of purposeful focus is by training teachers and principals to build their WSIPs by reviewing data and going through a "root cause analysis" to identify needs of concern. Then schools develop instructional action plans and identify goals that represent context-focused versions of the district goals.

Staff Selection, Leadership, and Capacity Building

One crucial factor in successfully implementing any curriculum, as presented by numerous Boston administrators and teachers, is having the right people in place to deliver it. The high value Boston places on human capital is evident in the document "Six Essentials for Whole School Improvement" (the "Six Essentials"), which drives the goals for the district. It specifies that the district will do the following:

- Use effective instructional practices and create a collaborative school climate to improve learning
- Examine student work and data to drive instruction and professional development
- Invest in professional development to improve instruction
- Share leadership to sustain instructional improvement
- Focus resources to support instructional improvement and improved student learning
- Partner with families and community to support student learning

Each of the Six Essentials either directly or indirectly involves getting the right people into place and developing and supporting them as a means for increasing student achievement. To this end, the district has developed a multipronged approach for building an ample supply of effective teachers and principals, as well as assisting with replacing its numerous retiring principals and teachers. The two tenets that drive its human capital strategy are that (1) instruction must improve in every classroom, and (2) leadership drives improvement. The three areas of focus to achieve these goals are the reinvention of their human resources department, creation of the Institute for Professional Development, and provision of direct leadership support to individual clusters and school leaders.

In 2004, Boston engaged in a three-year process of restructuring their human resources practices to create a data-driven system that would manage, coordinate, and improve human resources processes. Led by a new director, the HR department streamlined electronic hiring processes (before, there were twenty-nine steps to be completed on paper), established an earlier hiring timeline, and implemented numerous stakeholder surveys to determine district and school needs. With these new processes, the district has been able to hire better principals and teachers and be more responsive to existing staff requests for support. The significance of this change in the district is illustrated by one principal's comment:

> Changing the human resources department has been key to developing the correct benchmarks for hiring the best teachers out there in the field. It used to be that even late in August we didn't have staff. We had to hire at the last minute. With the HR changes, we now have a much more capable system. We used to come into central office and walk out with a hundred-resume pile we had to sift through. The new system helps us look at good candidates, interview them early, and offer them incentives to stay in the district.

The HR director also saw the need to add diversity to her central office HR team, so she worked hard to hire staff members who were more reflective of the city's population. This was an important step, because an extensive review of the district completed in 2005 by an external team cited the lack of diversity in the central office as a problem in the district.

Follow-up surveys conducted in 2005 yielded many positive responses throughout the district regarding the new direction taken by the HR department. Principals in particular believed that the HR enhancements were helpful, especially for the hiring process. However, the survey also revealed a continuing need to focus on providing more timely responses to schools and letting new principals know about the function of each subdivision within the HR department.

In addition to the improved hiring and tracking systems, the district pulled its long-standing leadership and teacher development programs together under one system called the Institute for Professional Development in 2005. To develop more leadership, the district is replacing retired principals with external candidates through its Leadership Institute (part of the Institute for Professional Development) and growing its own internal candidates through the Boston Principal Fellowship. The Fellowship involves a year-long residency with participants "living the life of a principal" for approximately eighty-five days. Both programs are cited as important sources of support for new and prospective principals and have helped the district develop administrators who are "instructional leaders." In 2006, central office leaders stated that about a third of the district's new principals were coming from the internal programs, another third from assistant principals and curriculum leaders, and the remaining third from outside the system.

These programs have been important to Boston since, during Payzant's tenure, 70 to 75 percent of the principals were either no longer in the principalship or had been moved to other schools because of their successes. Amidst this district-generated leadership turnover, Boston has gradually built a stable cadre of principals and leaders for its schools through its internal leadership programs.

Retention is also an important focus for building stable leadership in Boston. New principals are provided with mentors and intensive "nuts and bolts" training during their first two years. Additionally, all principals have the opportunity to collaborate with each other during monthly meetings and are frequently visited at their schools by the deputy superintendents, whose roles have shifted to working directly with principals rather than in central office. Shifting the deputies' roles was motivated partially by the internal stakeholder survey mentioned earlier that outlined the need for more responsiveness to the schools.

Following a similar grow-your-own format, the district increased its pool of teacher candidates through the Boston Teacher Residency (BTR) program, created in 2003 to counteract heavy teacher turnover along with a shortage of specialists and teachers of color. The BTR is a thirteen-month training program that follows a medical residency model and puts its candidates in the field on a weekly basis to work side by side with experienced teachers. In addition to working directly in classrooms four days a week, the residents also receive training on BPS's culture, curriculum, and unique instructional techniques through the year-long placement in a "successful" classroom. This key element of the program is important for BPS, as this information is not something that schools of education would be able to provide in their training programs. BPS's instructional programs are difficult to implement and require dedicated training and practice.

Once the program is completed, candidates earn a master's degree, a teaching license, and a "forgiveness loan" of $10,000 for tuition. Additionally, BTR residents are provided with a $10,000-plus stipend for living expenses during their course of study. In return, candidates make a three-year commitment to teach in the district. The ability to directly award participants with teacher certification is an integral part of the program, made possible through the district's partnership with the Massachusetts State Board of Education.

The BTR has gained a lot of attention over the past few years as an innovative program that drills down into the unique instructional practices and contexts of a particular school district while providing numerous hours of direct contact and field observation that district leaders often clamor for in new hires. According to a study conducted by the Aspen Institute in 2008, the BTR has been effective in recruiting teachers who are knowledgeable about instruction, are certified in hard-to-staff subjects, and represent minority populations. Specifically, the survey results revealed that 88 percent of BTR graduates seemed to be more prepared to implement Boston's curriculum and instructional program than their counterparts; 55 percent of BTR residents are minorities; 57 percent of the residents teach mathematics or science; and every resident receives a dual certification in special education. Regarding retention, the study found that after three years, 90 percent of BTR graduates are still teaching. The survey results attribute the successful retention rates to the high quality of the preparation program, ongoing support, and the upfront commitment made by residents to teach in high-needs schools.[14] Principals and teachers we interviewed for The Broad Prize corroborated the report's findings; several stated that the program prepared teachers well for the district's unique culture and specific instructional practices.

As mentioned earlier, concerns expressed by the schools about central office responsiveness were addressed through the HR department's third reform strategy of shifting the role of the deputy superintendents away from a traditional centralized position to working on a daily basis directly in the schools. In this new role, the deputies spent time shadowing principals, observing instruction, and making sure principals and teachers felt well supported and connected to the central office. Through these daily duties, the deputies asserted that they gained a much deeper understanding of what was happening in the schools, enabling them to identify school needs and report their findings back to the central office. Central office leaders, in turn, noted that the deputies have been able to provide much more insight on what is going on in the daily operations of the schools. Many principals affirmed the utility of the support provided by the deputy superintendents in the form of finding resources, analyzing data, or helping solve problems as they arise.

Ramping up support to retain personnel is another important step in Boston's human capital strategy. Teachers and principals are well supported through mentors, professional development, and numerous mechanisms that develop collaborative communities at different levels. Teachers at different schools in Boston mentioned that they were provided mentors located within their schools who often taught the same subject they were teaching. The teachers asserted that their mentors met with them frequently to provide instructional feedback and answer questions. New teachers also mentioned meeting with experienced teachers weekly to ask questions and gain insight from various teachers with different backgrounds and levels of expertise.

When asked about their main source of support, teachers most often cited the district's mandated professional development model, called the Collaborative Coaching and Learning (CCL) model. The CCL model involves an eight-week teaching cycle, during which teachers work in weekly study groups to set instructional goals and expectations for the next week. Teachers having trouble meeting a specific goal or learning a new skill can have a coach observe their lesson, give them feedback, and offer support. Coaches meet and observe in several classrooms each day.

The district has invested in master teachers who serve as literacy and mathematics coaches. These coaches may be former teachers or principals, higher education students, or adjunct professors at local colleges and universities. BPS has seventy-five full- and part-time literacy coaches and approximately forty mathematics coaches, some of whom are funded by the Boston Plan for Excellence (BPE).[15] In 2006, central office leaders stated that they were planning to move the coaches from the central office to campuses to provide principals with the power to control their own instructional supports. While they felt the shift would be difficult and cause anxiety among the coaches, they felt it was important to respond to the principals' request for more autonomy over that resource.

Overall, principals and teachers spoke favorably about the CCL model. One unique feature mentioned frequently was that it made teaching a much more "public act," which provided a great mechanism for creating alignment across classrooms, as described by one teacher:

> The CCL . . . helps you learn from others how to teach. We have the door open and are sharing both across and vertically through the grades. It helps me see how we grow and how the curriculum moves from one year to another. It also helps us build a common language. The kids even remember from one grade to the next since the teachers often use the same instructional techniques and vocabulary.

One elementary principal and her team of teachers described the model as being very teacher driven, since teachers are able to select their own topic of inquiry. Teachers select the topic based on their WSIP, focusing particularly on their instructional weaknesses. Several teachers felt the CCL model provided a unique opportunity for them to work with a trained literacy or math coach who could help them through demonstration lessons and by providing feedback to them on their instructional strategies.

While most teachers in interviews seemed to agree that the CCL was a more effective delivery of professional development than the typical static workshop models, central office leaders mentioned that its implementation was met by some resistance, primarily from the union. One central office leader told us about some conflict that occurred over requiring teachers to complete a demonstration lesson, an element in the model that leaders felt was important to the program. However, the union declared it would not support the district's mandating the demonstration lesson. Eventually, BTU allowed district leaders to encourage the model lessons, as long as they would not be tied to teacher evaluations. District leaders found a silver lining in the compromise, as they felt removing the connection to the evaluation made it easier for principals to also participate in the CCL progress. Overall, the elementary schools easily embraced the demonstration lessons, while middle and high schools were more resistant, with the exception of teachers in certain subjects, including English, math, and social studies.

In addition to professional development, the CCL also provided a vehicle for studying and solving instructional deficits within the district, as its collaborative structure went well with the problem-solving process. The district conducted several CCL cycles that focused on its growing achievement gap. The gap CCLs involved numerous teachers and principals, who analyzed disaggregated data together to identify where to target instructional interventions that would reduce ethnic- and income-group achievement gaps. In our district interviews, we were told the process worked so well within the schools that it surprised central office leaders.

Other retention strategies included the creation of leadership opportunities for teachers, the provision of time for teachers to collaborate and observe each other teaching, and the distribution of useful curriculum documents to aid instruction. Focus group interviews with teachers during the 2005 and 2006 site visits elicited far more positive comments regarding district and school supports provided to them than in our first visit in 2002. Both new and experienced teachers emphasized that they had many opportunities to meet with and learn from each other, and they felt that the professional development they received was accessible and useful to their instruction. These numerous investments in teacher supports may be one reason the district is finally seeing lower rates of teacher turnover.

Instructional Programs, Practices, and Arrangements

Boston's program selection is implemented through a districtwide process that engages representative teachers and administrators. The process entails conducting research on prospective programs, getting information from vendors, and often piloting programs for a full year before a purchasing decision. The district evaluates programs continually through feedback from principals and curriculum coaches. Curriculum directors investigate potential problems and request additional support from the central office, if necessary. One of the most impressive features of Boston's program selection process is the thoroughness of the research phase. In this step, the selection committee develops a detailed rubric on the type of program desired, any specific requirements, desired implementation effects, and so on. The committee then reviews numerous programs, rates each specification on the rubric, and moves the three top-rated programs forward to consider for piloting.

Regarding instruction, the district mandates the amount of time to be spent daily in two core academic subjects. Elementary schools have 120 minutes per day of language arts and 70 to 90 minutes per day of math. Double blocks of math and reading in grades 6 and 9 (the transition grades) are implemented and exceed the instructional time required by the state. The Reader's and Writer's Workshop and TERC's Investigations curriculum for math, both inquiry-based models, are programs that are mandated districtwide. Central office leaders felt the implementation of these uniform programs was important for meeting the district's instructional goals, providing alignment across schools, and for coordinating the professional development program.

The Reader's and Writer's Workshop and the various investigative math programs were selected to promote literacy across the curriculum and "break teachers from the mold of standing in front of the classroom," according to several district leaders. The inquiry-based literacy models are designed to personalize reading and writing for students by prompting interactions between students and text, with each other, and particularly with teachers. Through multiple instructional arrangements, including whole-group instruction, small-group mini-lessons, independent reading, wrap-up and sharing, and conferencing with students on their work, teachers are better able to gauge how well each student is doing on various tasks.

Investigations, developed at TERC in Cambridge, Massachusetts , is a K–5 mathematics curriculum designed to help students understand fundamental ideas of number and operations, geometry, data, measurement, and early algebra. Departing from traditional math textbooks, Investigations comes as a kit containing teacher guides with individual units for the year, posters, overhead transparencies, worksheets, and manipulatives. A second inquiry-based model, Connected Mathematics, is implemented in BPS middle schools. Connected Mathematics lessons provide a sequence of connected problems that are to be solved through inquiry methods.

Inquiry-based instructional programs are difficult to implement. To plan lessons that address different types of student grouping arrangements, teachers must assess student needs quickly and be well organized and prepared for several "lessons within a lesson." The Reader's and Writer's Workshop requires that teachers learn not only how to counsel students individually about their work, but also to teach students of all ages to be positive constructive critics of their peers' work. Imagine how difficult these programs would be for teachers who are wedded to their textbooks;

they require quite a shift in planning and teaching lessons. It is because these programs require a lot of training that the BTR is an ideal place to prepare future teachers using the district's actual programs.

Although these programs are difficult to implement, the district feels they provide an important emphasis on the process of learning. As one veteran teacher described it, "These programs make sure children understand what they are learning, that they can articulate it, write about it, and draw models, rather than just memorize facts and spit them back out." Other teachers voiced similar opinions about the importance of students becoming more involved in instruction and being able to discuss what they are learning. One principal felt the workshop models provided an important opportunity for students of all ages to read and write every day.

Not everyone was on board with the district-mandated programs, however, as there were some concerns mentioned by several teachers that the programs lacked appropriate coverage of important basic skills. Referring to the TERC math program, one elementary teacher stated:

> We find gaps in the program. It's a great program—kids can have fun with it—but the basic skills can get lost in there. That's huge, especially when parents are expecting to see the basic skills; they say, "This is great, but you guys are forgetting something."

As soon as this particular teacher had voiced her concerns to her math coach, he helped her figure out how to incorporate what she felt was missing from math instruction in her classroom. Another middle school teacher mentioned that she initially resisted the Connected Mathematics program because she did not think that she was allowed to modify it. However, she reported that over time she saw that the students' attitude toward math changing. She felt her students were not as afraid of math as they were in the past because, as she put it:

> You can see them thinking in so many different ways, whereas in regular math, they just memorized it one way. They are really figuring it out. It's difficult for

the specialty population, but once you master how to break it down, it's great because you can see these kids applying all the strategies in all areas.

Another principal described the difficulty he experienced in shifting to the Investigations math program five years prior to our discussion with him in 2006. On his campus, the program "sent everyone kicking and screaming, saying 'Oh why do we have to make this change?'" However, this principal felt the shift was important for getting everyone on the same page, to provide program continuity across the district, particularly for high mobility students. He also felt the uniform professional development that came along with the shift was also helpful. Eventually, he said, his teachers became comfortable with the inquiry models and agreed that their students were "being asked harder questions and having more academic demands made upon them."

To add another element of instructional alignment, several teachers mentioned using interdisciplinary units to connect different subject areas. From 2002 to 2006, and particularly since the last site visit in 2006, there was increased evidence of instructional uniformity across schools. This may be partially attributed to progress made on further defining the curriculum and the curriculum guides being provided to teachers. Another explanation could be the work of the local Instructional Leadership Teams (ILTs) that were placed at each school and comprised teachers and coaches from various grade levels who worked together to discuss instructional concerns and student work. One principal felt the teams were particularly useful because, "We have these difficult conversations about everything from instruction, curriculum, to scheduling. It all comes together with one purpose; for the success of our students."

The district's instructional program was further enhanced with several major changes in 2006, including creating a more inclusive special education model, developing a more aligned ESL program and creating more high school academies, as well as a plan to add seven hundred seats to its current pre-K program by 2010. The high school academies, which have been a main reform in Boston for the past few years, followed a model of breaking down large comprehensive high schools into small learning communities. The district is also moving to create more K–8 schools, converting former elementary and middle schools. All of these instructional programs were selected based on the district's review of research, data, and pilot programs.

Many interviewees felt that the district had shifted more attention to improving instruction over the past five years. Several principals mentioned that point in interviews, particularly in 2005 and 2006. Many of them attributed the focus and improvements in instruction to the support they gained from HR, the deputies, the training on instructional leadership, and improved responsiveness from central office leaders. Illustrating how his own work was changed, one principal stated:

> Really, I think the district is set up to focus on instruction, which is not the case in other places. This is the focus here; that was made clear. Yes, there's tons of silly little administrative stuff that I guess in the end is important, but the bottom line is, if kids are not achieving, you are not doing your job.

Along similar lines, a new principal mentioned how his deputy superintendent helped him balance his operational work with instruction. When she visited him and found him doing "operational stuff," she would tell him "give that to your assistant principal, and be sure this person and this person are doing this and this." He said she emphasized that he did not "have to be Superprincipal." Another new principal agreed that his deputy superintendent was very helpful and clear about where his focus should be. He said he would show her the bulletin boards, discuss the climate of the school, discuss how well the teachers were doing, and she would say, "Yes, yes that's fine. Let me see the students' reading notebooks and their writing journals; those are the window into the classroom." These evolving conversations about instruction were found throughout interviews in all levels of the district.

Monitoring, Analysis, and Use of Data

As in Aldine, every conversation about decisions and practices in Boston began and ended with data. The district's powerful data management system and numerous structured monitoring procedures help keep the system aligned and informed about its strengths and weaknesses. Boston developed MyBPS in 2003 as a means of making data useful to administrators and teachers. The secure web-based system contains student performance information on formative and summative assessments, as well as report cards, tips on how to use and interpret the data, links to state standards and learning objectives tied to assessment questions, and copies of students' writing compositions and scores. Interactive graphs displaying student performance data linked to specific questions on the state assessment are also available.

Through MyBPS, users can query the database to answer questions such as, "How did my students perform on the English language arts multiple choice questions?" or "What was the distribution of student responses on a specific test item?" One administrator commented:

> It's remarkable! You can sort your own class by different subgroups, and people who work across the school can look at it. We can see how the district data brings us all back to the school plan. Instead of requiring every teacher to be a data analyst, the tool does it, allowing teachers to focus on learning objectives.

Teachers in the district also spoke favorably of the usefulness of the system. One teacher offered the following example of how data is used in her school:

> We look at a lot of the formative assessments, as well as our assessments based on performance of the students, and we are able to see the weak areas. For example, we know that the students did not do well on nonfiction pieces, so that's one of our focuses. We also wanted to make sure that the students could become independent learners and thinkers. Now we are trying to use assessments in our classrooms with the students to show them,

"This is where you are," and question them about why they chose certain responses on particular tests.

Similar examples of teachers using data to drive instruction were abundant throughout the district.

Formative assessments are an important tool for tracking student performance in Boston. The district requires quarterly assessments in all subjects and grade levels, as well as midyear and end-of-year open-response assessments. To ease implementation, the district provides schools with large banks of test items and Scantrons, so that the assessments are easy to create and score. Having real-time, ongoing performance feedback is important for ensuring that students stay on grade level. To this end, benchmarks are reviewed every four to eight weeks. Although the formative assessments are included in MyBPS, they are in a static format and thus cannot be queried. That capability, however, is in Boston's plans for the near future.

In addition to the benchmark tests, school instruction and performance are monitored through "cluster walkthroughs," with a *cluster* being defined as a feeder pattern. Principals in each cluster decide at the beginning of the year which schools to target for walkthroughs. These walkthroughs are also used as a means for sharing best practice instructional strategies across schools and for viewing model programs.

Teachers use data in grade-level meetings to review results from both formative and summative assessments. Instructional coaches from the district help determine alternative instructional strategies. Individual teachers report using data to assess whether students are mastering the skills being taught.

Responses from the focus groups with principals and teachers confirmed that most school personnel were using MyBPS to a certain extent. Almost every principal and teacher interviewed seemed enthusiastic and comfortable with using data to guide daily decisions. Nicely illustrating the spirit in which data is used and its growing prevalence, one principal commented,

We monitor performance in many different and exciting ways with whatever data is available. The conversation trickles on down to the deputies, who are in the buildings more frequently, and they have conversations with the principals about the data. The conversations are very specific and focus on ownership rather than blame. "What haven't I done as a teacher? Where am I missing? As a teacher, I have a gap." It's not "Children have the gap," but "I have a gap."

Quite a few teachers mentioned liking being able to look at test-item analysis to determine specific areas where instruction needed to improve. One teacher described how she could look at a particular skill like "making inferences" and find what percentage of her class did not master items under that skill. She found this to be particularly helpful because she felt prepared to make appropriate lesson adjustments and to have focused discussions with grade-level teams and with students on how to improve. Another teacher mentioned that midterm results were posted on MyBPS, along with the Massachusetts Curriculum Framework code. Through the posting, teachers could see a particular question, its concept, and the strengths and what the students needed to master. The information is posted at the classroom level, so that teachers can pinpoint their incoming classes' strengths and weaknesses. Teachers reported that this part of the system was clickable and easy to use, as it provided clear instructions and useful visuals to make data points stand out on reports.

While there was less evidence of data use in 2003 and 2004, the site visit teams began to see an increase in data use across the district in the following two years. These conversations seemed to drill down much farther into what data results actually meant, particularly in 2006, as the district began to focus intently on narrowing its existing ethnic- and income-group achievement gaps. One principal mentioned that the district's accessibility and focus on disaggregated data was "vital in creating conversations and rapport about student achievement." The principal said that he and his colleagues spent time examining student work, "using real numbers about real people to focus on what we were really talking about." The district training was particularly helpful to this principal for drilling down and interpreting what his data meant for different student groups. Agreeing that the district was helping principals and teachers increase their skills in reading and interpreting data, another principal stated:

> Now we can read it [the data]. Five years ago you would just say, ok, I see what's going on. This year we've gotten to a point where we can sit down and say, we know what the needs of the kids are, and we know how to plan for their success.

Adding one more level of nuance to their data interpretation, several principals and teachers made very similar comments about the importance of using data to diagnose exactly what and where their focus should be, and that the midyear assessments were particularly helpful for addressing the issues earlier in the year. Principals and teachers knew they had to drill down when examining student results to determine whether their focus should be on individual students or particular groups of students; whether the problem is related to curriculum alignment or the curriculum maps; or whether the issue is an instructional or assessment issue. Interviewees mentioned that they gain much more insight from data when they analyze it with their colleagues to share ideas and theories about what it means.

As mentioned earlier, the district keeps track of its overall performance through the Whole School Improvement Plan (WSIP), which measures performance on the Six Essentials. Similar to Aldine, schools in Boston develop and measure progress on their WISPs, which feed into an overall review of district performance. Based on the data, district priorities are set and action plans are formulated to address performance gaps and concerns.

Recognition, Intervention, and Adjustment

The data and monitoring systems described above help the district respond quickly and early when weak areas become apparent. The district has numerous interventions to address the needs of struggling schools, teachers, and students.

Schools undergoing corrective action, or schools determined by the state to be underperforming, are involved in an intensive performance improvement mapping process that occurs in partnership with the state. Through this process, the district and state officials carefully review data and build a detailed improvement plan, focusing on achievement gap issues and identifying interventions based on root cause analyses. Within the district, under contract with the teachers' union, the superintendent can request an audit when a low-performing school is identified. The district and a team from the union assess the needs of low-performing schools to determine appropriate interventions, which may include reconstituting the staff, moving to a small-school model, sending in an intervention team, and/or providing additional professional development.

To assist teachers, the district is currently reforming its overall teacher evaluation and support system to align with its new teachers' contract. Currently, struggling teachers receive support from their principal, the Collaborative Coaching and Learning model, instructional directors, mentors, and additional professional development. Recently, the superintendent had teachers trained in Jon Saphier's Skillful Teacher model, which provides a repertoire of teaching strategies that are matched to student needs. Using the model, principals are trained to document the physical classroom environment and the teacher's practice and learn how to provide useful and sometimes difficult feedback to teachers. Although the process involves many hours of documentation for the union, the district feels it is important for teacher development.

Boston's numerous interventions for struggling students are also seen as helpful to teachers. In addition to before- and after-school programs and tutoring from Boston teachers, parents can choose from tutoring provided by Kaplan, Princeton Review, or other supplemental programs. Also, students who do not meet proficiency standards on the state norm–referenced test are provided with Individual Student Success Plans. These plans help document individual student needs and services and function somewhat like an Individualized Education Plan. In addition to these optional programs, the district mandates summer school for students in grades 3, 6, 7, and 8 who do not meet benchmarks in reading, writing, and mathematics.

Focus groups with principals and teachers confirmed the belief that Boston provides ample support for struggling schools, teachers, and students. The majority of the principals interviewed felt they were receiving more support from central office after 2005. In addition to the individual support they received from the deputy superintendents, the principals felt their cluster team meetings provided them regular opportunities to discuss "fixes and frustrations" with colleagues experiencing some of the same struggles. Because curriculum departments also attended the cluster meetings, principals asserted feeling more connections to the overall district instructional practices.

One new principal who was hired to work at a campus in corrective action said that he was provided with "a phenomenal school support specialist" through the district. Additionally, this principal felt his cluster leader was particularly helpful, and always got back to him "in seconds flat" whenever he needed anything. When he experienced "serious newsworthy things that just fell into your lap," the principal had support from someone in central office operations, as well as the director of public relations. Another principal mentioned receiving immediate assistance from the HR department when he was having a difficult teacher issue. She received assistance in completing the teacher evaluation and was able to resolve the situation in a timely manner. Principals even mentioned the curriculum implementation reviews as being very helpful in keeping them appropriately focused on student results and aligning professional development with teacher needs.

Teachers felt well supported through the coaching model and believed the professional development they received was relevant and useful to them. Several teachers felt that their most powerful resource of support was the ability to meet and plan with other teachers and to have opportunities to observe other teachers during classroom instruction. One teacher mentioned that some of her colleagues in her school initially were uncomfortable and resisted having coaches and observers in the classroom; however, she said that eventually they learned that the act of "opening up the classroom door" provided an important avenue for receiving support. One of the veteran teachers mentioned that one of her current challenges was balancing her duties as a classroom teacher with the obligation she felt to share her skills and successes through modeling and training other teachers.

Most conversations around student interventions contained references to their "assessment-driven model of instruction," which allows teachers to group students according to skills needs. Teachers felt that the data and tools provided to them through MyBPS were integral to helping them intervene early and frequently to ensure students were successful. Thus, interventions are a natural and ongoing part of everyday instruction.

INFLUENCING FACTORS

District governance, the union, and the business community all play important roles in Boston's successes and, in some cases, in its frustrations. The district is organized as a department within the city and has strong support from the mayor's office. The Boston School Committee (the district's board of directors) is appointed by the mayor. Details on these various stakeholders are outlined below.

School Committee

The seven-member Boston School Committee serves as BPS's governing body. Appointed by Mayor Flynn in 1989, the Committee serves four-year staggered terms. Since July 1993, Mayor Thomas Menino has appointed members from a list of candidates recommended by the thirteen-member Citizens Nominating Panel composed of parents, teachers, principals, and representatives of business and higher education.[16] For each vacant seat, the panel provides three names to the mayor from which to make the final decision. The chair is elected on an annual basis by members of the Committee, and the chair we interviewed during several separate site visits, Dr. Elizabeth Reilinger, had served since 1996, adding stability and consistency to the committee's work.[17] When asked whether there was a lot of competition for Committee seats, Dr. Reilinger told us that Committee seats were perceived as desirable, resulting in what she felt were higher-quality candidates over the years. She mentioned that in earlier years, there was some perception that members were tied to politics and special interest groups. However, when the panel expanded the network of eligible members, that perception no longer prevailed. The current Committee represents a wide range of ethnic and professional backgrounds, with some members serving in higher education, some in business, and others in community organizations, such as Head Start.

According to the district's Web site, the Committee is responsible for the following functions:

- Defining the vision, mission, and goals of BPS
- Establishing and monitoring the annual operating budget
- Hiring, managing and evaluating the superintendent
- Setting and reviewing district policies and practices to support student achievement

The committee evaluates the district's goals by collecting and reviewing outcome data, reviewing student dropout and retention, both aggregated and disaggregated, as well as student achievement data. As far as getting involved in program implementation or instruction, the chair was very clear that the Committee's role is to support and monitor policies and practices, but that implementation was not within its purview. In fact, she felt that it was important that new members clearly understood the role and purpose of the Committee as a governance board, not an operating board.

Dr. Reilinger described the Committee's relationship with the superintendent as "very collegial," as they spend a good deal of time discussing and setting the district goals and outcomes to ensure that their final product is something that can be translated and understood throughout the rest of the system. She also described the Committee's relationship with the mayor as very positive and supportive and mentioned that she personally had gotten to know the mayor quite well. She voiced appreciation of the mayor's conviction and focus on the district's success and stated that the mayor viewed the district as one of his number one priorities. Overall, she felt that a good system was in place for all the governance pieces to work well and that those pieces were filled with the right personalities, and concluded that the key to success is "to have the right people in place, and to have continuity where you can build credibility and trust in working relationships."

In 2005, one of the most active years in reform for Boston, the Dr. Reilinger observed that the district's focus was improving performance for all students, bridging achievement gaps, increasing community and family engagement, and providing supplemental services in classrooms. When asked to reflect on the reforms that most greatly affected student achievement, she referenced several instructional practices, including the district's literacy initiative, curriculum and instruction alignment across the district, improved accountability systems, and clearly articulated outcomes for students.

Regarding the superintendent's relationship with the Committee, Tom Payzant frequently voiced admiration for the wealth of professional expertise brought in by Dr. Reilinger, who had had years of experience as a CEO and had served on numerous boards. Payzant felt she was tough on accountability in a way that was productive for him and showed vigilance in ensuring that no members of the Committee micromanaged the district's work, which, according to Payzant, "is huge from a superintendent's perspective." Agreeing, key central office leaders reiterated that the Committee is focused on policy but does not get into personnel issues. The operations manager additionally asserted that the presence of an appointed governing body is a factor that makes the BPS superintendent position attractive, as it provides "the ability to work with a board that really has taken all the nonsense out of the school operations and focuses neatly on the mission."

School leaders also agreed that the School Committee was a supportive body that understood their role within the district. The principals mentioned having a connection to the Committee through the deputy superintendents who attend Committee meetings and present issues and concerns voiced by school leaders when they arise. Even teachers, who often have little connection to school boards, voiced some opinions about the board. One teacher who served in the district under the elected board spoke favorably about the appointed Committee. As she explained:

I was around when we had an elected board and it was a lot of politics. It was all about who you knew and what you gave or, you know, who you campaigned for; that's how you got somewhere. I like the appointed school board because I think they're more interested in education and the children. I think they're more focused on the curriculum and they're more focused on how the schools are run.

Union/Association

One challenging relationship that BPS had was with the Boston Teachers Union (BTU). BTU is the largest bargaining unit in the city, with over eight thousand members, forty-five hundred of whom are teachers working in the school system. The BTU is the exclusive bargaining agent for teachers, as well as some support personnel, paraprofessionals, substitute teachers, and nonadministrative staff.[18] The organization is affiliated with the American Federation of Teachers (AFT), AFT Massachusetts, and the Greater Boston Labor Council (GBLC).

BTU contracts with the district are renegotiated every three years in an ongoing process executed through meetings between the district and BTU leaders, where they exchange proposals outlining points for the contract and iron out conflicts. The district's negotiating team includes the chief operating officer and several principals. The union team includes the union president and several elected members. The superintendent and school committee enter the process only at the end of the negotiations. In addition to the typical district-union disagreements, several school leaders interviewed in early Broad site visits mentioned that the negotiation process was sometimes slowed when the union had to "respond to the concerns of a few individual members."

BTU has a strong voice in several key areas that affect instruction, including hiring and firing teachers, scheduling professional development for teachers, evaluating teachers, and intervening in the management of low-performing schools. Over the past fifteen years, the BTU and the district have resolved disagreements about pilot schools, seniority transfers for teachers, implementation of the CCL model, and provisions of the Whole

School Improvement Plan. The resulting compromises have provided the district with more flexibility on hiring and training decisions.[19] Additionally, some parents asserted that the union has helped the district gain more professional development time than is typical for most districts, as well as some autonomy for flexibility under the pilot or charter schools.

From the early 1960s through the 1980s, the union played a more traditional "trade union role," which created considerable friction between BTU and the district.[20] However, a union rep noted that in the 1990s the union's role shifted to "function more as a professional union." From that point forward, the interaction between the union and the district over educational policy increased. Interviews with the current BTU leader in 2005 and 2006 (the latter being the year the new contract would be implemented) revealed that he had some disagreements with some of the district's practices, but overall he seemed to appreciate his relationship with and the clear focus provided by Superintendent Payzant. When asked about the district's priorities, this leader mentioned teaching and learning and referenced Payzant's determined focus on achievement gaps. He felt that Payzant extended open lines of communication to him and his members, and he approved of the superintendent's ability to create a structured plan that would be in place once he left the superintendency. His main disagreements with the district in 2006 included the strict structure of the curriculum and pacing guides, the teachers' inability to select professional development content, and the lack of extra compensation for teachers who worked extended hours in pilot schools. In principle, the BTU leader understood the utility of having uniform instruction across the district, but he felt the outcome was not worth what he perceived as a loss of instructional flexibility and creativity for teachers.

For his part, Superintendent Payzant felt his relationship with the union president was positive, which he partially attributed to their three- to four-hour meetings held every two weeks. The meetings helped Payzant and the union leader discuss their differences and begin to iron out details on the contract within ample time; the goal in 2006 was to have it completed before the arrival of the new superintendent. Payzant felt the only continuous source of disagreement was having flexibility on the implementation of the pilot schools.

Leaders and teachers from schools had mixed perceptions about the union; however, the comments were more positive in 2005 and 2006 than they were in earlier site visits. In the earlier interviews, several teachers voiced frustration with the union; one teacher commented that she was given grief if "she did more than she should have been doing." Another teacher felt that the union was more interested in "the well-being of the teachers" than of the students. Despite some negativity, many teachers felt optimistic about the new union leadership that came into power in 2003.

Under that new leadership, interviews were more positive, yet still remained mixed. One teacher was pleased that her pilot school had autonomy from some district policies, but she also appreciated that, over time, she and her colleagues felt the union also "provided a safety net by keeping us tied to the system." However, another teacher opined that the union was not seen as a partner in core educational issues because "it does not hold itself accountable for student performance." Several principals and teachers also felt that BPS students needed more instructional time, which would mean a longer school day. They felt the union represented an unyielding obstacle in a much-needed intervention for students. Providing a more specific example, a high school principal mentioned problems he encountered with the union over a scheduling issue that would have provided students more flexibility with the testing schedule. After being turned down several times by union leadership, he eventually gave up. Although there were some negative opinions made about BTU, many teachers felt the union provided them support, and several leaders felt the union offered some "cutting-edge solutions" to some of the districts more complex challenges.

In 2007, Paul Reville documented many aspects of Tom Payzant's decade of reform in BPS and his experience as a district leader in general. In a chapter written by Payzant himself, he reveals how unions (in several districts he served, not specifically BPS) affected him personally and professionally as a leader and as a parent of children attending public schools.[21] On a personal level, Payzant states:

> My family and I witnessed pickets at our house, saw teachers wearing "Payzant Buster" buttons in classrooms where my children were learning, and even had our own children cross picket lines to go to school during a strike.[22]

Despite the personal conflicts, he stated that he still believes teachers have a right to be represented and to bargain the terms and conditions of their employment. However, his concern is that the union role continues to broaden to the extent that it impedes the flexibility needed to make necessary reforms for instruction. In his words, "Too often I found myself at odds with union leaders determined to protect the working conditions of their members at the expense of legitimate reforms needed to transform schools for the benefit of children."[23]

These comments do not reflect directly on BTU. Payzant does not reference the union in that section of Reville's book; rather, he is discussing his union experiences over his entire leadership career. However, he does mention that the lessons he learned over time in dealing with unions helped him work collaboratively with BTU, and he felt that the agreements reached between BTU and BPS, such as with the creation of pilot schools, represented what can be accomplished when both sides work together with student outcomes in mind. He stated that he hoped BPS and BTU would continue their work with "unprecedented collaboration and innovation to focus on the improvement of student achievement."[24]

Community

As mentioned earlier, BPS has a long history of partnerships with the community and businesses through the Boston Compact, prompted by the recognition by key business leaders that an economic link exists between successful public school students and future business employees. In addition to the Compact, the Boston Plan for Excellence represented another business-sponsored coalition that was highly involved with the district.

The plan began in 1984, when the Bank of Boston established a $1.5 million endowment to support innovative teaching and curriculum in BPS schools.[25] The plan drew other sizeable sponsors and contributions such as $1 million from John Hancock Financial Services for middle school programs and $1 million from a law firm for teacher development.

Several other key business and community partners appeared in the community focus group interviews each year to tell us about their role with the district and to discuss similar partners that helped them support BPS. The Boston Private Industry Council (PIC) is a public-private partnership that connects business, BPS, higher education, government, labor, and community organizations. Its activities within the district are almost too many to list; however, their main initiatives are with the Boston Compact, the Workforce Investment Board, and the Plan for Excellence. One interesting project the Council supports is collecting follow-up data on graduates three to four years after high school.

Another key community partner we interviewed was the director of the Boston Parent Organizing Network (BPON). BPON started in 1999 as a network of six community-based organizations within Boston's immigrant and minority communities. Its mission is to organize, develop, and support parents and families in working productively with BPS for "an excellent education for all students." In 2006, BPON had thirty-two member organization partners working directly with families. The organization pushed for the district to hire a deputy superintendent for family and community engagement, and was key in advocating for the implementation of the Individual Student Success Plans.

We heard about and talked to many other community partners associated with the district and its schools. Other frequently mentioned partnerships were Countdown to Kindergarten, Boston Children's Museum, Boston Youth Foundation, and Home for Little Wanderers, to name a few. Countdown to Kindergarten consisted of a partnership between BPS, the mayor's office, and twenty-six community partners, along with the museum, to reach out to young parents before their children entered public school. These numerous community and business partners supported the district in many aspects affecting students and their families, from providing outreach to pre-K students, supporting after-school activities for youths, to advocating for professional development for teachers.

When asked about the district's key priorities, the community members referenced the district's focus on student achievement, community engagement, and parent outreach. Interviewees voiced appreciation for having an additional full-time BPS liaison working with them, and several asserted that the district had made a "cultural shift looking toward the community to show them how to conduct change." They felt this shift demonstrated an increase in community engagement for decision-making processes affecting the district and public school students. When asked what districtwide reforms made the most positive impact on student achievement over the past three years, the answers primarily focused on implementing higher levels of accountability, the availability of more data, better professional development for teachers, and the creation of the pilot schools like the International High School with tailor-made programs. One community member said he could feel and see the tension when the district first implemented many of its formative assessments. However, he said, he saw the district trying to support the teachers on making the changes and he heard from teachers that they eventually grew to appreciate the additional data, as it was necessary for creating meaningful Individual Student Success Plans.

When asked about the district's biggest challenges, community members mentioned resources, Boston's continual influx of immigrants with unique language needs, improving high school performance, and tackling achievement gaps. When the achievement gap topic came up, several community members felt the district was doing a good job of putting the issue on the table. They pointed out that Dr. Payzant was a visible member at many community events, not because he was expected to, but because "he wants to hear what community groups discuss and think is important." The community members also agreed that Dr. Payzant brought stability to the district with his long tenure and steady focus, and they hoped that the incoming superintendent would keep the consistency laid out over the past ten years because "we are just beginning to see the fruits of that labor now."

Parents

The desegregation law that created districtwide busing is referenced in BPS as a "controlled choice plan" or "school assignment policy." Although it will be discussed in greater detail later in this chapter, it is important to understand the basic premise behind the student assignment policy in schools, as it is frequently identified as influencing parent involvement in the district. The district is divided into three very large geographic zones, and students do not attend their neighborhood school, which poses a number of logistical and social challenges to parents with children in BPS. While parents would prefer for their children to attend neighborhood schools, they did not want to do so until "they [the schools] were all of equal quality." In several interviews, particularly those prior to 2005 and 2006, several parents mentioned feeling disconnected from their school, and school personnel felt the logistical distance between parents and schools added an extra challenge in creating closer relationships with parents.

In parent focus groups, most of the parents had some knowledge of the district's goals and its Focus on Children reform plan, but had more knowledge about individual schools than district work. In addition to geographic challenges, many district and school interviewees cited the district's high percentages of single-parent families as a factor affecting parent involvement. Many parents felt these single parents could at best help with checking homework and reading to their children, but would likely have little time to attend school events.

The parents saw the principals and teachers as hardworking and the schools as being welcoming to the parents. Almost every parent interviewed agreed that parent involvement was an issue of concern, and that the availability of activities for parents often depended on someone at each school focusing on parent outreach. Before 2004, the district had parent liaisons as paid positions. However, those positions were cut after 2004 and were subsequently covered through existing positions. Parents missed the outreach personnel and some claimed that the district and schools were not communicating well with them. In 2006, the district created a new central office–based position called the Deputy Superintendent for Family and Community Engagement. The position seemed to improve the parents' perception about their connectivity with the district and schools, which helped increase their knowledge about district initiatives relating to student achievement and closing ethnic and income gaps.

Governance, Organization, and Decision Making

BPS functions as a department within the City of Boston. This structure adds another layer of governance to the district, putting district activities within the greater context of the city. According to the superintendent, this arrangement allows the city's three largest unions—police, firefighters, and teachers—to play effectively off one another for items of negotiation. The superintendent attributes some of the success of the district to the support of the city leadership. Several different sources mentioned that Mayor Thomas Menino treats the public schools as a priority that gets "stronger as years go by." "Our schools are making progress," Menino said in his 2001 State of the City Address. "The long slide down is over."[26] As part of the city, BPS can be affected by other city politics. The superintendent serves on the mayor's cabinet and, after being approved by the BPS School Committee, the district budget must be approved by the thirteen-member City Council. BPS represents about 36 percent of the city budget, so the superintendent often spends more time with the City Council than do other city department leaders.

Dr. Payzant reiterated in several interviews that the district's tight connection to the mayor's office, combined with the stability afforded by the "right" appointed board, has added great continuity, focus, and support to the district's work. In a 2005 interview, Payzant stated, "I've got public health, the fire chief, and the police chief—all the key city agencies—to connect with in terms of supports for schools." Given the needs of the students in BPS, the potential for coordinating services for students and schools makes this an ideal arrangement.

Under Dr. Payzant, the schools in BPS were organized administratively in three triads and nine clusters. The triads had mixed school levels: elementary, middle, and high. They were overseen by a deputy superintendent, and clusters were organized geographically within the triad and mentored by an active principal who leads each cluster. There were twelve to seventeen schools in each cluster. Several administrators noted in interviews that the three triads were very large areas geographically; thus, even though there was a mix of school levels, they were not organized in feeder patterns, since the student assignment policy basically eliminates neighborhood schools and predictable school placements. To connect to the district, cluster leaders served on the superintendent's leadership team as liaisons to the superintendent for the principals in their cluster. Additionally, cluster leaders stayed connected through MyBPS and e-mail, although many mentioned the need to refer to both systems daily or "you'll have trouble keeping up with all the information."

School leaders at all levels seemed to feel relatively connected to other schools and the district through cluster and principal meetings and professional development opportunities. One middle school cluster leader described how his cluster focused on middle schools within the entire district, so they could bring information from cluster meetings back to school instructional teams, which involved coaches (located at central office at that time) and other relevant instructional personnel. He felt the meetings between various stakeholders that trickled both up to central office and down to teachers was important because "that's how you align your resources." He mentioned that he sometimes combined various meetings if they had a common thread, like a cluster and a principals meeting, so that "you can be efficient, get the biggest bang, and everyone has the same information."

Principals in focus groups in both 2005 and 2006 asserted that their opinion and expertise were often solicited by the central office, and most felt that the district and schools engaged in "two-way communication." The principals also found Tom Payzant to be visible and accessible. Illustrating the point, one principal stated, "If all the principals are gone, the superintendent is the one sitting up front [in the classroom]." Another mentioned, "It's different than a district where you may see the superintendent once and that's it. People are used to him being around in Boston." A third principal chimed in, "I've seen him three times this week!"

One mechanism used to connect stakeholders across the schools is the local Instructional Leadership Team (ILT). Members of ILTs include teachers from every grade level and administrators and coaches who meet on a regular basis to discuss how to improve instruction. While several schools found ILT meetings to be useful, one high school principal was having problems with the ILT structure because his school, as with most high schools in BPS, had been restructured into four smaller learning communities. In a traditional school, ILT teams could easily discuss specific shared students in their conversations about instructional planning. However, this principal asserted that he faced constant tension between meeting with his smaller community teams and meeting with teachers across content areas. But another administrator found the ILTs to be very useful for connecting teachers; he described the process as being exciting:

> Before, the doors were closed, and teachers thought, "This is my own thing. I don't have time to go to another classroom." But now, especially through the ILT, teachers are visiting each others' classrooms. They're sharing and they're doing grade-level team meetings. They're giving suggestions and some are mentoring other teachers. It's just a wonderful, open process which has benefited everyone.

Regarding decision making, central office leaders seemed to have autonomy to implement the district's strategic plan to a certain extent, but always within the confines of their city, community, and union partnerships. Interviews in 2006 found that the union, sometimes interpreted as an obstacle, had made some concessions that gave the district important flexibilities that were not present in earlier years, such as the ability for principals to hire their own teachers rather than inherit them through transfers.

One interesting change being instituted in 2006 was the movement of the instructional coaches from central office to specific schools. The change was made in response to requests by principals to have more control over school instructional resources. Described by one key central office leader,

> We had a principal call us on it. He said, "Either you don't trust us, or you can and give us the resources. See if we do a good job. If there are concerns about effectiveness, you can always take them back."

The chief operations officer at that time, Mike Contompasis, mentioned that the change would pose quite a challenge to the district, mostly because of the anxiety voiced by the coaches at changing their home base. The coaches would need to build a closer relationship within one particular school rather than serve as an itinerant in several schools; this made them nervous about where they would be placed. However, despite these concerns, Contompasis felt the move was important because, "it is the right thing to do, because we expect principals to operate as instructional leaders, so we need to give them the resources to do it." This shift in support resources directly to the schools illustrated the district's willingness to make a difficult change to address the needs of principals.

While principals acknowledged that their budgets were relatively rigid, they still believed they had enough room to allocate resources as needed for their schools. Principals and teachers both asserted that they felt they had enough flexibility to enhance the curriculum as they saw fit and that their requests for curricular or programmatic changes were heard and addressed. Teachers felt they were somewhat constrained by the pressures of covering a lot of instructional objectives within short periods of time, but they did assert that they were given support and were heard when needed.

The manner in which students were assigned to schools in BPS had a big impact on the district's ability to keep schools, parents, and students connected to the district at times. The policy also complicated decision making and resource allocation and overall created a great deal of tension for many BPS stakeholders. Prior to 1999, the assignments were made to achieve racial balance reflective within a given zone. However, a federal court case addressing the challenge of a BPS parent resulted in the School Committee dropping race-based school assignments in 1999. Under the basic plan, parents could choose any elementary or middle school within their geographic clusters, and high schools were open to all students regardless of their home neighborhood. The resulting formula attempted to fill seats in schools through a more "fair" process completed through a computer-generated mathematical formula that assigns students to their highest choice (parents are encouraged to identify and prioritize three choice schools). When a school is full and cannot meet a parental choice, the computer generates the assignments based on choice and priorities. The priorities are sibling plus walk zone; sibling; walk zone (a priority for 50 percent of available seats); and random number. Walk zones are defined by school level, with one mile or less designated as an elementary school walk zone and two miles or less for high schools. Random numbers are used to "break ties" between students who have the same priorities for the same school. East Boston high school, which is located on the other side of a tunnel that poses great logistical challenges, guarantees a seat to any student who lives in the neighborhood.[27]

Student assignment has always been a very emotionally charged issue in Boston, and continues to fuel the city's ongoing undercurrents of racial tension. To ensure that these issues were understood and addressed, Mayor Menino, the Boston School Committee, and Superintendent Payzant launched a community task force to study the assignment system and generate recommendations for modifications. Their various recommendations included changing the assignment algorithm, creating a "buffer zone" that would allow families living close to a zone to choose schools on either side, and restructuring the number of zones.[28]

Although the task force report did shed some light on the desired outcomes of a new assignment system—namely, to have students attend schools closer to their neighborhoods and provide a variety of schools for families to choose from—a study by the Center for Collaborative Education provided additional information about the issues, creating tension with the assignment process. The authors' findings reported that pilot schools were most frequently chosen for high school, demand for pilot schools far exceeded availability, and families who did not receive their first school choice in transition grades (K, 1, and 6) were twice as likely to leave the district.[29]

BPS stakeholders also voiced a variety of complaints about the student assignment process during interviews. These problems included dissatisfaction by parents that their first or second school choice often was not fulfilled, inability of some schools to nurture close relationships with parents who live far away from the school, inability to organize students and schools in a consistent feeder pattern cohort, lack of alignment between resources flowing to schools and the neighboring community, excessive transportation costs, long commutes for students, and an increase in student absences. In addition to these challenges, a former central office leader stated in a follow-up interview that the assignment policy greatly reduced opportunities for the district and schools to tap valuable resources within parent and community groups, due to the lack of cohesion created through distance and logistics.

In a 2009 letter to the *Boston Globe*, a former co-chair of the BPS Assignment Task Force argued that the entire practice of busing should end in the district, since the assignment practice cost the district $72 million a year to "bus children across Boston to schools that are not demonstrably better than schools near their homes."[30] He felt the money saved, which he estimated to be about $40 million, could be better spent on teaching and learning. Additionally, he lamented that students do not learn much from long bus rides and that the bus routes were not updated; thus, many buses were only half-filled, adding to more fiscal waste. He also pointed out that the numerous buses traveling twice daily greatly added to the "carbon print" left in the city. He concluded with the point that the city's demographics had changed to the extent that the original intent of the policy was no longer relevant, and that focus needed to be made on improving all of the neighborhood schools.

In April 2009, new BPS superintendent Carol R. Johnson presented a proposal to replace the three-zone student assignment policy. The new model expands the choice area from three to five zones, where parents of students in grades pre-K through 8 may choose schools within one of three assignment zones, as well as any school within a certain distance of their home. The plan is intended to expand choices for parents, create more walkable communities, and reduce transportation costs. The announcement came with instructions on the public engagement process, including a series of community meetings until the end of June 2009 to gather public comment.

Resource Allocation

The district budgeting process in early site visits (2003) was described as being very centralized; all money, with the exception of pilot schools, was allocated by the central office. The pilot schools (which were considered charter schools) were given lump sums through an agreement with BTU and two Horace Mann charters. During that time, schools had few discretionary dollars. To help them, the superintendent shifted the responsibility for paying for materials from the schools to the district, enabling the district to pay for adopted texts with outside funding rather than with the typical instructional resource budget. This practice helped the schools retain those dollars for additional materials. One central office administrator stated that about 80 percent of the school funds were designated for personnel. School budgets were based on the number of students, and school site councils controlled the budget at the school level. Schools had the ability to convert positions into other types of positions and use the average full-time employment salary to determine the dollars they had available.

In 2004, the district began having more budget issues. Superintendent Payzant referenced one problem he had with how the state interpreted BPS's budget allotment, resulting in an $18 million difference "between average per-pupil cost and regular pupil average." At that time, Payzant explained, 35 percent of the city budget went to BPS and 30 percent of BPS funding came through the state, but was given to the city to allocate to BPS. Additionally, property tax funding provided another budget resource, and categorical state grants went directly to the district. Several other partnerships help determine budget spending and fund-raising as well. REACT, a group comprising members of BPS and the Boston Plan for Excellence, helps the district weigh the costs of its different types of innovations and practices, such as making the high school start time later. The Boston Compact creates additional budget support through the mayor and various partners, including a practice industry council that looks at district goals and helps raise grant dollars for the district.

Despite these valuable supporters, Payzant cited budget cuts made in 2003 and 2004 as being the toughest in his career, noting, "We cut over seven hundred positions over two years, and four hundred of those had impact on our work focusing on transitional instructional years—grades 3, 6, 9." The budget reduction made it difficult for schools to fund additional student support programs, such as summer school classes in core courses. Some schools were able to use outside funds to keep those programs intact, but others could not. Payzant continued, "Adding 470 new four-year-old seats [pre-K] without additional state funds slowed us down as well." During lean times, Payzant said it was important to "make the best of what you've got and have aligned resources and high priorities." Payzant's priorities were to let the impact of funding deficits rest on the district infrastructure, in order to keep the instructional programs intact. One follow-up interview conducted in 2009 also revealed that an increase in student flight from the district to private schools also hurt the district's fiscal picture.

When asked in 2005 how much discretion schools had over their budgets, Dr. Payzant cited several constraints to providing significant budget flexibility at the school level, one being that staff allotment was based on enrollment and needs, and staff represented 80 percent of the budget. Moving staffing allotments around in schools is not easily accomplished, due to constraints caused by class-size policies. Payzant mentioned that schools had flexibility on external funds, which were sizeable, since most BPS schools have 40 percent or more students receiving free or reduced-price lunch, meaning those schools received a fair amount schoolwide Title I funds.

Budgeting and resource allocation descriptions from principals agreed with information we obtained from district leaders. An elementary school principal mentioned that each school's budget is set by the number of students in the school and while there are items that can be shifted to different categories, "ultimately, you have a set amount to work with." Echoing frustrations with budget reductions, this principal said that her school had lost $260,000, resulting in the need to cut their librarian, a teacher, and two paraprofessionals. Discretionary funds for supplies and books are "very, very, tiny," she asserted. This principal also received about $157,000 in Title I funds, which she used to pay for a full-time reading teacher and a transition teacher, with the remaining leftover funds to use for a summer training institute. When asked how the funding issues affected her school, she stated, "It seems as if the system is counterintuitive; if you do well and make annual yearly progress with the MCAS, then you don't get extra money, even if your students need it." She wished that the district would spread the wealth "rather than take money from Peter to pay for Paul."

Providing similar responses about budget flexibility, a high school principal said he had little discretion over his budget because his school was small so that, "When staffing is taken out, there is not much left." He was appreciative that the district paid for copies and leases, which left him more funds to pay for textbooks and supplies. This principal did feel he had some flexibility in spending professional development funds, which he felt was "a step in the right direction." When asked how the availability of funding affected his school, this particular principal mentioned that he was no longer able to fund the school's transitional math and English program for incoming ninth-graders, and he had lost ten positions over the course of a year.

Several principals did mention, as did Payzant, that the district attempted to put back lost funds in small percentages each year, with the goal of gradually helping schools rebuild the losses they had experienced over the lean times. In 2006, we continued to hear frustration from the district and schools over budget losses.

Climate/Culture

Interviews with various BPS stakeholders illustrate that, while the climate of the city and district still challenges the ability to build an open and trusting climate, the district is making progress in how leaders and teachers approach instruction and student expectations. The shift to higher expectations for students and collective accountability by the adults in the system for student performance came about through intentional focus on reciprocal customer service between the district and schools. Citing size and the existence of "pockets of resistance" as a challenge, district leaders mentioned that they spent "a lot of time and energy" working to change the climate in the schools to function under the belief that all students can learn. Key factors in nurturing that belief were having a clear, focused, and consistent message communicated across the district and using data as a mechanism to diagnose instructional issues, discuss interventions, and acknowledge successes. The common mantra we heard from all levels of the system was, "There is no longer anywhere to hide," suggesting a level of transparency around student performance. In addition to the shift of the deputy superintendents to directly supporting principals, and principals becoming instructional leaders and supporters to teachers, many stakeholders saw data as a useful diagnostic tool that led to necessary supports and resources for both teachers and students. A quote from one principal illustrates similar statements made by several principals about BPS's cultural shift to being more open and honest about performance issues brought out by data:

There is a culture of not giving up for anything. The data doesn't lie. You have a lower performing group, you develop a strategy. We can say we are not doing well and ask for help. That culture is building into the classrooms also.

Making a shift to higher expectations across an entire system is difficult. Several principals felt they had heard similar conversations about raising expectations "thirty years ago," but that now "the difference is, everyone is buying into it." Principals particularly felt they could see the shift in teachers, who were "no longer blaming the students" and were working together to improve instruction for students. Several referred to a change in "the open classroom door" where teachers were honestly sharing and saying, "I don't know how to do this" to their peers.

Unusual as it may sound, teachers also often stated, "You can't hide in the classroom anymore. You can't say 'you don't know.'" The "open door" and data were key, according to teachers, to focusing on the wide gaps existing between different student groups in the district. Teachers said that, to varying degrees, their schools were very open and honest about their gap issues in an attempt to drill down and understand causes and solutions behind performance disparities. The frequency of teacher references to achievement gaps was surprising. One teacher helped us better understand the presence of the issue:

> Now there is more dialogue where people are frank and honest and also educated about what you're talking about and looking at, and having students thinking about it. I think there's sometimes danger that this is not the only world you live in. Everybody here, it's not necessarily painted the picture of Boston as a whole, you know, in the classroom. It paints a picture of, for many of my kids, Dorchester and Roxbury. But, you know, there are different parts of Boston; I can help them out on that. They [teachers and students] can help me out on knowing about their neighborhoods and things like that.

Some teachers mentioned that their schools were not discussing issues of race and gaps as much. One teacher felt the racial tension in the district was a product of deep-seated conflict between different ethnic groups that have long existed in the city:

> You have to understand the city that we're in. You know, I teach and then I also coach basketball. Just being in a different area, there is something always under the surface to some extent. I think people walk on eggshells almost more with adults than with students. I probably walk much more on eggshells with adults than I do with my students because, I know them, I understand.

Most conversations at the schools and with principal and teacher focus groups eventually turned to discussions about the gap in the last two years of site visits (2005 and 2006), confirming a concerted focus on the issue over prior years. In 2006, we learned that the BPS principals were attending an annual three-day institute every August to closely examine gap issues in partnership with community members. Payzant mentioned that they learned in those meetings that "the key element is what the expectations are in the achievement gap, and the policy commitment to moving those expectations forward." When asked how to specifically raise expectations in a system, Payzant responded, "You start with very clear, high expectations for the kids, then the schools get the message out." Because kids come into the system often with a gap, one strategy in the district has been to focus on investing in early childhood education to help students begin school with the right skills. Payzant also emphasized that each school carefully reviewed its data for achievement gaps and then had conversations about the root causes for performance differences; based on those conversations, it built its intervention plans. While many principals and teachers believed they had not figured out how to make measurable changes in the size of their gaps, they believed the conversations were an important impetus for starting the process.

A follow-up interview with a former central office administrator shed some light on why Boston was so challenged by achievement gaps and pockets of tension and mistrust. In his opinion, "The scars of segregation are still very evident within Boston." He felt that members of the African American community still felt disenfranchised from their schools and frustrated with the imposition of having to travel outside of their neighborhoods to attend an appropriate school. However, they did not want to move back into their neighborhood schools until the district "fixed them." The administrator also pointed out that Boston's racial tension was misconstrued at times as just a white–black issue, and because of that, many other groups—in particular, the growing Hispanic populations and the increasing number of diverse immigrants coming to the city—felt left out of conversations addressing their needs and opinions about creating equity across the district.

Principals and teachers described the climate within their schools as being very positive and supportive, with good relationships between the school leadership, teachers, and parents. Reiterating the importance of the "relationship" corner of the triangle described by Payzant in his reform approach, one teacher said:

> Relationships are very important in a positive school climate. That goes from administrator to teacher, administrator to student, teacher to student, student to teacher. Everyone in the building—the nurse, custodian, cafeteria workers—we're all working together. We believe in one another and everyone has to be consistent. Most people in this building believe in what they are doing; they have pride in the building and they are working hard. That makes it easier for all of us. We all work hard because we don't want to let anyone down. The students know we have expectations here. They come here to learn, so they know when they come here there are certain standards, certain things they have to do. So they just do it.

Believing relationships to be very important, school principals saw teacher support as a priority, and the teachers invested time in communicating and visiting with parents. Teachers asserted that they worked hard and were proud of their schools, and the collegiality they modeled with each other seemed to transfer to their students, who also voiced pride in their schools.

REFORM AND STUDENT ACHIEVEMENT—BRINGING IT TO SCALE

BPS provides a wealth of information about long-term reform in a complex urban school system through its unique willingness to keep and support one leader to implement a focused plan for an entire decade. In 2005 we asked Superintendent Payzant what his main focus was for BPS and how he saw education reform. His answer:

> I believe there will be systems of schools [in the United States] around for a long time, and we won't be able to reach the goals that standards-based reform have for all students by having ninety thousand schools bloom by themselves. I came to Boston set to see if you could take a midsize urban system and have impact on a system of schools, not just a few good ones.

Outlining the reform process, Payzant mentioned that the district started with very clear expectations about what students needed to learn, adjusted the curriculum to give students the ability to meet those expectations, and then focused on the other crucial elements: instruction and leadership. "All of that has to be connected and aligned, using a laserlike focus on teaching and learning," Payzant stated.

Given the complexity of BPS, one must wonder how a leader could walk into a system that has a long history of dysfunction and complications and figure out the right levers to pull to penetrate its culture and implement a very different and focused plan. Reville and Coggins's book on Payzant's decade of reform describes how he prepared to become the system's leader.[31] He appointed a transition team several months before he began as superintendent to help him gain information about the key issues in BPS and to make recommendations on building a reform plan and identifying where to begin the work. When Payzant explained his vision of focusing on instruction, training and support, and the use of data and accountability, he told BPS stakeholders not to "view each component as a separate initiative, but rather to make connections among them and ensure that the whole was greater than the sum of its parts."[32] The resulting "road map" was key, according to Payzant, for keeping focus and leading the work during his first year.

The second important initial step taken by Payzant was to dig in and really learn about the system, particularly the schools, by visiting every one of the 125 schools his first year. What was unique about those visits was that he did not just visit with the principals; he actually spent time in classrooms speaking to students and observing instruction. As noted earlier in this chapter, his presence and interest sent a message to stakeholders that he really wanted to understand and know the system he was leading. Reville and Coggins's book records that his presence was particularly a surprise to teachers, who at that time viewed their classrooms as "their private domain."[33] Thus, his actions facilitated the transparency he set out to establish within instruction and accountability; this would eventually be key to creating alignment across the system. The need for alignment become particularly important, Payzant recalled, when his initial visits also revealed to him just how different the expectations, instruction, and climate were in each school—a problem not only for students who tend to move around within the district, but also for creating a seamless K–12 instructional program for students.

A second interesting point that came out of our last interview with Payzant was about the pace of reform, a topic that often comes up when researchers and practitioners scrutinize the work of urban district leaders. Payzant stated that he had overheard conversations speculating that he had been in BPS for a long time, so, why didn't he get "get it all done?" Addressing that question, he asserts, "I am viewed as an incrementalist by some, yet others postulate that I have moved too fast." Balancing the urgency of poor student performance with ensuring that reforms take hold is challenging. Payzant added, "[They] would have taken root better if we had more time." He felt a lot of groundwork had been laid, but that the next superintendent would have a lot of challenges.

Clearly, BPS began pulling its system together by hiring a superintendent who stayed for the long haul, thus providing a clear, well-coordinated vision and consistency to the district. In the early site visits between 2003 and 2005, when we asked about which reforms were the most powerful, many leaders pointed to the district's clear vision and use of data as improving student achievement. Some leaders also mentioned the extended process of refining and aligning their curriculum, but that strategy was not mentioned as consistently.

In 2006, two key central office leaders identified the "Six Essentials" as being crucial for the district's improvements in student achievement, as well the fact that they spent each year drilling down and better refining the elements. Many other district and school leaders mentioned the improvements made in the human resources practices, the district's focus on literacy across the curriculum, and the improved responses they received from the central office through the deputy superintendents. The district also continued to refine its curriculum by making each subject clearer and more explicit, paying particular attention to outcomes in literacy, math, and science. The reconfiguration of its large comprehensive high schools into smaller thematic academies was also discussed as an important reform having measurable impact on student achievement.

Principals and teachers at the schools mentioned the availability of more and better professional development, the increased focus on literacy, and the use of the workshop model as significantly affecting student achievement. One teacher voiced the conviction that the workshop model helped students become more involved with subject materials at higher cognitive levels and that writing, reading, and math scores had improved in his school as a direct result of that model. In addition to the workshop model, another teacher said that the benchmark assessments were very helpful for guiding teachers in adjusting instruction according to student needs.

While many BPS constituents feel the district is moving in the right direction, there still remain a number of challenges on the road ahead after its Broad Prize win in 2006. Tom Payzant was serving his last year as superintendent that year, so one of the foremost challenges on the minds of district leaders was finding his replacement. The other major challenges discussed had to do with serving students in special education and in ELL services within the mainstream population as continuing to pose a challenge to the district.

Central office leaders felt that the district was serving too many of the students in special education in separate pull-out classes. They were looking closely into the issue because they believed "if you have an issue in special education, it means you also have problems in your regular education program." To reduce the identification of students for pull-out classes, the district started focusing on providing more supports, training, and coaching for regular education teachers to ensure they had the skills to differentiate instruction in their classroom. Additionally, the district identified fifteen schools with high numbers of students in special education to closely study and provide additional instructional supports.

The issue with English language learners (ELL) is more complex. In 2003, the state passed a referendum to end transitional bilingual education and move to a sheltered English instruction–only approach.[34] By state law, ELL students would have 2.5 hours of ESL instruction; however, they would be missing another subject in their instructional day. Additionally, in 2008 regular education teachers were required to have additional certification for ELL instruction, resulting in seventy-five extra hours in training, straining the district's time and money resources. In addition to addressing the needs of students in special education and of those receiving ELL services, BPS leaders voiced concerns about maintaining balance between raising academic achievement in core subject areas and keeping a variety of electives available for students to squeeze into their schedules. One potential solution mentioned was extending the school day and working with the union on how to compensate teachers for additional time.

Elementary school principals and teachers were worried about a potential change to the current student assignment policy. Their primary concern was that students be able to remain at their current school under the new policy. Middle school staff members were concerned about maintaining positive relationships with the union while negotiating the time school leaders wanted teachers to attend professional development. Staff members were worried that the two extra hours of professional development time they had earned in a hard win over the union would disappear in the near future through union intervention. At one high school, leadership team members found it a challenge to get their students more actively engaged and to be responsible for their academic performance. Teachers and leaders felt that the performance plateau they had hit over the previous three years could be addressed through increased student investment in school. Overarching all these conversations about ongoing challenges were concerns about continual budget constraints within the district.

A case study completed in 2005 by the Aspen Institute and the Annenberg Institute identified some of the same challenges as above and added a few additional ones, such as inconsistency in math, the perception that some departments in the central office operated as separate "silos," and an ongoing perception by some schools that they did not receive timely responses from the central office.[35] In 2006, several central office leaders practically quoted some of the findings in that report, suggesting that the district paid a great deal of attention to the report's findings and suggestions. In fact, many of the suggestions and some of the district's own remedies had already been instituted during the year following the release of the report. To address the math issues, the district began working with several math professors, and district curriculum leaders were engaged in reviewing their math programs. Central office positions were reviewed and reconfigured to increase efficiency, and the central office team met more often to improve departmental connectivity. Additionally, deputy superintendents were working harder on responding to schools, and the district went one step further by shifting the instructional coaches to single schools, as discussed earlier, to provide principals with more control over their instructional supports.

Current Performance and Practices

This case study captured a decade-long process initiated by Superintendent Tom Payzant in an effort to reform BPS to scale. Although many of the same systems and practices are still in place, BPS also has a lot of new changes in their system. In August 2007, BPS hired Dr. Carol R. Johnson to be the superintendent of schools. Dr. Johnson previously served as superintendent in Memphis City Schools (Tennessee), a district with 119,000 students. Prior to her work in Memphis, she served as a superintendent in the Minneapolis Public Schools, where she was named Minnesota's Superintendent of the Year in 2002. She also has experience as an administrator, principal, and teacher.[36]

In January 2008, Dr. Johnson presented her "Acceleration Agenda" to the Boston School Committee. The plan appeared to address many challenges and areas of concern voiced by various BPS stakeholders and cited by the review completed by the Aspen and Annenberg Institutes. Highlights of the plan include realigning the leadership structure by hiring a new chief academic officer; creating an Office of Accountability; restructuring the existing Family & Community Engagement Office into the Family & Student Engagement Office; separating special education from other support services and hiring a director who will report to the superintendent over that function; improving support for English language learners; expanding the school choice marketing strategy to inform parents of their options; and exploring new school models, such as International Baccalaureate, an elementary Montessori program, and gender-specific programs. Regarding operations, the plan proposes to assess BPS facility needs, analyze transportation to find opportunities to maximize efficiency, institute a multiyear budget-planning process, and establish an Institutional Advancement Office to secure additional resources for the district.[37]

Follow-up interviews in 2009 with various BPS stakeholders revealed some concern that hiring an African American superintendent might disenfranchise other groups, such as the Hispanic population. Additional concerns were voiced that the new organizational structures put into place created overlap in some job responsibilities, potentially creating a lack of clarity within different BPS departments.

Student performance in 2007, the most recent year of available comparable data, shows that BPS achieved some small gains across grade levels and within subgroups. In elementary and middle school reading, aggregated proficiencies rose by at least four percentage points, and each minority ethnic and income subgroup increased as well. In high school reading, scores fell back down by a few percentage points, except for low-income and Hispanic students (figure 3.13).

Figure 3.14 shows a slightly different picture in math. The largest gains found from 2006 to 2007 in mathematics was in the middle and high school levels, with the fewest gains found in at the elementary level, except in the "all students" category. Both minority and low-income students improved in 2007 at the secondary level. Math performance is also relatively higher over the lower grades at the high school level.

FIGURE 3.13

District reading proficiencies for 2006 and 2007 by student group

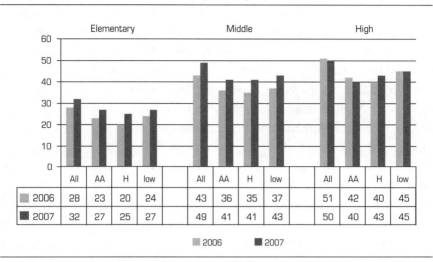

FIGURE 3.14

District math proficiencies for 2006 and 2007 by student group

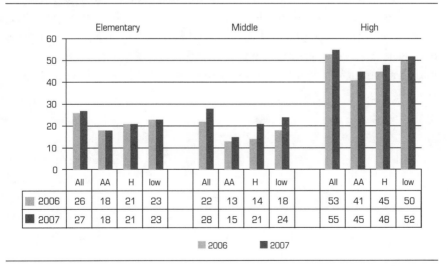

CONCLUSION

Despite numerous challenges, BPS has maintained relatively high levels of student achievement, as compared with similar districts in Massachusetts. Our last site visit (2006) confirmed the strength of Boston's student data system, its Collaborative Coaching and Learning professional development models, and the benefits of stable leadership under Tom Payzant's eleven-year tenure. In addition, the site visit team found marked progress in curriculum alignment and benchmark assessing. Teachers and principals spoke favorably of the curriculum and supporting documents in most of our school interviews, and district interviews confirmed that most core subjects now had aligned curriculum guides, pacing charts, and assessments. Teachers also felt that the district's use of the workshop model provided an effective means of helping students make better connections to what they were learning and at higher cognitive levels by incorporating more critical thinking, problem-solving, and communication skills into their lessons.

The most noteworthy improvements—those having the biggest impact on student achievement—were the "reinvention" of the district's human resources department, the redefinition of the role of deputy superintendents as campus support, and the marked increase in using data to drive decisions. Many conversations with principals and teachers led to an explanation about how a problem was identified or solved by reviewing data.

4

Garden Grove Unified School District

Garden Grove Unified School District is one of the growing number of "urban suburban" districts in the United States, serving 50,030 students in parts of seven municipalities in the Los Angeles area. The district covers twenty-eight square miles of territory and serves most of Garden Grove, California, and portions of six surrounding cities—Anaheim, Cypress, Fountain Valley, Santa Ana, Stanton, and Westminster.[1] The Garden Grove area saw a significant increase in its Asian American population (primarily Vietnamese and Korean) in the late 1970s and 1980s. Recently, Garden Grove has grown in the areas of entertainment and tourism, including nine high-rise hotels. According to the most recent census, in 2000, 43 percent of the population have children under the age of eighteen living with them, and the spread of the age groups is relatively even. The median income in the city is $47,754 for a household and $49,697 for a family. Roughly 14 percent of the population lives below the poverty line.[2]

Garden Grove USD's demographics are urban: 61 percent of the district's roughly fifty thousand students qualify for free and reduced-price lunch, 53 percent are Hispanic, 31 percent are Asian American, 15 percent are white, and 1 percent are African American.[3] The district is heavily populated by families who immigrated recently to the United States. English is the second language for approximately 75 percent of the district's students, who speak sixty-eight different languages.

After being named a finalist for the first three years of The Broad Prize, Garden Grove won the award in 2004. Highlights contributing to its 2004 win showed that Garden Grove had:

- Met its Adequate Yearly Progress (AYP) targets in 2004 for 100 percent of its schools
- Consistently performed higher than demographically similar districts between 2001 and 2004
- Narrowed the external gap (the gap between the district's disadvantaged group and the state's advantaged group) for all groups in reading and for low-income and Hispanic students in math

DISTRICT DEMOGRAPHICS AND ACHIEVEMENT LEVELS

Data from Broad Prize report cards indicate that Garden Grove showed strong performance throughout its Broad Prize years from 2002 to 2004, and afterward up to 2007. In fact, Garden Grove outperformed the state in many subjects and grade levels between those years, despite differences in student demographics. Compared with all California student enrollment percentages, Garden Grove enrolls more than three times as many Asian American students (many of whom are first-generation immigrants), slightly more Hispanic students, fewer African American students (consistent with the city's population), and fewer white students. More Garden Grove students qualify for free and reduced-price lunches (60 percent) compared with the state (47 percent). There are also twice as many English language learners (ELLs) in Garden Grove USD—51 percent, compared with 25 percent in the state.

Garden Grove outperformed the state over a consistent time period at all grade levels in math. Figure 4.1 illustrates the district's middle school math proficiencies compared with the state between 2003 and 2007. While both the district and state show similar increases over time (including a slight drop in 2007), the district consistently outperformed the state by at least 11 percentage points between 2003 and 2006.

FIGURE 4.1

District and state middle school math proficiencies: All students

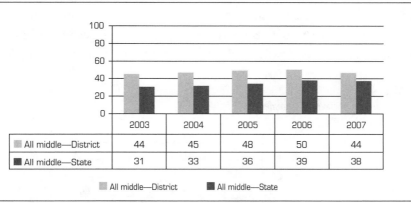

	2003	2004	2005	2006	2007
▨ All middle—District	44	45	48	50	44
■ All middle—State	31	33	36	39	38

▨ All middle—District　　　■ All middle—State

In reading, the district performed the same or slightly better than the state at every grade level except at the elementary level (defined as grades 3, 4, and 5 in the Broad analysis) in 2006 and 2007. Figure 4.2 illustrates that the district maintained slightly higher proficiency rates than the state between 2003 and 2007 in high school (defined as grade 10 in the Broad analysis) reading. The district's scores in reading are particularly impressive, given that its ELL population ranged from 53 percent to 47 percent during that time.

FIGURE 4.2

District and state middle school reading proficiencies: All students

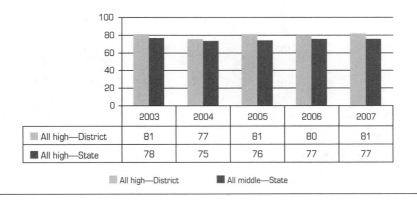

	2003	2004	2005	2006	2007
▨ All high—District	81	77	81	80	81
■ All high—State	78	75	76	77	77

▨ All high—District　　　■ All middle—State

Figures 4.3 and 4.4 illustrate performance in both math and reading at the different grade levels over time. Contrary to what is typically found in districts, the high school consistently outperformed the other grade levels, with a difference of over 30 percentage points or better in reading. The differences between grade levels are slightly smaller in math, but the el-

FIGURE 4.3

District math proficiencies: All students

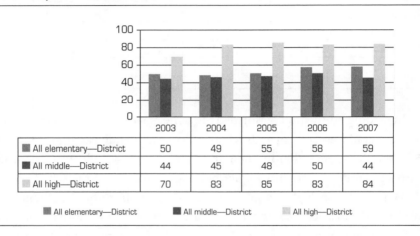

	2003	2004	2005	2006	2007
■ All elementary—District	50	49	55	58	59
■ All middle—District	44	45	48	50	44
All high—District	70	83	85	83	84

■ All elementary—District   ■ All middle—District   All high—District

FIGURE 4.4

District reading proficiencies: All students

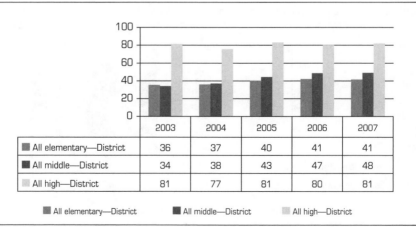

	2003	2004	2005	2006	2007
■ All elementary—District	36	37	40	41	41
■ All middle—District	34	38	43	47	48
All high—District	81	77	81	80	81

■ All elementary—District   ■ All middle—District   All high—District

ementary schools performed slightly better than the middle schools in all five years.

The main ethnic gap of interest in Garden Grove is between Hispanic and white students, since Garden Grove has an extremely small African American population. Figures 4.5 and 4.6 illustrate that the district had a narrower Hispanic/white gap than the state over time in middle school math. While the district's Hispanic/white gap widens slightly after 2007 (figure 4.5) due

FIGURE 4.5

District middle school math achievement gap between Hispanic and white students

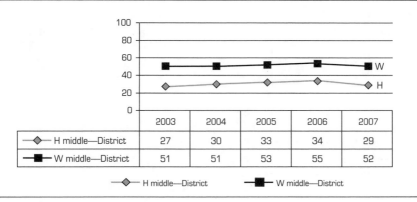

	2003	2004	2005	2006	2007
H middle—District	27	30	33	34	29
W middle—District	51	51	53	55	52

◆ H middle—District   ■ W middle—District

FIGURE 4.6

State middle school math achievement gap between Hispanic and white students

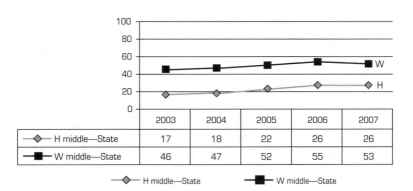

	2003	2004	2005	2006	2007
H middle—State	17	18	22	26	26
W middle—State	46	47	52	55	53

◆ H middle—State   ■ W middle—State

to a slight drop in Hispanic performance, the district still has a narrower gap between Hispanic and white students than the state (figure 4.6), and higher performance with its Hispanic students in middle school (defined as grades 6, 7, and 8 in the Broad analysis) math than the state.

High school achievement gap performance is difficult to view over time, as there was no gap data available in 2003 and 2004. However, figures 4.7 and 4.8 illustrate that the district consistently maintained a narrower gap

FIGURE 4.7

District high school math achievement gap between Hispanic and white students

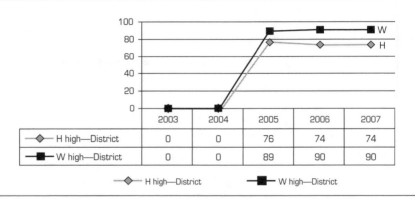

	2003	2004	2005	2006	2007
H high—District	0	0	76	74	74
W high—District	0	0	89	90	90

FIGURE 4.8

State high school math achievement gap between Hispanic and white students

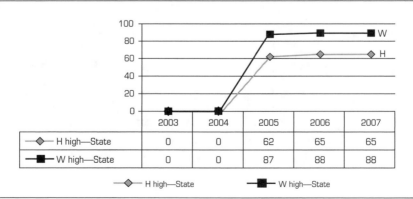

	2003	2004	2005	2006	2007
H high—State	0	0	62	65	65
W high—State	0	0	87	88	88

between Hispanic and white students between 2005 and 2007 compared with the state, and both groups in the district maintained higher proficiency rates than the state as well.

Where the district consistently appears to be making headway in achievement gaps is between low-income and non-low-income students. Figures 4.9 and 4.10 illustrate that Garden Grove has a smaller income gap in high school reading proficiencies compared with the state. Though the

FIGURE 4.9

District high school reading achievement gap between low- and non-low-income students

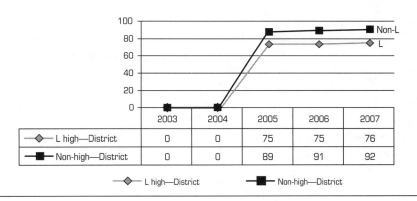

	2003	2004	2005	2006	2007
◆ L high—District	0	0	75	75	76
■ Non-high—District	0	0	89	91	92

◆ L high—District   ■ Non-high—District

FIGURE 4.10

State high school reading achievement gap between low- and non-low-income students

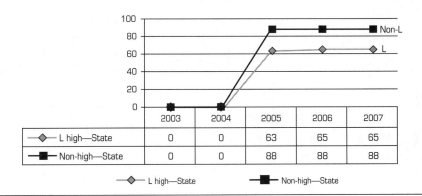

	2003	2004	2005	2006	2007
◆ L high—State	0	0	63	65	65
■ Non-high—State	0	0	88	88	88

◆ L high—State   ■ Non-high—State

district's gap widens slightly after 2005, it still remains narrower than the state's income gap, and performance for both low-income and non-low-income groups in the district remains higher than the state between 2005 and 2007.

When comparing the district (figure 4.11) and state (figure 4.12) low-income and non-low-income students in middle school reading over time, the district shows a narrower gap between its low- and non-low-income

FIGURE 4.11

District middle school reading achievement gap between low- and non-low-income students

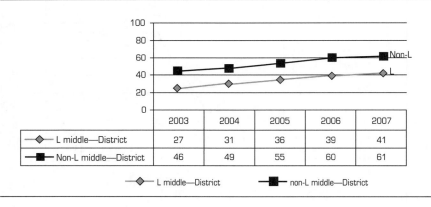

	2003	2004	2005	2006	2007
L middle—District	27	31	36	39	41
Non-L middle—District	46	49	55	60	61

◆ L middle—District   ■ non-L middle—District

FIGURE 4.12

State middle school reading achievement gap between low- and non-low-income students

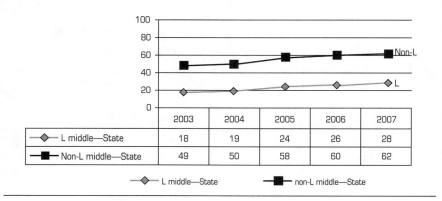

	2003	2004	2005	2006	2007
L middle—State	18	19	24	26	28
Non-L middle—State	49	50	58	60	62

◆ L middle—State   ■ non-L middle—State

students than the state, and shows higher performance in its low-income students between 2003 and 2008.

Garden Grove's performance looks particularly strong when compared to districts with similar demographics within the state. Figures 4.13 and 4.14 illustrate all positive residuals in both reading and math across all grades

FIGURE 4.13
District reading residual analysis: All levels

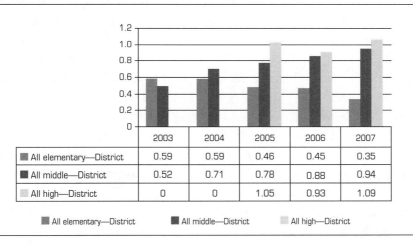

	2003	2004	2005	2006	2007
All elementary—District	0.59	0.59	0.46	0.45	0.35
All middle—District	0.52	0.71	0.78	0.88	0.94
All high—District	0	0	1.05	0.93	1.09

All elementary—District   All middle—District   All high—District

FIGURE 4.14
District math residual analysis: All levels

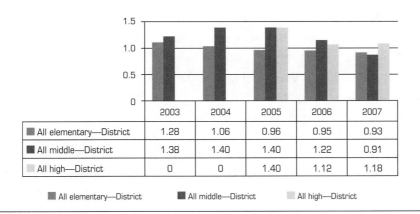

	2003	2004	2005	2006	2007
All elementary—District	1.28	1.06	0.96	0.95	0.93
All middle—District	1.38	1.40	1.40	1.22	0.91
All high—District	0	0	1.40	1.12	1.18

All elementary—District   All middle—District   All high—District

levels between 2003 and 2007. Noteworthy residuals above 1.0 are found in high school reading in 2005 and 2007, and in most levels in math except in elementary school between 2004 and 2007 and middle school in 2007.

High School and College Readiness Data

The Education Trust has recognized Garden Grove as having relatively high graduation rates for an urban district.[4] In 2004, the year it won The Broad Prize, the district had a graduation rate of approximately 77–78 percent, according to the Manhattan Institute and Urban Institute methods, and 80 percent under the averaged freshman graduation rate (AFGR). Disaggregated graduation rates showed that the district's largest minority group, Hispanics, had a graduation rate of 62 percent according to Manhattan at the lowest, and 71 percent under the AFGR at the highest rate.[5]

Garden Grove also performed well on Advanced Placement (AP) exams. In 2006, 57 percent of the juniors and seniors who took any AP test received a score of 3 or above (which is considered a desirable score for college).[6] Fifty-two percent were at the same standard in 2007. Disaggregated AP data shows that 57 percent of Hispanic students also performed at the same standard in 2006, but showed a decrease to 46 percent in 2007.[7] Despite the slight drop between years, these numbers still mark strong performance on AP exams; AP results for high school students scoring a 3 or better on AP exams were 20.2 percent in California and 15.2 percent nationwide in 2008.[8]

Our 2005 retro study of past Broad Prize winners found Garden Grove a heartening example of sustainability. Since winning The Broad Prize, Garden Grove has maintained high performance while continuing to close income and ethnic achievement gaps. In fact, Garden Grove has smaller income gaps than the state and continues to close them at a faster rate. Laura Schwalm, who has served as superintendent of Garden Grove for about ten years, attributes Garden Grove's success to slow, intentional, strategic reform, though she maintains that there is no *reform* in Garden Grove; instead, there is *refinement*. To her, "reform" connotes a major discrete event;

Garden Grove strives to drill down further to refine its strategies toward its two stable goals. This is not to say it does not make changes; it does. However, the district prefers to see "reform" as a verb describing something one does to make improvements, rather than as a noun that suggests a single event or practice. For example, when district leaders decided to try a successful math initiative used by Long Beach, they had trouble finding language to describe it. They didn't want to use the word "initiative," according to Dr. Schwalm; she did not want to give it a name at all because "a name can cause an entire change of idea." Rather, district leaders wanted to show how the program would improve upon what teachers were already doing in math. Making improvements without layering on the next greatest program or making drastic changes is not what Garden Grove does. It continues to approach its work carefully and strategically with sensitivity to its stakeholders within the system.

As in the other districts featured in this book, Garden Grove's leaders believe in setting a clear course and staying on it—refining rather than changing goals. Although Dr. Schwalm much prefers to have her team referenced rather than herself, one cannot resist the impulse to share the many great metaphors the straight-talking superintendent provides as she paints vivid, honest pictures of their struggles and successes. When discussing how Garden Grove approaches student achievement, Dr. Schwalm very matter-of-factly states, "It's not complicated, but is difficult to do. If we teach right, they'll learn it." When asked about challenges, she mentions there are always some, but that her main challenge is "working on people's comfort levels and being patient." She further explains, "We need to make sure to push people to the edge, and hold them until they are ready, then they can be pushed some more." Dr. Schwalm's frequently used "edge" metaphor describes the district's approach to "stretching people to meet their potential" while respecting the feelings of discomfort and lack of confidence that often accompanies making changes. Her yardstick for ensuring she is asking for reasonable "stretches" is to ask herself, "If it were me, could I go one step further?" The challenge, she states, "is how you do it; the timing and strategy you need to bring people along so it goes beyond the surface."

Preparing for College and Skilled Careers

Between our site visits and the retro study, Garden Grove implemented two major "refinements." The first was the process of improving and aligning the curriculum and goals, and then focusing every district activity and practice on the goals. The second refinement was made after The Broad Prize win; district leaders realized that "it was not enough to just focus on graduation," according to Dr. Schwalm. Despite success in increasing the number of students receiving diplomas, leaders felt they were not doing enough to prepare students for life beyond graduation, for college and skilled careers. Thus, district and school leaders drilled down to improve their practices to not only raise rigor, but to align the system to even higher standards.

Getting students prepared to succeed in pre-college advanced classes is difficult; many districts continue to struggle with helping all student populations access advanced college-level opportunities. In 2005, I coauthored an article with Chrys Dougherty that highlighted Garden Grove as a rare example of a district that focused its entire system on preparing its students for college and skilled careers.[9] In the article, we explain the many ways the district is approaching this work from a true preK–12 view. Referring to the growing practice of focusing on "bridge building" courses in high school, Dr. Schwalm explained, "You cannot build a bridge long enough to get from grade 3 skills to college in a four-year time span. It has to start earlier."

Garden Grove's focus on college readiness goes beyond the surface level by actually increasing rigor throughout the entire preK–12 system. The district does not simply file students into AP classes and then proudly quote how many minority students are enrolled in those courses. It actually prepares its students to successfully pass the AP exam and leave the system ready for college or skilled careers. The district's focus on moving its target and goals beyond graduation was partially a matter of raising rigor throughout the system—eliminating most remedial courses, providing innovative supports to help students with challenging courses, and overall "doing a few things but doing them well, with meticulous and consistent implementation."

DISTRICT PRACTICES BY THEME

When other districts visit Garden Grove to find out how they built their well-coordinated system, Dr. Schwalm reiterates a message she often states and believes to be important, "There is no silver bullet. There is nothing fast about it. It's slow, hard work that takes patience and persistence." Additionally, Schwalm has mentioned that she always had great people in place, but that the district needed to put the systems in place to sustain their work over time. To design those systems, district leaders began with focus, a clear, consistent message, and explicit goals that would drive a better understanding about what had to be taught and learned.

Curriculum and Academic Goals

Dr. Schwalm recalled that when she became the superintendent of Garden Grove in 1999, the district was not as focused as it needed to be on an academic mission, a state exemplified by unaligned programs, a lack of strong academic focus, and little use of data. Recognizing the need for change, district leaders developed two consistent goals to drive all district activities: (1) students in Garden Grove for five years or longer would meet or exceed state standards in core academic subjects, and (2) English language learners in Garden Grove for five years or longer would attain the state-defined early advanced level in overall English language proficiency.

The first goal requires some explanation. The expectation for academics in Garden Grove is that students will move up one performance category or "band" per year, as well as transition to the next grade level per year.[10] Thus, if a student is performing at the Below Basic level in third-grade math, the district expects that student to move up to the next "band" (Basic) *and* grade (fourth-grade math) the next year. District leaders explained that this approach means students often must achieve more than one year's "growth" under this goal.

To meet these goals, the district divided the state standards into specific "focus standards" supported by curriculum and pacing guides, which are continually revised using student data and current research on best practices. The focus standards further specified what students should be able to do in each grade, keeping alignment in mind by mapping backward from higher to lower grades to ensure that instruction would neither be skipped nor unnecessarily repeated. The guiding principles behind the development of the focus standards, according to central office interviewees, were that "what is being tested is not all of what kids need to know" and that teachers' input on the standards was critical.

The specific pieces of the curriculum were developed by groups of teachers and district administrators who worked with experienced consultants to construct the curriculum guides, quarterly benchmark assessments, and pacing guides for all grade levels.[11] Having test-writing experts help develop the benchmarks was very important, according to Dr. Schwalm, for ensuring proper correlation with the standards. She felt their expertise added more usability and validity to the end product and was a worthwhile investment. In addition to the benchmark tests, many Garden Grove schools have developed common units and assessment pieces to customize instruction based on the unique learning needs of their students.

To ensure "faithful implementation" of district standards, the district provides intensive training for teachers and principals in the use of curriculum guides and research-based instructional strategies. Training is offered throughout the year and often includes opportunities such as Learning Walks, the district's term for a structured walk-through process developed by each campus to observe and discuss classroom instruction. Additionally, principals and department chairs monitor curriculum implementation through classroom walkthroughs and assessment data culled from their data monitoring system.

The communication of standards from the district to schools appeared to have been effective, as several principals asserted that articulation from district to schools was in place. For example, when the language arts focus standards were introduced, principals were trained in the standards so they "knew what to look for in classrooms." To ensure the standards contained the correct elements, one teacher from each school served on a literacy implementation team that collected feedback from teachers on the standards and discussed details such as writing and student scoring guides. These teams met monthly and generated in-depth conversations about the standards as well as feedback for future revisions.

In 2003, not all teachers seemed to embrace the increased focus on standards and adherence to the instructional pacing guides. While some teachers felt they saw improvement with the level of preparedness students had for the next grade, others still believed that many students were not improving, particularly in high school. Teachers did, however, note a marked improvement in math skills, which they attributed to improved alignment in the math curriculum. When we returned for the retro study in 2005, teachers seemed to find more consistency across subjects and grades in the schools. A team of teachers interviewed mentioned that the pacing guides helped create a common vocabulary, which seemed to help them work more effectively together to create instructional consistency. Illustrating more confidence in the preparedness of students, one teacher noted, "If a student moves anywhere in the district and is in Algebra I, I'm confident that child will know 'XYZ' because the teachers all follow the pacing guide."

Site visit and retro study interviews with teachers found a sense of satisfaction with their involvement with the development of the focus standards. Because teachers work in teams to develop and revise those standards, they believed the revision created a more seamless and aligned district curriculum. As one teacher described it:

> Being able to get into vertical teams and talk to your grade levels helps to actually create an effective plan. In that way, you are able to remind [other teachers] about current skills to be addressed and then go on to the next skill and spiral instead of spending more time teaching what they already know. We are trying to meet the background knowledge of our kids.

This process has been very effective for helping teachers view the curriculum in larger pieces across numerous grade levels. Another teacher who has been involved in the curriculum revision process said:

> We look at the results of the California STAR test and also look specifically at the weak areas. At a grade level, we look at those results and decide what we need to emphasize for the year. We also look at the standards that have changed over time so that it is not just a set of standards. We see what it looks like from kindergarten to sixth grade, so we take a strand, like "word analysis" and talk about how that strand looks at different levels so that every student is receiving the standards, but it may be at a different level, depending on where their ability is. Everyone is always going to have word analysis and comprehension, literary response, etc. However, the *depth* of that standard is different.

The clarity created by better defining what was to be taught and learned was eventually translated to communicating that information to parents. To help parents understand how well their children are mastering the standards, the district developed a standards-based report card for kindergarten through sixth grade. Instead of using simple letter grades, the report cards detail the specific skills that students have or have not mastered. This helps parents and students know exactly what has been learned and where there may be cause for concern. In 2004, Garden Grove was piloting an electronic version of these report cards translated into the major languages spoken in the district in preparation for a districtwide implementation.

Staff Selection, Leadership, and Capacity Building

District leaders interviewed by the site team in 2006 said that they had no problems attracting principal candidates because "people want to come to the district." These leaders attributed this to the district's strong record of academic performance. At that time, the district was filling around 50 percent of vacancies with external candidates for principal positions. Since then, in an effort to maintain its culture and build a strong instructional team, Garden Grove has focused its efforts on building principal candidates internally. One internal development method has been the provision of numerous professional development opportunities for teachers, leading to leadership opportunities at their campuses. Additionally, leadership team members have the opportunity to attend leadership academies as a first step in exploring the principalship. Both internal and external principal candidates are interviewed by district and school administrators, along with the president of the local teachers union. Once selected, all new principals are provided ongoing training for the first two years of service in conjunction with any and all training provided to veteran principals.

As for the teacher pool, the district believes that its extremely selective hiring practices have increased its pool of highly qualified teacher candidates by enhancing Garden Grove's reputation among professionals. Additionally, the district recently developed a brochure outlining the specific qualities it seeks in potential teachers, helping attract appropriate candidates. Central office leaders assert they are seeking candidates who know instructional strategies, who are team players, and who are "teachable." They also seek teachers who "represent the face of the community," according the district leaders. This does not necessarily mean candidates will match identically by race, but rather that they are teachers who can relate to the students and the families within a given school. Because the district feels its professional development program is strong, its initial hiring approach focuses on the "core principles" it finds in potential teacher candidates.

The teacher hiring process involves three steps: an initial screening at an interview or job fair, from which candidates are recommended for the second step, involving interviews with central office personnel. Candidates who pass the second interview are allowed to interview with a principal at a school. From there, schools engage in different hiring processes. One high school principal said that she felt the hiring process needed to be viewed partly as "marketing" because "outstanding teachers are shopping, so I'm trying to sell my school." This principal, along with her assistant principal, interview the candidates, take them on a tour, and let them observe a class. If there is mutual agreement that the school's needs and culture match the candidate, then the candidate is offered the position. To ensure they can obtain the "best" teachers, several principals mentioned that they push their hiring process to the earliest they can in the spring, to avoid competition from other schools. Overall, many principals asserted that there were ample candidates, as teachers were attracted to the district for its successful performance and reputation of being supportive to teachers.

Once in the district, teachers are well supported. The district provides appealing compensation packages, an attractive union contract, numerous staff development opportunities, and many instructional supports from principals, other teachers, and coaches assigned to help new or struggling teachers. Some of the instructional training is provided districtwide, such as training in reciprocal teaching, a technique used to build reading comprehension skills.[12] District and school leaders mentioned that teacher training activities are covered through the union contract, which provides a monetary stipend for fifteen hours of training. Training is often supported with follow-up visits to help teachers implement new techniques in their classrooms. In 2004, a high school principal mentioned that she had seen improved focus in teacher professional development over the past few years. She partially attributed the improved focus to the district's shift in directing schools to select teacher training activities based on needs identified by their school data. This was an improvement over the past "random selection," the principal stated. Several other principals observed that new teachers were well supported through the state-mandated induction program that provided training and support to teachers through their first two years of teaching.

Teachers also serve as an important source of support to each other, as they have many opportunities to meet and learn from one another. They meet on a regular basis both vertically and horizontally to review data, discuss specific students, share materials, and plan instruction. Additionally, teachers participate in two Learning Walks per year, during which they observe instructional and classroom management strategies.

The ability to meet with other teachers and collaborate has been particularly helpful to new teachers in the district. One new teacher said,

> I'm totally dependent on the other teachers to help me, since I'm a new science teacher. They pull out all their lessons and teach me their lab tech-

niques. My help to them has been the writing portion. They have the experience to tell me how to pace my instruction and the best ways to approach a topic. We were doing a chemical reaction lesson and one teacher had all the activities down, while I made sure it sequenced to cover the scientific method. We put our classes together to learn from each other.

As one can imagine, scheduling collaboration time at the high school level can be challenging. One high school principal's solution was to reduce the number of large faculty meetings by disseminating more information via e-mail. This allowed the school to reallocate the regular 1.5-hour block as time for teachers to meet. The district provided an additional solution by moving district-based trainings to more site-based trainings at schools. Regardless of the grade level, teachers often described the atmosphere in their schools as being very open to sharing ideas, reviewing data, and discussing instruction.

Instructional Programs, Practices, and Arrangements

The program-selection process in Garden Grove provides another leadership opportunity for teachers. Programming decisions, revisions, and supplements for all grades (K–12) are made through a highly collaborative and structured process called a Consult. The number of participants in a Consult depends on the decision for which it is being convened. A Consult may have from twenty to fifty participants and includes representatives from special education, gifted and talented education, ELL, and "all groups that would represent the district as a whole." The teachers' union assists the district with selecting teachers who will participate in these research and decision-making groups.

Programs and textbooks considered in Consults come from state-recommended or state-approved lists. Consult participants review research on programs for effective practice, "high-yield strategies," alignment of the materials to district standards, and "available support for faithful replication of the program." After this initial Consult process, the district conducts pilot studies in all subject areas for the programs it is considering.

For example, at the secondary level, the district first chose four program vendors to speak to the Consult about their programs. The Consult decided to pilot all four at each high school, used an extensive matrix to evaluate implementation, and solicited feedback from all pilot teachers after implementing the programs. Participants in Consults also consider local assessment data before making a final decision to adopt a program districtwide.

The Consult model works well because it makes program selection a joint process between schools and the district, strengthening alignment and support. The district is able to guide selection by providing the research base, connecting teachers and administrators across schools, and providing direct support for implementation as needed. District administrators characterize the process as "a site-level decision with a lot of guidance from the district."

The district evaluates programs and instructional models as soon as they are introduced. There is a strong focus on faithful replication and intensive instructional training. Materials and programs are constantly monitored by teams of multiple stakeholders to ensure alignment with the standards-based curriculum guides. Leadership teams conduct similar evaluations at the school level to ensure that implementation meets the needs of their student population.

Instructional schedules are determined by individual schools, which use student achievement data to create schedules based on the students' individual needs. Common instructional arrangements include providing advanced classes, summer bridge classes, and double blocks of core classes for students in need of intervention. For example, a student might be enrolled in a regular Algebra I course as well as a supporting companion class (thus, the double block) that focuses on pre-teaching and reviewing Algebra I concepts and providing general instructional support.

Garden Grove does not offer below-grade-level courses in many of its core academic subjects. This does not mean there are not any intervention courses available. It means the district does not by default offer a "fundamentals of mathematics course" that houses numerous students. The philosophy is that intervention should be provided when needed, however, students should be in courses that are either at or above their appropriate grade level. In essence, the district has eliminated the "non-college-preparation track" in favor of a single-track college preparation course of study. The district offers courses to get students "on the freeway," but no longer offers a "parallel country road that runs alongside the freeway but never meets it," is how Dr. Schwalm explains the approach. The district calls its efforts to move kids up to appropriate grade levels "up-leveling." To do this, it provides students with numerous supports, such as graphic organizers, rubrics, preview and review, and other strategies, to help them make sense out of the standards. Once students are comfortable, the supports are phased out. Teachers are also trained in research-based techniques that have a reputation for high-yield results, such as direct instruction and reciprocal teaching.

Garden Grove's approach to the classic tension all districts face between keeping students moving forward academically while addressing instructional gaps seems to work well. This is particularly apropos in high school, where learning gaps can become larger and more challenging. Dr. Schwalm describes this tension and Garden Grove's approach:

> At high school, a lot of the talk is about up-leveling kids into higher-level courses and how you provide the scaffolding so they can be successful. You can't just throw them in there and think they are going to succeed. If they can't multiply, throwing them into Algebra II isn't going to be something they can successfully access. Your teacher needs capacity building and your kids need a lot of scaffolding to get them there. So we talk a lot about what are we going to do to accelerate and to up-level [students] and focus on that, not just on remediation. Because remediation really only gets you maybe to the middle. Remediation isn't going to get you to the next step.

That "next step" is where Dr. Schwalm believes her district and others get stuck. Garden Grove does well moving students from the bottom to the middle rung of achievement. The real struggle is moving students from the middle rung to the top rung, where students have met the standards, or ideally, in Dr. Schwalm's words, are "ready for college or skilled careers."

To this end, the district is placing more students in higher-level courses by removing entry requirements for those courses and providing counselors with placement guidelines using individual performance data. An important focus of that performance data is the collection of evidence "based on what students know instead of on how much homework a student turns in or if they sit in the front row," according to one administrator. To create more objective data, the district has embarked on an extensive study comparing course grades assigned by teachers to benchmark results. Discrepancies have resulted in frank discussions about grading criteria and improvement in the match between the two data points.

California also has systems in place to help promote and prepare students for college readiness. In addition to graduation requirements, the state implements A-G subject requirements to ensure students are ready to participate in a first-year program in the University of California system or at California State University.[13] For example, for a regular diploma, students would take two math courses, whereas students would take three courses (including geometry), under the A-G requirements. Districts can receive feedback on their students' progress toward college readiness through assessments that measure mastery toward those requirements.

In a follow-up interview during our retro study, we heard from several principals that schools were working on solving instructional issues by meeting together in feeder-pattern groups called "think tanks." One example involved a high school that convened a group of the schools that feed into them to resolve a particular instructional problem in algebra. The problem had been uncovered through a voluntary audit completed by the district, so the team came to that meeting with several ideas in mind to address their issues. After three hours of meeting, they left with a concrete plan for solving the problem. The middle and high school principals said they were surprised that the meeting was so productive and thought it provided a viable model for other schools to solve problems together across vertical teams.

In a follow-up interview in 2008, I asked Dr. Schwalm exactly how the district was working to raise rigor in the earlier grades. She explained that academic expectations for kindergarten students had increased greatly over the past several years; previously, kindergarten students used to write just a few words, but now those students are writing two- and three-word sentences rather than just single words. Dr. Schwalm cautioned that it is important to be "careful" about setting high enough expectations for students without "getting too carried away." "You would not walk a block and then instantly think you are prepared for the Boston Marathon," she said. To ensure that students meet their instructional targets, the district aims for sixth grade and moves backward because "students that are far below grade level in sixth grade have [a] very small chance of going to college." While this method worked for most teachers, Dr. Schwalm mentioned that some balked at increasing rigor at the lower grades. However, she would simply say to them, "It's in your hands whether your students go to college." She gave teachers the same message whether they taught high school or pre-K students. The message seemed to make sense to teachers and they seemed to embrace it. According to Schwalm, "It made the connection to a higher moral purpose of giving kids the chance to access the things they want for their own children."

Monitoring, Analysis, and Use of Data

The district maintains tight focus on managing and monitoring district and school goals through the use of data. Since winning The Broad Prize, Garden Grove has started using DataDirector, a Web-based platform that uses preset queries to build multiyear custom reports with assessment results and classroom-level item analysis. Teachers and administrators have access to the system 24/7, and testing results are typically available the next day. The district moved to the new system to make it more accessible and user-friendly. Before DataDirector, teachers or administrators would have to request that the central office data department run specific queries, or principals would spend time themselves figuring out how to program the queries, cutting into time better spent in classrooms. One administrator describes the previous system as "like the hospital administrator has the data but the doctors never get it." The end result of the new system is real-time data available to principals and teachers. The addition of color-coding and pivot tables, which connect data from previous years to create a longitudinal view, has also helped make the system easier to use and to connect to different programs.

As with all initiatives in Garden Grove, training for the new data system involved carefully rolling out the same message and process gradually down to the teacher level. In the initial stage of implementation, site administrators were trained by consultants from Achieve, Inc. Training sessions lasted 3 or 3.5 hours, long enough to help the administrators become knowledgeable on how to weave through the system. From there, they branched out to train assistant principals and then anyone they felt needed to access the system immediately, like counselors. Teachers were trained through data teams of four or five teachers from a particular school and their principal. Half-day teacher training sessions were made possible through the use of substitute teachers.

A second important enhancement to Garden Grove's monitoring system, just under development during the site team's 2004 visit, was the addition of quarterly assessments in all core subjects. Developed through Consults with the help of professional test writers, the quarterly assessments, or benchmarks, were intended to measure progress on the standards. Prior to quarterly assessments, student performance had remained somewhat of a mystery until the end-of-year summative test results came out. The benchmarks were necessary, according to Dr. Schwalm, because previously, "it was like the autopsy at the end of the year, without having any diagnostic tests in the middle."

At first, the benchmarks were difficult to introduce. To alleviate some of the anxiety surrounding them, district leadership provided a "road show" for department chairs, who in turn introduced the benchmarks at their schools. When teachers first received poor performance results from the assessments, they blamed the test, leading to what district leaders described as "painful conversations revealing the problem as instruction, not the test." Despite the pushback, district leaders kept working with teachers to help them become more comfortable with the benchmarks. Dr. Schwalm described the process as building a platform from a cliff:

> There they were backing up, saying, "We can't go here. The kids all are going to fail." So you hold them while you build the cliff out further, and then you push them some more and you hold them again and you tell them it's going to be okay, and that's why it takes so much time. But if you push too fast, you push them all over the edge—then you've got to go down, pick them up, dust them off, apologize, and bring them back up. Then they don't trust you anymore and you've got to start all over again. So it's that kind of timing. But I think what's really been very effective is that we've listened and we've made adjustments.

Each year, the teachers have become more comfortable with the benchmarks, which the district leadership and teachers attribute to the trust that leadership stability helped build within the district.

Another strong selling point for the benchmarks with teachers was the speed at which they received the results. The benchmarks are sent to the district office where they are immediately scanned and loaded into Data-Director. This way teachers do not have to hand-grade tests, and they can look at item analyses the next day to find out exactly how well their students performed on each particular standard.

Teachers also have assistance interpreting the data and using it to inform instruction through a protocol developed by the "Leadership Academy," the district's training program for principals. Central office leaders explained that the protocol provides a helpful tool to guide questions and reflection through collaborative data review processes. In these meetings, "data teams" meet to compare and discuss data and "ask the tough questions." One principal said there is usually at least one teacher who speaks up to acknowledge an instructional problem revealed by the data, and then voices appreciation for having the data to pinpoint the problem. One central office leader stated, "It is nice to have those voices come up and say they appreciated having the data and the ability to slice and dice it. The negative ones are the quiet ones now." Another principal thought that the protocols were helpful for providing structure and a level of "comfort" to the data review process. One teacher used the protocol to develop a three- to four-day lesson sequence to teach her students how to analyze selected benchmarks. The lessons were taped and are now used to train other principals and teachers to use data to inform instruction.

Overall school performance is monitored through the Single School Plan, which is written at the beginning of each school year by principals and submitted to their supervisors. The plan outlines the school goals for the year and is monitored through ongoing formal and informal Learning Walks to measure progress toward the school and district goals. Administrators say the walkthrough process provides another trust-building opportunity:

> We're talking about tough stuff, such as the student work that you have displayed that doesn't really show the rigor of the standard and why. What do we need to do about it? But it's during that informal discussion where [teachers] begin to feel comfortable in talking about it as team members.

Teachers felt that the Learning Walks, done at least three times a year, helped them talk about student performance and instruction. Occasionally, teachers participate in Learning Walks in other schools, which not only helps them gain new ideas about instruction, but also adds another level of alignment across schools.

In retro study interviews in 2006, we found a deeper commitment to using their data system to diagnose issues and plan instruction. Several central office leaders and principals mentioned comparing formative and summative data results to classroom grades to see if the two correlated. Leaders said that the comparisons "really open up teachers' eyes and start some good discussions." The district also uses data to track students who were retained in earlier grades, and has added the ability to link students to particular teachers to see where assistance and support might be needed. While the district believes it is using the system in better ways to "answer more questions," many interviewees say they are still working to find more ways to use the system to improve their instructional program.

Recognition, Intervention, and Adjustment

The availability of real-time data combined with frequent monitoring has helped Garden Grove focus on keeping schools, teachers, and students on track. The district intervenes in the management of a struggling school before the state identifies the need for intervention. All identified schools write a Program Improvement Plan and set aside 10 percent of their budget for professional development. The district collaborates with external consultants to build appropriate staff development for each school. Recently, the district targeted six schools for improvement. The schools were pulled into a systemwide comprehensive intervention, during which their data was closely reviewed throughout the year to make sure they had appropriate supports and were showing acceptable improvement. Follow-up interviews in 2006 with principals of those six schools found that they were making improvements, and that the principals felt they had an additional resource for ideas and support by being pulled together in a group of schools with similar concerns.

As mentioned earlier, classroom monitoring occurs on an ongoing basis through both formal and informal walkthroughs. Teachers in need of extra help are paired with mentor teachers for coaching. Teachers on Special Assignment (TOSA) specialists work directly in classrooms and are also available to model research-based classroom management practices and demonstrate well-designed lessons. TOSAs are selected through a competitive process by central office and school leaders. They are selected by different subject areas as well as by particular skill needs, such as classroom management. At the school level, principals refer struggling teachers to participate in staff-development activities most appropriate to their individual needs. They also release teachers to observe classrooms in their own or other schools. Teachers with unsatisfactory evaluations are referred to the Peer Assistance and Review program to work with district mentors throughout the year.

The district has numerous interventions to address the needs of struggling students. Most of these interventions are implemented through flexible grouping, a process used to identify individual student needs through data and then match those students to teachers showing strong perfor-mance in the targeted area. Vastly different from the practice of tracking students, flexible grouping in Garden Grove means that students move flu-idly based on subject-specific needs instead of staying within one type of performance group. One specific format of flexible grouping, the School Wide Intervention Model, or SWIM, groups students by reading level for intensive, uninterrupted two-hour instructional blocks. Through this model, students are assessed frequently to monitor and adjust their pro-grams. Additionally, all students in grades K–6 are offered extended-day intervention using research-based programs. Frequent assessment guides the teaching and the adjustment of student groups. High school students who need extra assistance and/or would benefit from a comprehensive college culture/character-building program can enroll in the district's Ad-vancement Via Individual Determination (AVID) program, which helps them prepare for four-year college eligibility.[14]

To provide accelerated interventions for students, the district provides numerous Advanced Placement (AP) and honors courses. In our retro study we found out that the district was sending its teachers for AP training to a fellow Broad winner, Long Beach, to take part in intense AP training.

Many districts, when discussing interventions, reference remedial pro-grams implemented outside of instructional hours; but when Garden Grove leaders and teachers discussed interventions, they primarily mentioned strategies provided during regular school hours that helped keep students within their grade-level classes. Dr. Schwalm said of Garden Grove's inter-vention philosophy, "Interventions should be a ramp to help students get on the highway. The alignment has to be there with your curriculum, sup-port for teachers, the data, and ongoing capacity building."

INFLUENCING FACTORS

Dr. Schwalm characterizes the overall district climate and relationship with different constituents as "solid and stable" and on the correct path for improving student achievement. Her statement is supported by various stakeholder groups within the district.

School Board

Garden Grove USD is governed by a board of education consisting of five elected members who serve four-year terms. The superintendent is considered to be the chief executive officer of the district and serves as secretary to the board. Interviews with district leadership and the board president revealed a healthy, respectful relationship in which everyone agreed that the board's charge was to "set policy and direction," and the district's job was to provide quantifiable evidence of student progress. The board represents a wide range of experience, including a current principal from a neighboring district, a former mayor, an attorney, and business professionals.

In 2004, the board president described Garden Grove as a "very conservative district that believes children must have a strong foundation to prepare them for the future." She appreciated that the district goals did not "move around a lot," and believed that a district's culture is best maintained through a leader who "came through the ranks" like Dr. Schwalm. The president voiced appreciation for Dr. Schwalm's long-term experience in the district and her open and honest approachability. She also mentioned the importance of accessibility in superintendents, as well as their ability to focus on being instructional leaders rather than being "plant managers." Agreeing that the district's relationship with the board is positive, Schwalm concurred that "relationships take time" and that she highly values her relationship with the board. She felt the board did well in focusing their role on setting policy, and asserted that they do not "micro-manage."

Union/Association

The Garden Grove Education Association (GGEA) represents teachers, nurses, and librarians from Garden Grove USD. GGEA is affiliated with the California Teachers Association and the National Education Association.

GGEA supports the state union organization and serves as a collective-bargaining unit and advocate for teachers. The union has the legal right to negotiate and consult. The goal of the union is to provide the best possible environment and support to teachers and students.

According to interviews with union leaders in 2003, GGEA has a strong relationship with the district and in classrooms, as several past presidents have returned to the classroom after serving their terms.[15] In subsequent interviews, the union president characterized his relationship with the district and superintendent as a partnership of mutual respect. When asked if there were ever a threat of union strike, the president in 2004 stated that nothing remotely close had ever occurred, owing to the high level of trust between GGEA and the district. When asked how they built that level of trust, the president asserted that he and Dr. Schwalm had "lunch or dinner on a regular basis; sometimes on the record, sometimes off the record." He appreciated her accessibility and willingness to involve the union in district goal setting, curriculum revision, and program selection (the Consults). In fact, he mentioned that Dr. Schwalm always attends the first union association function each year—orientation. He felt this was another symbol of the district leadership working with them on common goals.

Dr. Schwalm asserted that the district tries to keep reform issues out of the teachers' contract and avoids bargaining around it. She partially attributes the strong union-district relationship to the fact that teachers and the union are involved as much as possible in work that will affect teachers, such as developing benchmarks and curriculum guides. As she puts it, "The no-surprises approach has served us very well."

Interviews with central office leaders and various union members confirm that the union sees its role as supporting teachers to help forward the district's goals for students. Teachers described the union as a positive force that supports them, while also serving as a partner for the district. One principal described the union as being very "progressive and open to change." Principals also felt the union served as a good resource for supporting teachers when needed.

Community

Garden Grove has approached its relationships with the local community and businesses in a very selective manner that is similar to their grant-procurement process. Its reluctance to rely on outside monetary support is due to Dr. Schwalm's concern that the district remain as self-sufficient and focused as possible. In a 2003 interview, the union president agreed that Garden Grove typically did not solicit outside fiscal dollars, unless it was for the purpose of providing support and outreach rather than revenue generation. These services typically came in the form of noneducational services such as after-school care, mentoring, and family support.

Interviews with groups of community members often referenced the district's strength in bringing various communities together to "work on behalf of student success." One member elaborated, "There is just a philosophy written into everything here, whether it is classroom activities or extracurricular activities—everything is tied to student success and to students having a constant learning experience." Further attesting to the district's openness, another community member stated, "The district opened [its] doors to us [his organization] and gave us the tools to support what is happening in the classroom." He was referring to training the district provided to his business for its work in the district.

Several key community partnerships were noted in the community focus group interviews. The police department and the Boys and Girls Club have partnered to create a truancy-reduction program. Additional collaboration with the Boys and Girls Club and community agencies provides focused after-school programs as well as parent education, adult ESL instruction, and school-readiness programs. Because the district is the largest employer in the city, large-scale business partnerships are restricted. More notable are partnerships that individual schools have with local businesses.

Parents

Focus groups with parents confirmed that the district's efforts to partner and communicate with parents were also successful. The parents showed an awareness of the district goals and felt they were valued partners in their children's education. One parent commented, "The district recognizes that the family is more important than school and is very conscientious about the connection with families. My son's teacher calls me if there are concerns, and also when he made an A+ on a project." When asked how the district involves parents, one said, "The district draws you in. They send a contract to the student's home defining the roles of student, teacher, and parent. They make you sign it and take responsibility. They involve you."

Nearly three-fourths of the families with students in the district speak a language other than English as their first language. The district supports them by providing all written materials in English, Spanish, Korean, and Vietnamese. Translators are present at all school events and during visits to families. Interviews with different district members describe various levels of success with parent involvement, with a greater degree of success predictably occurring in elementary and wavering at the high school level. One elementary school principal explained her school's definition of parent involvement and its subsequent impact on students:

> More than the teacher saying what little Johnny needs to do, but about the parent and the child coming to an agreement about where he is going, what his strengths are, where he has been, and where he is headed. Parents who have not seen their child succeed are thrilled to have their child take ownership of what he will do.

That principal's school hosts walkthrough days when parents can go to the elementary school and see what is going on in classrooms. At the high school, teachers and principals mentioned that their high number of limited English–speaking parents required careful attention and focus on providing adequate solutions to various communication needs. Additionally, the schools showed sensitivity to the issue of working parents not being available to attend meetings or parent nights.

In a discussion in 2008, Dr. Schwalm spoke about making gains in parent involvement at the high school level. She attributed the increase to approaching parents directly in their homes and working through parent-neighborhood networks. The power of that intervention is evidenced by one high school that had only five parents in attendance at a family event at the beginning of the 2008 school year, but had an "entire gymnasium full" at another event near the end of the same year.

Governance, Organization, and Decision Making

Each time we visited the main central office team at Garden Grove, we found the same small, consistent team of six. Each member was equally knowledgeable about their teammates' specific duties and focus within the district, to the extent that they seemed ready to step into any position or situation. They even frequently finished each other's sentences in interviews. Many central office teams are larger; this one remains small. During one interview in 2004, Dr. Schwalm said she had considered adding one more team member to alleviate some of the workload, but decided against it due to worry about diminishing the tight alignment of her small, efficient team.

When asked how authority is distributed in Garden Grove between the district and schools, Dr. Schwalm described the system as "centralized." She clarified that the district's standards are districtwide, and although instruction may be similar, implementing the standards is left to school discretion. She mentioned a "sense of trust that principals are going to be good to their teachers" because they were hired for that purpose. Each school has its own climate, and principals are given leeway to "run their schools for their student population." As long as alignment exists across the system, there are "a lot of checks and balances" and a lot of trust regarding authority and decision making.

When we asked at the schools how authority was distributed in the district, we received similar responses. Several high school teacher leaders noted that, as department chairs, they sometimes worried about losing individual freedom. However, they seemed to feel comfortable with their level of authority and felt the standards still allowed them "opportunities to do what we think," with the added structure of a time frame to follow. Several high school teachers mentioned that they felt some reluctance when they were first asked to follow common instructional goals. However, the teachers said they changed their minds over time as they felt they had been successful with their students because of the common goals, to the extent that they believed the high school to be "ahead of the curve" in buying into and successfully implementing the curriculum. They felt the collaborative approach with curriculum development and program selection through the Consults was particularly useful for garnering support for district initiatives.

At the middle school, principals and teachers also felt the district involved them in decisions that were important to them, and that they are able to select programs and plan academics appropriate for their individual schools. One principal commented:

> We are a centralized district, so we don't get to do whatever we want, but we have parameters and plan around it. We choose our strategies because we know what would fit our students' needs. We look at our data and look at the areas where students need assistance. The district allows us the opportunity to do what is best for our students.

At the elementary schools, teachers reported feeling involved in decision-making processes and pleased with the level of support they received both from their principals and from central office leaders.

Resource Allocation

Almost every stakeholder in Garden Grove describes the district as being "fiscally responsible." Despite a state budget crisis described to us in 2004 by several business members, the district has done well with cutting and trimming where needed but leaving instruction intact. Stakeholders believe the district does very well with "very little," invests its resources intelligently, and aligns its resource decisions to district and school goals. In 2003, the board president mentioned that the district does allow budgetary flexibility for schools as long as they justify how allocations will help reach district standards.

Dr. Schwalm agreed that resource allocation was a strong area for the district. Matching comments from other stakeholders, she stated in one interview:

> The district has always been extremely fiscally responsible. We set priorities in the classrooms and have held hard during tough times and not added programs or things we couldn't afford or sustain. We plan for lean times by saving during the good times.

Dr. Schwalm noted that the majority of the district's budget comes from state revenue, and that 90 percent of their funds "go straight into the classrooms."

The general fund in 2004 was $450 million, and the district received $30 million in categorical funds. Dr. Schwalm and the board president both stated that the district was very careful and strategic with categorical funds by funding positions with several sources, depending on regulations attached to the funds. The district also keeps costs down by maintaining as much work as possible "in-house" to avoid contract fees and give the district cash flow. Additionally, the district keeps an insurance reserve and a general fund reserve, which is spent only on "essentials." The district also conserves by "throwing nothing away."

These frugal practices are not seen as difficult or a burden within the district. Dr. Schwalm often stated, "It is amazing how much you save if you don't waste and how much you really don't need to get things done." Several other stakeholders also admired the district's determination to keep administrative costs down. The union president in 2004 mentioned that Garden Grove had "the lowest district administrative cost in the state." The only central office function that is outsourced is transportation for some special education students. District leaders also mentioned some practices around refurbishing their own school furniture, which was undocumented but added another illustration to how the district approached being "thrifty," or as Dr. Schwalm describes it, "running a very tight ship on the business side."

School budgets within the district are often developed through school site councils. One elementary school principal mentioned a desire to include more parents in that process, although in 2004 the district's timeline did not allow as much parent involvement as the school desired. The council develops an action plan and identifies what is needed for the educational program. When teachers make budget requests, they are required to fill out questionnaires that document the needs of their students in relationship to their proposed purchase. The action plan becomes the Single School Plan, which drives everything at the school level. Copies of the budget go home to parents in both English and Spanish. School personnel at the elementary school did not feel that funding was at all constrained, and they confirmed the belief that the district is very fiscally responsible.

The same belief was found at the middle and high schools. Principals and teachers asserted that they got what they needed as long as they could justify the expense. One principal mentioned that some administrators occasionally get frustrated with how strict the district is about funds, but acknowledged that the district's fiscal management had benefited everyone during budget crunches. Illustrating the purchasing process, a principal said:

> We have had a lot of support from the district. When a teacher wants equipment in science, they have to tie it to a state standard. This has helped cut down on a lot of over-purchasing. We've gotten everything we need.

Another topic voiced often in resource discussions was the appreciation by principals and teachers that no teachers lost their positions during the state's worst budget times, while some teachers in neighboring districts did. Overall, school personnel reported that they received what they needed, including superior building maintenance that helped their schools not only look good, but last longer.

Climate/Culture

District leadership described Garden Grove's climate as "healthy, solid, and stable." This statement was supported by the service longevity of many district and school staff members and their positive interactions witnessed by the entire site visit team. School leaders and teachers at all levels described the district and their school climate as being pleasant, collaborative, cohesive, and caring toward staff and students. Teachers asserted that other teachers come to teach in the district because "the students are pleasant and everyone knows what is expected of them." Principals and teachers at all school levels often referred to the climate of the district and their school as being tight-knit "like a family." Illustrating similar comments we heard throughout interviews, one principal stated,

> We have a real community, in spite of the size of the district, with that sense of family and belonging and taking pride in the schools and the district. It pervades the entire district. People are proud to work here and want to work here.

My personal observations from the 2004 site visit, the 2005 retro study visit, and more recent conversations with Dr. Schwalm support the district's ability to maintain its positive, caring climate over time. Staff members appear to really want to help each other and genuinely seem to like and respect one another. Even after ten years of service as a superintendent, Dr. Schwalm still sounds proud and enthusiastic about the work and success happening in Garden Grove. Passion for helping students excel to higher levels is felt at every level of the district system.

In addition to the organizational climate, the district has worked hard to make a cultural shift in its student and parent stakeholders to focus on college and skilled career readiness. Several principals mentioned that many parent and community perceptions about the possibilities of college for their children needed to change. They noted that the work was very difficult; creating the correct curriculum was easy compared with "building a college-going culture within a school," one principal stated. To this end, the schools were working very hard with parents, trying to make connections with them and having conversations about why college matters. Principals mentioned the challenge presented by the message, as many of the students would be the first in their families to attend college. When asked how they were approaching parents, principals responded, "Any way we can." One elementary principal described building trust and involvement with several parents by letting them assist with her first-grade class, which helped those parents not only observe their children but also learn missing skills along with their children. Another principal mentioned conducting parent meetings by feeder pattern so that parents could ask questions and discuss their fears and concerns about their children's school and about college in general. Other principals stressed the importance of building self-confidence in students so that they would understand that college is a possibility for their future. The principals felt the district's AVID program was successful in helping students gain confidence and also helped deliver the same college-going message across multiple grade levels.

REFORM AND STUDENT ACHIEVEMENT—BRINGING IT TO SCALE

Reform in Garden Grove means deciding what student outcomes ought to be at graduation, mapping backward to ensure the entire pipeline addresses those outcomes, and aligning all activities, supports, and resources to those outcomes. The district does not layer on discrete reform events; rather, it sees reform as building a systems approach, and then improving on pieces within that approach.

District leaders in Garden Grove felt that that one of the improvements that had the most significant effect on student achievement was the ability to provide a clear curriculum to teachers, coupled with a "no excuses" belief in student achievement and the availability of data to provide teachers with timely, detailed information on student performance. Additionally, district leaders mentioned the ability for "teachers to connect to students" as a crucial link to student achievement. Similarly, leadership teams at all school levels mentioned having high expectations for students, aligning the work around student needs, and having a positive school climate that transfers from the adults down to the students. Teachers cited the importance of showing respect for the school and students, exemplified by clean, well-maintained buildings and paying close attention to making sure that students felt valued and appreciated.

The many interviews conducted in Garden Grove over the years reveal a very tight, well-aligned system that continues to improve and refine its practices. How this district made measurable movement in both improving graduation rates and then in the number of students meeting the state's college readiness standards is interesting. The themes reiterated throughout this chapter have been clear focus, acknowledgement that the work is slow, supporting and encouraging the adults in the system, and increasing expectations from a strong foundational base. Additionally, Laura Schwalm talks about balancing their reform ("refinement," in her words) work in terms of short- and long-term goals and successes. To help jump-start the system, she mentions the importance of grabbing "low-hanging fruit." It is a quick fix, but establishes and encourages successes. What is important, according to Dr. Schwalm, is to "resist the temptation to get fast results that are merely a whitewash." While such results look good, she believes it is important to develop strategies that will lead to long-term, meaningful change.

In a recent interview, Dr. Schwalm and I discussed how the reform process is somewhat like weight loss. When you have a lot of weight to lose, you can drop quite a few pounds easily at first and look successful. The difficulty lies in the last five or ten pounds. In 2006, the district was still performing as well or better than the state in many areas. So, to reiterate one of Dr. Schwalm's observations, it is difficult to move a lot of students from the middle to the top rung of the ladder.

When asked about challenges, Dr. Schwalm responded that no challenge was insurmountable, but that she struggled with her own personal challenge of being patient and taking time to "get people comfortable." She said, "Knowing what to do isn't hard; the challenge is how you do it, the timing and strategy you need to bring people along so it goes beyond the surface." School leaders and teachers showed similar attitudes; they had to think hard about specific challenges and frequently cited a few "small things" they felt were issues. School leaders and teachers at the high school level mentioned class size as a challenge (I observed several classes with at least thirty-eight students in them), as well as keeping parents involved. The middle school leaders and teachers admitted that their ability to maintain their high performance levels was a slight challenge, but that, overall, "Most of the challenges are external and not something to worry about." Most teachers mentioned time as a challenge—getting in all the instruction while re-teaching when they needed to. Additionally, most teachers at all levels mentioned parent involvement as a challenge, both in keeping students connected to the school process and helping parents work with their children on succeeding in challenging academic programs. Another specific challenge mentioned was in meeting the needs of ELL students, given the varying language needs of the student population.

Current Performance and Practices

Because Garden Grove won The Broad Prize in 2004, it was not eligible again until 2008. The last Prize data available, from 2007, shows that Garden Grove's performance has remained relatively stable. Figures 4.15 and 4.16 compare district and state proficiency rates in 2007 for Asian, Hispanic,

FIGURE 4.15

District and state reading proficiencies for 2007 by student group

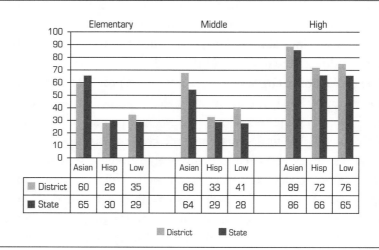

FIGURE 4.16
District and state math proficiencies for 2007 by student group

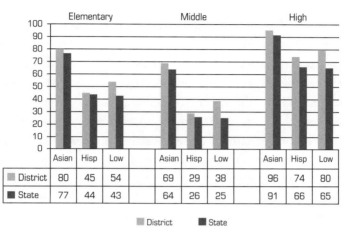

	Asian	Hisp	Low	Asian	Hisp	Low	Asian	Hisp	Low
District	80	45	54	69	29	38	96	74	80
State	77	44	43	64	26	25	91	66	65

and low-income students in reading and math, respectively. With the exception of Asian and Hispanic students in elementary reading, all student groups show higher proficiency rates in the district, compared with the state. The same charts show more consistent performance between the different student groups at the high school level, and that the district shows markedly higher scores, particularly at the secondary level, with their low-income students.

Another way to view academic performance in California districts is to look at their Academic Performance Index, or API.[16] Garden Grove has been a proud member of the "700 Club" since our first site visit in 2003. The 700 Club comprises California districts that have earned (and, in Garden Grove's case, maintained) an API score of at least 700. According to the California Department of Education, Garden Grove earned a base API of 767 in 2007, and a Growth API of 778 in 2008.[17] API scores are also provided for schools and even for student subgroups. In subgroup performance, every subgroup earned a "yes" for significant API growth. Noteworthy growth targets include: students with disabilities (API increase of

17), Pacific Islanders (API increase of 29), economically disadvantaged students (API increase of 11), and Latino students (API growth of 11).

A conversation in fall 2008 with Dr. Schwalm found her to be just as enthusiastic about the district's accomplishments as she was back in 2003. Their recent focus since we last visited in 2006 for the retro study had been on getting students into the correct courses, with a particular eye on sixth-grade performance. By focusing in the early grades, the district managed to get 80 percent of its sixth-graders to a level on the state test that puts them on the trajectory for college readiness. In addition to assessment scores, district and school personnel closely watched grades; students receiving grades of a C or lower were given additional supports, sometimes summer school. All of these efforts are geared toward ensuring students are on track to master the A-G requirements for enrollment at the state universities. What sets Garden Grove apart is that this college readiness view begins much earlier than high school; Garden Grove leaders have learned that student success is largely defined by the sixth grade.

In our 2008 interview Dr. Schwalm felt Garden Grove's early college focus was paying off well. Although their scores were not official, preliminary results showed that Garden Grove students had an increase in A-G course mastery. According to Schwalm, they moved from 31.7 percent in the 2006–2007 school year to nearly 35 percent in the 2007–2008 school year, although those numbers had not been officially confirmed by the state when we last spoke. Although the numbers are expected to lower slightly when the official state report comes out (they have not been officially announced at the time of writing), due to either a calculation or reporting difference by the state, Dr. Schwalm believed their official number would be very close to the state's average for A-G preparation. When I asked Dr. Schwalm exactly what the district was doing to improve college readiness and academic success for its students, she detailed several practices that encouraged a districtwide focus on college readiness. As mentioned before, monitoring and interventions for students begin in the early grades, partially prompted by conversations that occurred several years earlier in the district over grades and the creation of more uniform grading standards. The next focus was on placing students in the correct courses. This meant putting students in courses that would challenge them, providing interventions and support courses and techniques for succeeding in those classes, and retraining counselors on their approaches to placing students in courses.

The latter point was particularly important, since student placement was based more on perception by well-meaning educators than on data, creating what seemed from Dr. Schwalm's description as unintentional bias toward students who displayed certain behaviors:

> If you're quiet by nature and say "yes ma'am," the likelihood that you would be placed in a college-preparation or honors course was 85 percent. If you were did not fit that type of mold, the likelihood went down to 30 percent. Now the placement criteria are based on data rather than on unfounded perceptions about good students. If students meet the established criteria, they get placed.

In addition to the instructional supports provided to students, Dr. Schwalm mentioned that students were also taught "resiliency, self-regulation, study skills, positive self-concept, and asset building." Finally, the district continued to focus on adding rigor throughout its entire preK–12 pipeline and on viewing parents as an integral piece of the education process. The focus on parent involvement was important, as this area was frequently identified in earlier interviews as a concern to teachers, principals, and the parents themselves. Dr. Schwalm said that going to parents directly, instead of waiting for them to come to the district and schools, was found to be a more successful approach.

In the same conversation, Dr. Schwalm said she was excited to hear the conversations from teachers change, and apparently the conversations coming from the district changed as well. Principals and teachers were beginning to "see their numbers really go up," and they were recharged by their growing accomplishments of their students. Reflecting on this, Dr. Schwalm said that their steady focus and refusal to get distracted from their set course was important. She knows the work is hard, and there are times when parts of the system "struggle"; for example, when the district first implemented the elementary standards-based report cards. To this Dr. Schwalm says, "It's not a problem to 'hit plateaus.'" She continued:

> The problem is when you get over a plateau and you think you're done. You need to figure out where to go next and hit the next plateau, and continue to look at it that way. It's nothing fancy or glamorous. It works for us.

The district has done well and has enjoyed many successes, including the distinction of having one or more high schools featured in *Newsweek*'s list of top high schools in the nation. However, the leadership team continues to adamantly state that while they are on the "correct path," they "are not there yet."

CONCLUSION

Garden Grove began its journey to improvement by providing greater focus and alignment both instructionally and organizationally. District leaders characterize the district as operating in a "great culture of accountability" that has managed to "get beyond where other organizations have gotten stuck," according to Superintendent Laura Schwalm. When asked about improvements in student achievement results, Schwalm said,

> Although we have always had great people in this district, we have not always had a good focus. We needed to put the systems in place so that [increased student performance] didn't rely on just great people [but on] the systems that could help all teachers excel for students.

The work has taken a long-term view, a slow and patient approach, and a determination to "do a few things well," through refining instead of reforming.

Garden Grove's instructional approach has been to clearly define what is to be taught and learned, with the added goal of increasing rigor to prepare students for college and skilled careers. This has meant developing high-level "focus standards" and eliminating remedial courses. Organizational levels have been aligned through collaborative work between central office and schools, further bolstered by open collaborative relationships within schools focused on student achievement. The work is also supported by strong relationships with the board, union, community, and parents.

Data is an important element within each of the five Framework areas, as it is used to align and refine the curriculum; select professional development activities; place students in the correct courses and inform instruction; monitor student achievement; and match appropriate interventions to struggling schools, teachers, and students. In Garden Grove, data is used to inform decisions and spark honest discussions, not to punish or accuse.

5

Long Beach Unified School District

In 2003, the year Long Beach Unified School District won The Broad Prize for Urban Education, it served 97,212 students in 90 schools, making it the largest of the five Prize finalists during that year and the largest of the districts discussed in this book. Long Beach serves an extremely diverse student population; its student enrollment is 48 percent Hispanic, 19 percent African American, 17 percent white, 10 percent Asian American, and 6 percent other racial/ethnic groups. Of this population, 65 percent are eligible for free or reduced-price lunch, and 33 percent are English language learners.[1]

Being the third-largest district in California and serving one of the nation's most diverse populations, the district has received wide media attention for its many "firsts." It was the first district to establish a school uniform in grades K–8, first to require any third-grader reading below grade level to attend summer school, and first to end social promotion. The district also led one of the nation's first conversations about creating separate classes for boys and girls in middle school. As discussed in a later section on current performance, the district has again gained the media spotlight for having not one, but two high schools named in *Newsweek*'s annual rankings of the top 5 percent of public high schools in the United States.

Many of these "firsts" were implemented by now-retired superintendent Carl Cohn, who led the district from 1992 to 2002, marking the longest service in urban superintendency in the United States at that time. After Cohn retired in 2002, the board selected a twenty-year veteran "insider": The new superintendent, Chris Steinhauser, had served as a teacher, vice principal, principal, director of special project services, and then as a deputy superintendent in the district. Between Cohn and Steinhauser (who is still serving as the superintendent as the time of writing), the district has benefited both from long-term stable leadership and from a reform path that did not drastically change when Steinhauser became the superintendent.

Broad Prize performance highlights and practice details for Long Beach from 2003 are less specific than the other four cases in this book, since Broad Prize performance results were not made public until 2004. However, the recent publication of Broad Prize report cards containing longitudinal data has provided more details on the accomplishments that contributed to Long Beach's win, as well as to it's being named a finalist again in the three years from 2007 and 2009. Since Long Beach was the first past Prize winner to reemerge as a finalist after the required three-year hiatus, it gained media attention as an example of a district that proved that performance sustainability is possible, even for relatively large urban districts.[2]

DISTRICT DEMOGRAPHICS AND ACHIEVEMENT LEVELS

Similar to Garden Grove, Long Beach performed as well or, in some subjects, better than the state, despite having more than twice as many African American students, slightly more Hispanic students, almost half the white students, and slightly more Asian American students than the state. More Long Beach students qualified for free and reduced-price lunch (65.3 percent) compared with the state (47 percent), and the district served more ELL students (33.1 percent) than the state (25.4 percent).

Long Beach's best comparison to the state over time appears at the elementary school level (grades 3, 4, and 5). Figure 5.1 shows that math per-

FIGURE 5.1
District and state elementary school math proficiencies: All students

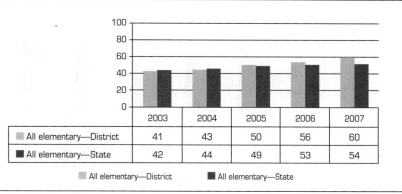

	2003	2004	2005	2006	2007
All elementary—District	41	43	50	56	60
All elementary—State	42	44	49	53	54

formance for the district remains very close to the state until 2006, when the district performance exceeds the state through 2007.

Figure 5.2 shows similar performance to the state in middle school math (grades 6, 7, and 8), although improvement is somewhat flatter both in the state and district compared with elementary math.

One of the highest performance areas for both the district and state is high school reading (grade 10). Figure 5.3 illustrates that while the district's proficiency rates remained close to the state's from 2003 to 2007,

FIGURE 5.2
District and state middle school math proficiencies: All students

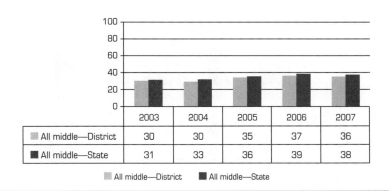

	2003	2004	2005	2006	2007
All middle—District	30	30	35	37	36
All middle—State	31	33	36	39	38

FIGURE 5.3
District and state high school reading proficiencies: All students

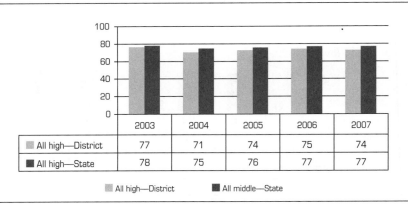

	2003	2004	2005	2006	2007
All high—District	77	71	74	75	74
All high—State	78	75	76	77	77

All high—District   All middle—State

both the district and state fell behind a few percentage points during those years, although the state regained most of its loss by 2006.

The district's math performance over time at all three grade-level divisions (figure 5.4), shows steady performance increases for each level, although the strongest gains are made at the elementary and high school levels. For each year between 2003 and 2007, the high school shows rela-

FIGURE 5.4
District math proficiencies: All levels

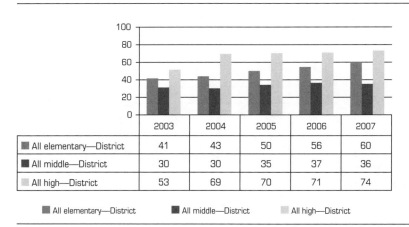

	2003	2004	2005	2006	2007
All elementary—District	41	43	50	56	60
All middle—District	30	30	35	37	36
All high—District	53	69	70	71	74

All elementary—District   All middle—District   All high—District

tively higher performance than the other grade levels, and middle school performance remains behind elementary and high school, showing only very slight improvement over time.

Long Beach exceeded the state in narrowing ethnic and income gaps in several grade levels between 2003 and 2007. Figures 5.5 and 5.6 show that while the state technically has a slightly narrower gap between white and African American students in elementary math (figure 5.6), the district's

FIGURE 5.5
District elementary school math achievement gap between African American and white students

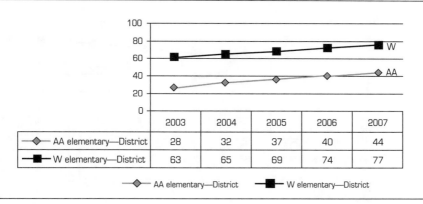

	2003	2004	2005	2006	2007
◆ AA elementary—District	28	32	37	40	44
■ W elementary—District	63	65	69	74	77

◆ AA elementary—District   ■ W elementary—District

FIGURE 5.6
State elementary school math achievement gap between African American and white students

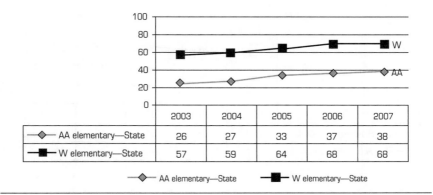

	2003	2004	2005	2006	2007
◆ AA elementary—State	26	27	33	37	38
■ W elementary—State	57	59	64	68	68

◆ AA elementary—State   ■ W elementary—State

white and African American students out-performed the state in that sub-ject and grade every year from 2003–07.

The next two charts illustrate how relying on gap-narrowing numbers alone would be a mistake. While figures 5.7 and 5.8 clearly illustrate that the district has a narrower gap than the state between Hispanic and white students in elementary math, in fact, both the district and state began with a gap of approximately –28 in 2003, but the district narrowed its gap by

FIGURE 5.7

District elementary school math achievement gap between Hispanic and white students

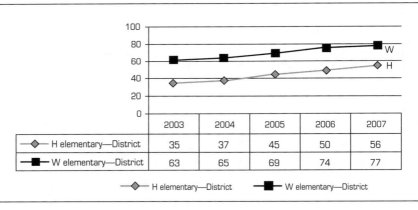

	2003	2004	2005	2006	2007
H elementary—District	35	37	45	50	56
W elementary—District	63	65	69	74	77

H elementary—District   W elementary—District

FIGURE 5.8

State elementary school math achievement gap between Hispanic and white students

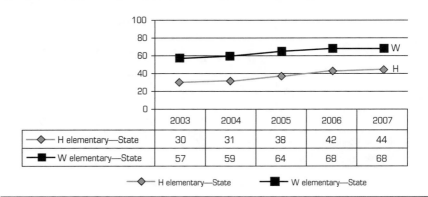

	2003	2004	2005	2006	2007
H elementary—State	30	31	38	42	44
W elementary—State	57	59	64	68	68

H elementary—State   W elementary—State

increasing achievement with both student groups, while the state showed less improvement with both groups.

Figures 5.9 and 5.10 illustrate a slightly wider gap between the district's Hispanic and white students in elementary reading when compared with the state's same groups. However, the district shows higher proficiency rates with both its Hispanic and white students than the state.

FIGURE 5.9

District elementary school reading achievement gap between Hispanic and white students

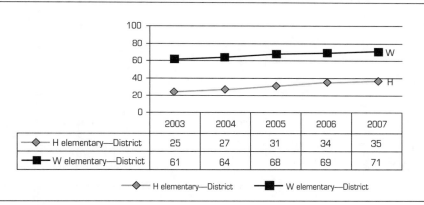

	2003	2004	2005	2006	2007
H elementary—District	25	27	31	34	35
W elementary—District	61	64	68	69	71

H elementary—District   W elementary—District

FIGURE 5.10

State elementary school reading achievement gap between Hispanic and white students

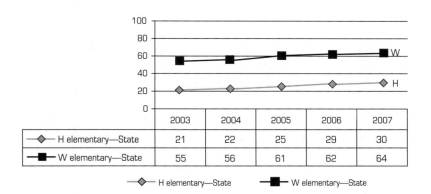

	2003	2004	2005	2006	2007
H elementary—State	21	22	25	29	30
W elementary—State	55	56	61	62	64

H elementary—State   W elementary—State

Regarding income gaps, the district narrowed the achievement gaps more between its low-income and non-low-income groups and shows higher performance than the state's low-income group in most grade levels. Figures 5.11 and 5.12 illustrate that the district narrowed the gap between low-income and non-low-income students at a faster rate than the state's same groups in math proficiency. The district also shows higher performance with its low-income students than the state consistently over time.

FIGURE 5.11

District elementary school math achievement gap between low- and non-low-income students

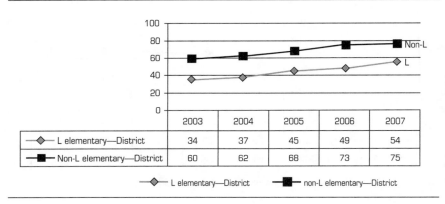

	2003	2004	2005	2006	2007
L elementary—District	34	37	45	49	54
Non-L elementary—District	60	62	68	73	75

FIGURE 5.12

State elementary school math achievement gap between low- and non-low-income students

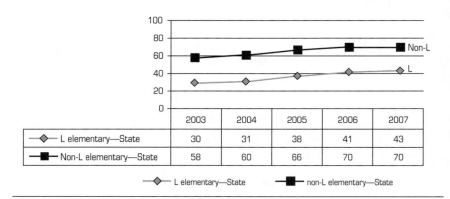

	2003	2004	2005	2006	2007
L elementary—State	30	31	38	41	43
Non-L elementary—State	58	60	66	70	70

The district's performance in the residual analysis used to compare the performance of the district to the expected performance of other California districts with similar demographics appears strong. All the residuals in math and reading in all grade levels are positive except in high school, as no disaggregated high school data was available between 2003 and 2005. Thus, the district performed better than expected in all grade levels in reading and math, with particularly high residuals shown in reading, as seen in figure 5.13. In the residual analysis, the elementary schools significantly outperform the middle and high schools.

High School and College Readiness

According to the national averaged freshman graduation rate (AFGR) numbers, Long Beach's graduation rate of 69 percent in 2003 has remained the same through 2005. Disaggregated graduation AFGR data was slightly lower for African American students, averaged between 60 percent and 62 percent for Hispanic students between 2003 and 2005, and was 80 percent for white students from 2003 to 2004, lowering slightly in 2005 to 78 percent.

FIGURE 5.13
District reading residual analysis: All levels

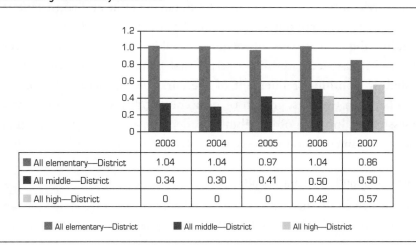

	2003	2004	2005	2006	2007
■ All elementary—District	1.04	1.04	0.97	1.04	0.86
■ All middle—District	0.34	0.30	0.41	0.50	0.50
All high—District	0	0	0	0.42	0.57

■ All elementary—District   ■ All middle—District   All high—District

Long Beach looks at college readiness in a similar fashion to Garden Grove, which may be partially attributed to the state's A-G subject requirements.[3] Also, like Garden Grove, Long Beach instituted powerful supports for students to prepare them for more advanced courses such as honors and Advanced Placement (AP) courses. In fact, Long Beach's AP training for teachers attracted many other districts, including Garden Grove, to participate in Long Beach's training to certify teachers for AP courses. The district's college-readiness efforts are observable; high percentages of its students pass AP exams with scores of 3 or above. In 2003, 58 percent of all students passed the exams with a 3 or higher, and Hispanic students were only slightly behind, with 57 percent. This number decreased steadily between 2004 and 2007, to 50 percent for all students and 45 percent for Hispanic students. For white students, the number remained slightly higher, starting with 66 percent passing with a 3 in 2004 and ending with 63 percent in 2007. Participation rates in AP courses remained similar for white and Asian American students, fell moderately for Hispanic students, and much lower for African American students.

DISTRICT PRACTICES BY THEME

The district attributed its win in 2003 to having clear and consistent academic goals that were supported by specific documents and training and by building the capacity of staff members at all levels. During the 2005 retro study visit, district leadership asserted that Long Beach's ongoing success rested on continual refinement of the curriculum, increased collaboration between teachers, growth of its accountability system and common assessments, infusion of distributed leadership, and the rejuvenation and exchange gained from visitors to the district sparked by the Prize itself.

Curriculum and Academic Goals

Long Beach established a standards-based curriculum in 1994 and has since aligned district standards to the state testing system and national standards.

Development of its content standards grew out of the district's strategic planning process and statewide concerns about student preparation for higher education. In 2003, the district developed course outlines and curriculum maps to clearly communicate the curriculum to administrators and teachers. During the 2005 retro visit, the team found that the district had further refined the curriculum and pacing guides to establish common academic language, increase instructional alignment, and add more elements of literacy into instruction. Responding to teacher feedback, the district made the guides more flexible by adjusting instructional pacing to cover three "instructional clusters" in a longer time span instead of adhering tightly to one specific objective to be covered in a shorter time period.

The addition of more common assessments, including trimester assessments in grades K–5 and quarterly assessments in grades 6–12, marked another powerful change in the district. Additionally, extensive efforts to create more cohesiveness between high school classrooms has resulted in common chapter exams and increased teacher teaming. Teacher discussions around chapter exams led to more in-depth discussions about the standards. One group of teachers recalled a science standard referencing cytoskeletons (structures inside cells) that was not addressed in any of their science texts except for an AP biology text. To address the gap, the teachers constructed a lesson about how cytoskeletons function "using [an] analogy to superheroes." The end result was useful lesson ideas that teachers were able to share across the district.

Curriculum implementation in Long Beach is monitored through the common assessments and through frequent walkthroughs conducted by administrators and subject-area coaches. According to district and school leadership, the coaches have been instrumental in creating consistency across classrooms through their work with teachers inside classrooms and through the process of sharing best practices across the district.

To maintain and improve alignment between grade levels, the curriculum is revised at least annually to address any gaps found in the state standards and to incorporate feedback gathered by teachers. Through curriculum revision, common assessments, frequent walkthroughs, and support from instructional coaches, teachers and administrators have observed that students are better prepared when they enter a new grade. Teachers assert that their feedback on the standards is heard by central office and incorporated when appropriate. One elementary school teacher recalled participating in council meetings between the district's fourth- and fifth-grade teachers and the superintendent. She described the process as being very effective, saying, "It's not like you meet and tell [district leaders] what you need and they don't do it. We are being heard and listened to."

Long Beach developed its districtwide goals based on the SMART concept—goals must be *s*trategic, *m*easurable, *a*ttainable, *r*esults-oriented and *t*ime-bound. Middle and high school educators said their success was directly related to district and school goals. They noted that goals create a shared understanding of the school vision, unite them in a common focus, and provide them with a means for addressing and evaluating school success. The superintendent's goals for the 2002–03 school year are:

- *Schools*—All schools will meet or exceed all their student performance targets.
- *District offices*—All district offices will support school personnel in their efforts to attain API targets.
- *Leadership*—All schools and offices will build on the leadership skills of their staffs to attain the goals of the superintendent and board of education.
- *Facilities*—All district facilities will be maintained to maximize student achievement and work productivity.
- *Communication*—All schools and offices will enhance their internal and external modes of communication to insure that accurate information regarding the district is communicated at all times.
- *School safety*—The staff of the Long Beach USD will develop structures to insure(ensure?) that staff and students work in safe environments that foster student learning.
- *Professional development*—All district employees will have opportunities to hone their skills through professional development in-services offered by the district.

Additionally, Long Beach has two primary districtwide goals—to improve teacher performance and to improve student achievement in reading, language arts, and mathematics.

Staff Selection, Leadership, and Capacity Building

Despite the challenges of being a large, diverse district, Long Beach's leadership reported low principal turnover and an ample pool of qualified candidates. For example, in 2005, the district's latest opening for an elementary school principal yielded over twenty-five qualified applicants. Finding that its strongest principals have come from within the system, the district has continued to focus on building and strengthening internal leaders to maintain program consistency and district culture.

Principal training has recently changed to focus on K–12 instruction, curriculum, and pedagogy. The "leadership modules" in principal development programs are designed to add greater alignment between school levels and are implemented at the elementary, middle, and high school levels at the same time to ensure consistency. This concept has been taken further in practice; now, all high schools have co-principals, meaning two administrators have equal roles as leaders within the same school. One innovative twist Long Beach has applied to this already unique leadership arrangement is to have one former elementary or middle school principal serve as co-principal in each high school. A principal explained that the practice was meant to add systemic alignment and bring useful instructional practices from earlier grades, such as creating print-rich classrooms, into high schools. However, a few principals reported that having two leaders within a building can sometimes cause confusion, and several implied that some schools had problems clarifying the role of each principal.

The district has experienced some turnover in their teaching force, because they have had to let uncertified teachers go to meet the requirements of the No Child Left Behind Act. In addition to being certified in their specified areas of instruction, all but a handful of Long Beach's current teachers are certified for working with English language learners (ELL), and many teachers are certified in gifted and talented education (GATE), so they can address differentiated instruction for accelerated students. Many Long Beach teachers came from California State University (CSU), which has been a strong and unique partner for a number of years. Modeling an atypically reciprocal district-university partnership, CSU professors and district leaders and teachers meet regularly to discuss issues affecting district and university practices. As a result of this partnership, the CSU teacher preparation program has changed based on district feedback, and the district curriculum has been adjusted based on CSU input. For example, the district recently worked with CSU to strengthen students' narrative reading skills. The combined work of professors, teachers, and district leaders led to the development of twenty units of study focusing on high-interest, high-level nonfiction text, complete with a template for creating future units. The inclusion of district leaders on CSU faculty search committees and the addition of a district evaluation of CSU teacher graduates mark additional joint activities that have benefited both organizations.

Teachers in Long Beach report having easy access to numerous classroom supports, including their principal, subject-area coaches, clear curriculum documents and model lesson videos, and collaboration with other teachers. Staff members at all levels attribute part of the district's continued success to effective communication, collaboration, and professional development opportunities. They believe the resulting sense of community contributes to the success of their schools. High school educators attribute success to opportunities and support for professional teacher growth and development. As mentioned, high school collaboration has greatly increased over the last few years as a result of the district's vigilance in "pushing the departments to work together." A secondary central office administrator described the process:

> We observe a lot of collaboration going on between the teachers and what's important in each unit that they teach. They're collaborating and talking about exam results, discussing what the kids missed, and sharing their instructional practices. There's much more talking about curriculum and strategies than ever before. It's very, very exciting to see that happening!

Teachers of all subjects throughout the district mentioned the help and support they get from their colleagues and the importance of working as a "team." One teacher described collaboration on her campus as "one big family that has erased the lines between subject levels." Even though she does not teach math, she often joins math team meetings to discuss ideas for working on particular lessons or with specific students.

Instructional Programs, Practices, and Arrangements

Textbook adoption in Long Beach is governed by the state, which uses a seven-year cycle to adopt basic textbooks. For K–8 textbooks, the state approves texts that meet requirements for appropriate content and align with state content standards. Long Beach establishes committees (composed of curriculum leaders, grade-level teachers, and other at-large members) to examine the matrix and review student data. These committees identify textbooks that will best meet student needs by examining student performance strengths and weaknesses. District stakeholder committees also select commercial instructional programs. These committees evaluate district needs and the scientific evidence on program success, determine alignment with district content standards, and explore how similar schools have implemented the programs. Administrators stress that final program decisions are based on identified needs.

The common instructional tools and programs in Long Beach have improved alignment and uniformity across schools. Instructional alignment is further enhanced by the requirement that teachers use Essential Elements of Effective Instruction (EEEI) to drive instructional pedagogy. The EEEI program helps teachers create and maintain effective classroom environments, engage and support all students in mastering the standards, plan instruction, assess and monitor student progress, and use effective strategies for small-group instruction. Through this program, teachers receive a total of eight days of training during the first two years, with continued training in core subject–driven sessions during subsequent years. Teachers noted that lesson plans and student interventions must use EEEI strategies, which are evaluated through walkthroughs and formal teacher evaluations. High school teachers believe that ongoing implementation of EEEI has made a difference in the achievement of high school students.

Programmatically, the district has been working to improve alignment in math instruction and begin algebra instruction in lower grades, starting with sixth grade. The district supported this process by providing Texas Instruments TI-Navigators—handheld devices that record instant assessment results on classroom math problems, allowing teachers to adjust instruction immediately. Additionally, to help ensure students stay on grade level, summer school instruction is strongly encouraged for students who do not pass all "basic math facts" in grades K–5.

Another district initiative that enhanced instructional alignment and improved student performance reporting was the development of a "standards-based" report card in elementary school. The goal was to provide much more detailed instructional information for parents and students.

Teachers assert that the curriculum guides and training, and particularly the instructional coaches provided by the district, have been extremely helpful for improving classroom instruction. One example that should not go unmentioned was the impact a district math instructional coach had on the performance of one of the schools the site team visited. Identified by the district for his strengths in math instruction, a teacher was pulled out of his position and appointed a math coach to help a school struggling with math performance. To help the school improve its low math ratings, the coach completely restructured its math scope and sequence, using strategies like those used by teachers in Asia, where he had learned mathematics.

The school's teachers explained that the coach grouped math facts by order of operation. Instead of teaching math in separate topics—multiplication, division, decimals, fractions, etc.—the coach taught everything under the four orders of operation, so when he taught multiplication, he would teach how to multiply everything, including fractions and decimals. He also had successful methods for helping students understand conceptually how the operations functioned and how to solve problems. The school adopted his approach and monitored his staff training sessions to ensure that a consistent message was being conveyed. A pilot in the lower grades showed a jump in math trimester exams from 30 percent to between 50 percent and 60 percent. The school principal voiced appreciation for the encouragement and support she received from the district in taking such a big risk in changing instructional pedagogy and sequence so drastically. Now that the program is fully implemented at the school, the same coach will work with another targeted school.

Monitoring, Analysis, and Use of Data

During the 2003 site visit, district administrators described their student assessment and monitoring system as "seamless." According to the superintendent, the district examined both "hard" and "soft" data to identify district successes and areas for improvement. For example, student achievement data revealed student reading difficulties, which prompted a districtwide focus on literacy. At that time, most of the district's student data was kept in a "static online notebook," used by a district data team to create snapshot and longitudinal reports. The retro study site visit in 2005 revealed a new Web-based data management system called ELROY that allowed principals and teachers to run their own queries and view numerous formative and summative assessments as well as demographic, behavioral, and attendance information. The additional nonassessment information is gained through an academic browser, which provides secure online student academic profiles that are accessible by teachers. Academic profiles include a student's entire course, grade, and discipline history, a list of interventions implemented, and the student's home contact information. The browser is set up with tabs to resemble an online folder.

Training for ELROY was rolled out from the central office to school administrators, then to department heads, and then to teachers. A district administrator described an example of the instant effect the system had on classrooms:

A department head went right back to her school, pulled up her classes, and she used the sort system to identify this year's kids and their quarter exams from last year's math tests. Then she identified misplaced kids from her class and got them moved the first week of school . . . right on time. So she could identify if a particular kid failed every exam and she knew this student did not have appropriate classes. We don't know how it happened, but it happened. Instead of waiting two, three, or four weeks before we say "What's this child doing here?" we can identify inappropriate classroom placements immediately.

The district has further aligned and increased its benchmark tests to include trimester exams for grades K–5, quarterly exams for grades 6–12, and common chapter tests. Many of these assessments are easily loaded into the data management system through electronic scanners located in every middle school and high school. The scanners have enabled teachers to obtain instant results from benchmark tests, and in turn provide those results to students so that they know exactly which questions are missed.

In addition to reviewing student performance by analyzing data reports, principals monitor classroom instruction and provide support to teachers through a uniform process called the Key Results Walk-Through Process. External teams composed of central office staff, school administrators, and consultants conduct a three-step process—pre-walkthrough, walkthrough, and debrief. During the pre-walkthrough, the school administrator and management team identify classrooms to be visited, clarify the walkthrough focus question, and define expectations and evidence for the external team. During the walkthrough, groups of external team members (usually three to five members on each team) conduct ten- to twenty-minute classroom observations and collect related evidence. The number of observations depends on the size of the external team and the time allotted for the visit. Observers use guides to focus their observations. After the walkthrough, a debriefing session is held between the external team, the school administrator, and the school management team. The external team provides feedback related to the walkthrough's focus, identifies key questions for the school to consider, and offers advice on improvements for teaching and learning. Targeted schools undergo three walkthroughs during the school year. Schools also self-monitor with internal walkthroughs.

The district provides comprehensive, hands-on training to prepare individuals for walkthrough team participation.

Teachers also use data frequently to monitor school performance. They meet routinely in teams to review data, monitor student progress, and target interventions for students. Administrators described teachers' conversations about data as sounding very informal, including questions like "How come you got those results [illustrating strong student performance]? What did you do differently? How did you teach that?" When asked if conversations around data were always comfortable, district administrators said that it was a gradual process. Before the availability of formative data, teachers often discussed student work products. Gradually teachers learned that the data helped them analyze lessons and improve instruction.

Students in Long Beach also analyze data and self-reflect to improve their learning. Using the Baldrige Education Criteria for Performance Excellence, students monitor their own progress in high school by keeping notebooks of their classroom work, data results, and individual academic goals. When they see performance concerns, they engage in conversations with teachers about how they can improve their academic performance.

The emerging trend in all the data processes in Long Beach, confirmed by district administrators, is to provide tools and training on data use to all levels of the system to build autonomy and frequency in data use. For example, the district has invested considerable time in training teachers to analyze data to ensure students are placed correctly in classes, instead of relying on counselors or administrators to do it. The above example illustrating how students are taught to analyze their own results further demonstrates this mind-set.

Recognition, Intervention, and Adjustment

Long Beach uses data on a daily basis to intervene with students before performance concerns become difficult to address. Some preventive measures have included ensuring students are in the proper grade level, making sure instruction is uniform and aligned across the district, and examining the overall academic program.

Struggling schools identified by the district receive first priority in support, resources, and academic coaches. For chronically low-performing schools, the district conducts either "soft" or "hard" reconstitutions. A soft reconstitution requires that the district replace only the school's administrator; a hard reconstitution requires that the district replace the school administrator and that all teachers reapply for their positions. If these steps do not improve school performance, the district designates the struggling school as a "focus" school.

During the 2003 site visit, Long Beach had identified two struggling high schools as focus schools. The district hired an outside consultant to collaborate with district staff to identify effective methods to improve school operations and student achievement. Long Beach allocates substantial resources for instructional development and delivery at focus schools. Teachers must attend a forty-hour math and literacy professional development institute and participate in eighty hours of follow-up training. The principals and assistant principals of focus schools must also attend professional development activities and follow-up sessions on instruction in the target area (i.e., the content area in which the school's student achievement scores lag). Focus schools participate in three "Key Results" meetings and monthly certification walkthroughs. District staff members conduct weekly on-site visits, and academic coaches build capacity in the focus area. The focus schools must adhere to strict goal targets with timelines and must submit monthly data analysis reports to the district to track progress.

Teachers in the district receive a wide array of supports to help with instruction, including clear curriculum guides, opportunities for professional development, and support provided by principals and instructional coaches. Teachers who require additional assistance receive support from the district's state-supported Peer Assistance and Review (PAR) program. Under PAR, teachers who receive unsatisfactory performance evaluations are required by state law to participate in the program. These teachers receive sixty hours of focused intervention from a consulting teacher who conducts multiple observations, models exemplary practices, and provides targeted assistance in classroom management, lesson plan development, and best practice implementation. Teachers may also request to participate in the PAR program and receive intervention based on their identified needs and goals.

Performance data clearly drives identification of students needing intervention in Long Beach. The district has developed an International Student Registration Assessment Center to properly assess and place new English language learners based on their English performance level. Teachers collaborate to identify the needs of struggling students and effective intervention strategies. Overall, differentiation of instruction and grouping students according to academic needs appears to be the district's most powerful method of student intervention. This focus is driven by the district's retention policy, under which students in grades 1, 3, 5, and 8 are required to meet certain benchmark standards in order to be promoted. Long Beach schools design individualized intervention plans to meet the unique needs of their student populations. The district uses the state-level Student Success Teams process "as part of [its] ongoing efforts to support the attainment of high standards by all students." Student Success Teams collaborate with classroom teachers to identify and implement structured, individualized intervention for struggling students. During the site team's 2003 visit, middle school educators emphasized that the school has a variety of safety nets to provide multiple opportunities to close the achievement gap and ensure that all students learn.

In addition to using instructional techniques and programs, schools implement a variety of extended learning opportunities for students needing additional assistance. These opportunities include three-week Kinder-Camps, Better Learning After School Today (BLAST) for high school students, and the Eighth Grade Academic Initiative, which requires any eighth-grade student receiving two failing grades to attend summer school, followed by a content-intensive transitional ninth-grade program (T-9) at one of five district high schools. Although many districts have similar programs, intervention programs in Long Beach are particularly successful due to the district's determination to ensure that its programs adequately address student needs. This is particularly important, since the utility of summer and after-school programs is often questioned. The success of Long Beach's summer school classes is illustrated by this administrator's comment:

> Over time we've seen [summer school] go from just something to do during the summer, to truly helping students that are really struggling. We changed the ways those programs look in order to meet the needs of the kids, rather than just having a program and funneling the kids through. We're working hard on the kids that get identified as a result of our data to change their results, by providing the right interventions.

Teachers reported to us that the district's wide range of interventions, including the retention strategies, helped raise the number of well-prepared students coming into their classes. One high school teacher commented, "I don't know what they are doing in elementary and middle schools, but this is the first time they've sent a cohort of kids to the high school this well prepared." So the long-term effect is that teachers believe students are showing up with the appropriate skills to succeed in their classrooms.

INFLUENCING FACTORS

Stakeholder focus group interviews were not included in The Broad Prize process until 2004, after Long Beach's win. However, individual interviews with various stakeholders did provide some information about the district's relationships with its board, union, community, and parents.

School Board

Similar to Garden Grove, the Long Beach school board saw its role within the district as setting policy, according to an interview with the school board president in 2003. Agreeing, Superintendent Chris Steinhauser and the union president of that time noted that the board set high standards and held the district accountable without micromanaging the actual work. Parents also saw relationships with the board as being positive and supportive. Our return visit in 2005 found that relationship still stable and positive. Board members were happy that the current superintendent was providing long-term stability; the two main concerns they voiced were the perceived divisiveness caused by a union president and budget cuts resulting from declining enrollments and reduced state funding. They felt the district was beginning to make progress in narrowing achievement gaps, but they were concerned that the progress would be difficult to maintain because their population "is actually getting poorer," according to one board member.

The board members also believed the district was doing a good job serving ELL students, and they were proud that Long Beach was one of the two districts in the state (out of over one hundred) to be in complete compliance with its ELL population. They felt it was an accomplishment, given that there are over forty-six languages spoken in the district, and that the accomplishment was partially prompted not only by Long Branch's instructional techniques for ELL students, but by its programs that were also working with parents of ELL students to improve their English skills.

Union/Association

The main union serving Long Beach USD is the Teachers Association of Long Beach (TALB), affiliated with the National Education Association. TALB serves as a collective bargaining unit that takes an active role in teacher salaries and benefits and state-level lobbying. In 2003, TALB interviewees reported having regular meetings with the superintendent, district leaders, and the board. The union interviewees described those meetings as collaborative and focused on student success. The only detection of any conflict in 2003 between the union and district was a miscommunication that occurred during contract negotiations, which spurred rumors that the district had "wiped out everyone's benefits."[4]

Our return back to the district in 2005 for the retro study found the relationship between the union and the district to have changed somewhat—for the worse, according to some. During the 2003 site visit, the district's relationship with the union was characterized as highly collaborative and supportive, but numerous interviewees voiced concerns about that relationship in retro study interviews. While specific details were not divulged, we were told there had been a change in leadership that was seen was more "distracting" than supportive. When asked about current district challenges, several school interviewees mentioned the growing contention with the union. One board member asserted that union leadership was changing the teacher culture in the district from a body that frequently referenced the "Long Beach family" and doing things the "Long Beach way," to a group that viewed administration as "them" and teachers as "us." This member believed this perception was driving a wedge between teachers that reduced the district's ability to address them as a cohesive group.

Community

Regarding external relationships, the school board president stated that Long Beach "has a tremendous relationship with the community." The district's relationship with CSU, mentioned earlier, is one of the strongest and most unique of those partnerships. Called the Seamless Education Initiative, the partnership was created as a collaborative K–16 effort to improve student achievement, teacher preparation, and faculty and staff capacity building. As part of this initiative, the district partnered with CSU and Long Beach City College to develop a standards-based teacher preparation program, aligning pre-service content standards and assessments with Long Beach's standards for students. In addition to the postsecondary partners, Long Beach is supported by numerous community organizations, including the Communities Organizing Resources to Advance Learning (CORAL) Initiative, Education Trust, Industry Education Council of Long Beach, Long Beach Chamber of Commerce, Long Beach Education Foundation, National Council of Jewish Women, Performance Plus Tire, Suzuki, and the YMCA.

Parents

As in most districts, parental involvement in Long Beach varies, and diminishes at the high school level. As a mechanism to connect to parents, the district employs a parent coordinator, who facilitates an annual Parent Institute. During the institute, district leaders work with parents on different methods for supporting their children in school. One obstacle to connecting to parents noted by district leaders was the district's school choice policy, which resulted in some parents living far from the school. To address that issue, the district provides free transportation so that parents can attend school events.

One elementary school we visited in 2005 felt that parent involvement was improving and that parents were aware of the school's goals. The teachers interviewed considered parents as important partners in student achievement. One teacher mentioned that she was hearing more from parents recently to thank her for helping their children improve grades and schoolwork.

Teachers in a middle school we visited in 2005 mentioned that they work hard to provide parents with information, partially through weekend-long sessions designed to explain to parents how to look for financial aid, make them aware of the A-G college-readiness requirements, allow them to listen to a motivational speaker, and provide time to network with other parents and ask teachers and the principal questions. To ensure high participation, the school invites a local celebrity like a well-known actor or baseball player. Teachers report a moderate turnout for these weekend events, and relatively high numbers for the annual open house events at that particular middle school. An additional intervention with parents implemented by the same middle school is to send a letter that requires a parent signature to permit a student to attend an additional hour of school for remediation. At the bottom of the letter are two check boxes: one box states, "Yes I want my child to succeed," and the other states, "No, I don't care if my child does not succeed." The teachers asserted that the letter sent a powerful message to parents.

Governance, Organization, and Decision Making

In the 2002 and 2003 site visits, we did not specifically ask about governance and organizational structures. From cross-interview analyses, we found that

Long Beach operates with a traditional model of an elected board, which has worked well for them thus far. Most district stakeholders agreed that Superintendent Steinhauser communicated well with both internal and external stakeholders, and they trusted his ability to provide leadership to the district.

In our 2005 retro study visit, we collected an organizational chart showing how the district central office was organized into two main divisions: instruction and support services. Three assistant superintendents provided leadership to each grade level (elementary, middle, and high schools), and the other main central office leaders provided oversight to support services. Those positions included the CFO; Deputy Superintendent of Curriculum, Instruction, and Professional Development; Assistant Superintendent of Human Resources; Assistant Superintendent of Research, Planning, and Evaluation; and Assistant Superintendent of School Support Services. Numerous positions served under these leaders to provide direct services to schools, teachers, and students.

The high schools were led by co-principals—one in charge of instruction, and the other of discipline and plant management. The high schools also had several assistant principals serving under the co-principals. In one high school we visited, the assistant principals served a section of students divided by the alphabet.

Regarding authority and decision making, the district appeared to be centralized in many practices, such as curriculum selection and development, goal setting, and monitoring. However, the district also appeared to give school leaders some level of authority to run their schools as they saw fit. District and school administrators partially attribute their success to their curriculum alignment, which was primarily accomplished through their centralized curriculum and instruction practices.

District and stakeholder interviewees also attributed their successes to what they described as "effective school leadership." Teachers and principals at all levels felt that their school leadership teams, which served as the primary decision-making body at the school level, worked collaboratively and effectively in moving schools toward their stated annual goals. Regarding authority, principals felt well supported and able to set appropriate goals for their schools. Principals at all levels felt they received useful feedback from assistant superintendents during walkthroughs, and many asserted they received whatever they requested from central office, within reason.

Similarly, teachers reported feeling very connected to their schools and the other teachers, and many said they felt empowered to make decisions. One teacher at a middle school commented that her school provided many leadership opportunities, which she described as "distributed leadership." She felt that everyone had something to do and, "everyone's empowered to do better and just take control the way they want to do it." The same teacher mentioned that her principal would always encourage her with her ideas and say, "Fly, go do it." This was important to her, as she said it made her "want to do a great job for this school." She continued, "I want to do it, I want to show everybody that this idea or that idea can help us."

Teachers also seemed to particularly appreciate the time they were allotted to meet collaboratively to plan instruction, review data, and solve instructional challenges. Teachers felt it was important that they create a culture of high expectations and support for their students, and provide them with numerous opportunities to "push themselves and perform at high levels."

Resource Allocation

The California school finance system has been in place for a number of years and is considered to be somewhat complex. The governor and the California legislature annually determine public school funding, including property tax revenue. The sources that fund schools (details are from 2007) are the federal government (11 percent), state budget (61 percent), local property taxes (21 percent), miscellaneous local revenues (6 percent), and the Lottery (1.5 percent).[5]

Stakeholders in 2003 interviews were worried about the state budget crisis and voiced great concern about budget cuts experienced by the district. A central office administrator reported that the district had been forced to cut $26 million from its operating budget and that another $9.5 million cut was still pending.[6] To manage the cuts, the district hired fewer teachers and reduced its overall central office budget by 45 percent. Additionally, the district received some much-needed financial support from other sources, including the Long Beach Education Foundation, Verizon, and Boeing. Many elementary schools were dependent on revenue received from Title I and Title III funds. The high schools also mentioned having several grants in 2003, including High School Outreach, AP challenge, High School Magnet, Digital High School, and Gear UP grants.

When developing the budget during the budget crunch in 2003, Steinhauser said, his priority was making cuts everywhere except "in the classroom." The drivers of the budget were the ability of the district to meet content standards, achieve district goals, and reduce student achievement gaps. Additionally, the district was working at that time to ensure appropriate investments were being made to support teachers, as they represented a key factor in student success. Funds were thus focused on teacher induction, professional development, and coaching for teachers.

Long Beach central office leaders describe school budget processes as being rather "decentralized." School site council teams work together on the budget and are given autonomy to make budget decisions, as long as they use their school data to support their goals and decisions. However, Chris Steinhauser did note that low-performing schools have less autonomy over their budgets than schools showing stronger student achievement.

During the retro study site visit in 2005, we found the district and schools still struggling with a declining budget, as well as concerns over rising costs in health care and declining district enrollments resulting in less funding from average daily student attendance. Specifically, central officer leaders mentioned an enrollment decline of eight thousand students, which they equated to a loss of $11 million in revenue that forced the district to cut over twenty-four central office and sixty-five management positions.

Interestingly, the two schools we visited during the retro study did not mention having made large cuts in their school budgets when we asked. One middle school had cut back on a before-school math and reading program due to loss of funds, but otherwise, interviewees in both schools asserted that they were not dealing with difficult budget issues. While this may have changed after 2005, these two schools reported that they were still able to deliver their instructional programs as planned, and asserted that they still received what they needed from central office.

Climate/Culture

District and school staff members all described the climate in Long Beach as being "collaborative" and "exciting." In our first site visit in 2003, interviewees at all levels felt the district had high expectations for students, a clear focus, and a commitment to raising student achievement and narrowing ethnic and income achievement gaps. When we revisited the district in 2005, members expressed feelings of pride in winning a nationally recognized prize and believed that the attention helped them meet and get to know educators from other districts. One fruitful connection from such a visit was a partnership that the Long Beach forged with Garden Grove USD. In addition to enjoying the collaborative team atmosphere, teachers felt well supported and valued as a key factor in helping students achieve. Additionally, teachers said they felt "empowered" by the ability to better address student needs with the data available to them. Interviews with teachers found them to be very appreciative and trusting of their principals, citing them as a major resource for information and support.

REFORM AND STUDENT ACHIEVEMENT—BRINGING IT TO SCALE

When asked in 2003 which reform had the most impact on student achievement, district leaders cited the value the district placed on aligning the system overall, better defining and aligning the curriculum, and using data to improve the educational program. The data piece was mentioned often by leaders and teachers, who felt the district's focus on continuous monitoring and analysis of student progress was particularly important for making appropriate responses to students' instructional needs. This monitoring came not only from formative and summative assessment data, but also from the district's well-structured classroom walkthroughs. Teachers in the 2003 interviews often mentioned that they found students to be better prepared for the next grade or subject than they had been in the past. Many high school teachers also observed that their students were demonstrating mastery of more prerequisite skills for algebra.

During our return visit in 2005, district leaders mainly spoke about high school improvements, which included a shift from typical high school department silos to more willingness to collaborate and embrace the benchmark assessments. The leaders felt that the increased collaboration and data use were major factors in recent improvements in high school math scores. In addition to district reforms, school leaders mentioned that winning the Prize also affected the district by sparking pride and providing affirmation that it was "headed in the right direction." Several principals pointed out that they had not made a lot of significant changes since winning the Prize, but were simply drilling down to refine the same goals and plans carved out prior to 2003.

Teachers agreed that winning The Broad Prize was exciting and affirming to students and to them as well. When asked what changes had been made since the win to improve student achievement, teachers answered that there were none, really, but rather a continued focus on using data to inform decisions and supporting teachers to strengthen classroom instruction. During the retro study, we kept hearing teachers refer to the "Long Beach Way." When asked to describe what that meant, one teacher replied:

> The Long Beach way is about accountability . . . It is this pride—a built-in compass that kids come first, no excuses. We are constantly looking for new and better ways to do things. Our curriculum department is so superior that when we ask our staff to do things, there is no argument. Everything is piloted and tested and we are sure of the things we are asking. We all know what quality looks like.

Although the 2003 and 2005 site visits yielded great enthusiasm from stakeholders about the district's accomplishments, the interviews also contained recurring challenges as well. Concerns about a dwindling budget were mentioned both in 2003 and 2005 interviews with district leaders. In addition to budget shortfalls, several school staff members mentioned that families were moving away from Long Beach due to rising housing costs. According to one real estate–tracking Web site, the median price for a house in Long Beach in 2002 was around $200,000; in 2006 it had risen to $525,000.[7] Teachers also referred to the continuing challenge of keeping transient students connected to and attending school. Although they received help from Student Success Teams, they still felt concerned that they could not do more with those students.

Probably the biggest concern voiced by staff members at all levels across the district in 2005 was the deterioration of the relationship between the district and the union. One principal mentioned that he and others were frustrated that the district had been "moving in the same direction with the same passion for years," only to have that relationship hampered by a leadership change in the union. Another central office leader referred to the existence of both union contention and mounting budgeting challenges as "the emergence of the perfect storm." In one principal focus group, a principal described himself as "appalled" by the current union leadership, because he felt union leaders were providing different messages to teachers, causing a huge distraction and contention between teachers and district leaders. Agreeing, another principal voiced concern that the divisiveness was creating a situation where "teacher's voices are not heard," implying that their opinions were not fully represented by union leaders. Another principal opined that "the union leader is more about creating strife than working for the kids."

CURRENT PERFORMANCE AND PRACTICES

By rule, Broad Prize winners remain out of the Prize competition for three years after their win. Long Beach was the first Prize winner to reappear in the finalist list, and did so the first year they regained eligibility in 2007. The district stood out from among the one hundred eligible districts each year from 2007 to 2009 because of its continued strong performance in student achievement. Not only has its student achievement increased over time, it has also continued to do well with minority and low-income students.

Figure 5.14 compares the district's reading proficiencies at all three grade levels with the state's for the 2007 school year. In all levels (although narrowly in high school), the district's African American, Hispanic, and low-income students outperform the state. Figure 5.15 illustrates even higher performance with the same groups compared with the state in math, especially at the elementary level.

In 2009, Chris Steinhauser was still the superintendent at Long Beach, sustaining the stability and vision set forth when he began his leadership there in 2002. When we revisited the district in 2005, it had not engaged in a lot of new work; it was primarily drilling down to improve the work already set in motion years ago. The district had invested more time in training leaders and teachers, improving its data system, and refining the curriculum, instructional techniques, and interventions for students and schools.

FIGURE 5.14

District and state 2007 reading proficiencies: All levels

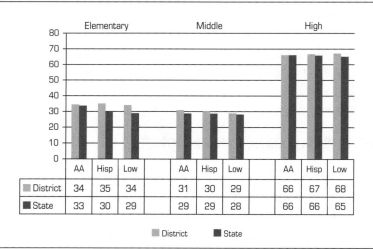

	Elementary			Middle			High		
	AA	Hisp	Low	AA	Hisp	Low	AA	Hisp	Low
District	34	35	34	31	30	29	66	67	68
State	33	30	29	29	29	28	66	66	65

District　State

FIGURE 5.15
District and state 2007 math proficiencies: All levels

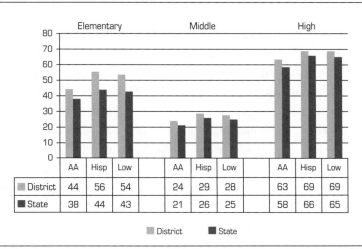

	Elementary			Middle			High		
	AA	Hisp	Low	AA	Hisp	Low	AA	Hisp	Low
District	44	56	54	24	29	28	63	69	69
State	38	44	43	21	26	25	58	66	65

District State

The recognition that came with winning the Prize has helped the district as declining enrollments, budget constraints, and the rising costs of housing and health care exerted pressure. Though the district lost 325 out of 5,000 teachers in 2005, it managed to attract and hire qualified candidates mainly through the newly gained prestige resulting from the Prize and its partnerships with CSU and the University of California. In a district-developed survey of new teachers, district leaders found out that many new teachers were advised by their college professors to apply for teaching positions at Long Beach. One district leader described the professors' recommendations as "another illustration of the two-way communication between us and the two universities."

Two relatively new programmatic focus areas the district discussed at length during our revisit in 2005 were college readiness and improving special education programming. To help ramp up student preparation for college, the district wanted to develop college-level coursework for its high schools. During the previous summer, forty teachers had attended an institute for AP training, and the next year all students took the PSAT to assess potential for college-level courses. When the district found a lack of diversity in that student group, it worked to develop and implement summer bridge programs to prepare more students for advanced courses. The district was planning to conduct research over the next summer to compare and assess the impact of summer bridge programs and student tutorials. Additionally, district leaders mentioned adding Advancement Via Individual Determination (AVID), Gifted and Talented Education Program (GATE), and International Baccalaureate coordinators.

The district also wanted to improve the academic success of the students served in special education, since 50–70 percent of those students were failing, regardless of whether they were served in pull-out courses or within regular classrooms with co-teachers (inclusion). Deciding that something different was needed, the district developed a Strategies for Success model that would provide students with the study skills they were missing. In middle school, the model included pacing guides, course outlines, and mini-assessments to ensure students were progressing at an acceptable rate. Students who were not doing well on the mini-assessments were given an additional action plan for every grade period. Finding the model to be a success, as evidenced by the assessment data, the district expanded it by developing course outlines and pacing charts for all middle and high school classes, making sure the courses were parallel to the state standards for each course. Being a former special education teacher myself, I was impressed with the amount of structure and detail contained in this program. Many such programs are not as vigilant about keeping courses for students in special education aligned to the state standards, nor do they do as good a job of monitoring academic progress on an ongoing basis.

CONCLUSION

Like Garden Grove, Long Beach started its journey by operationalizing the vision that all their students could achieve at high standards and by clearly defining what that meant for teachers and students. Along with clarity came the provision of a multitude of supports throughout the system to ensure student success. The use of data in a trusting and collaborative manner to identify supports for schools, teachers, and students has been an integral part of that progress.

Leadership stability and positive relationships have also been important for Long Beach to sustain and spark current and future successes. Chris Steinhauser took leadership of the district from another revered leader, and he came as a product of the system he is leading. One key partnership that has benefited both higher education and Long Beach is the reciprocal relationship with California State University.

The next step in the district's plan is to continue to focus efforts at the high school level and aim for the goal of preparing its students for college and/or skilled careers. Its continued focus on the Seamless Education Initiative will remain an important part of that goal.

6

Norfolk Public Schools

Norfolk Public Schools (NPS), a three-time Broad Prize finalist and the 2005 winner, is a moderate-sized district with 36,724 students, 57 schools, and 3,363 teachers. The diverse student body consists of 68 percent African American students, 3 percent Hispanic students, 27 percent white students, and 2 percent Asian American students, with 60 percent of students eligible for free or reduced-price lunch.[1]

NPS is located in the Norfolk, a major port city in southwest Virginia that hosts the region's international airport and one of the busiest international ports on the east coast of the United States. It is also home to the world's largest naval base and NATO's North American Headquarters.[2] According to the 2000 census data, the major population groups in Norfolk are whites at 48.7 percent, African Americans at 44.2 percent, with the next largest group being Hispanic at 3.8 percent and Asian American at 2.8 percent. According to the 2007 American Community Survey, the median household income was $40,701 and the median family income was $47,504.[3] The area includes five centers of higher education, and the military employs 25 percent of the local workforce.

NPS was a Prize finalist in 2003 and 2004 and won the Prize in 2005. Since winning, the district has gained numerous distinctions. In 2006, it was recognized by the National School Boards Association as having the top school board in the country. In 2007, Norview High school earned a bronze medal in *U.S. News & World Report*'s annual ranking of high schools, and Taylor Elementary School was named a Blue Ribbon School by the U.S. Department of Education. In 2008, Maury and Granby high schools also appeared in *Newsweek*'s ranking of top high schools.

NPS has done well with a challenging student population. The district's results demonstrate higher levels of achievement than demographically similar districts in Virginia. Highlights contributing to their nominations for and win of The Broad Prize in 2005 include:

- Met Adequate Yearly Progress (AYP) targets in 2004 for 76 percent of schools.
- Increased the number of elementary students who reached proficiency in reading by 14 percent between 2001 and 2005, and increased the number of middle school students who reached reading proficiency by 12 percent.
- Increased the number of elementary students who reached proficiency in math by 14 percent from 2001 to 2005, and increased the number of middle school students who reached proficiency in math by 23 percent.
- Reduced achievement gaps in elementary reading for Hispanic students (by 11 percent) and in middle school math for African American students (by 10 percent).

DISTRICT DEMOGRAPHICS AND ACHIEVEMENT LEVELS

Detailed data from NPS's Broad Prize report card shows that the district performed well in comparisons with the state over time, showed steady improvement, and did well in narrowing ethnic and income achievement gaps in certain subjects and grades. These results are impressive, since compared with the state, NPS enrolls over three times more African American students, twice as many (6 percent compared with 3 percent) Hispanic students, and almost twice the number of students who qualify for free or reduced-price lunch (60 percent compared with 34 percent).[4]

It is important to note when reviewing NPS's Broad Prize data and charts that the tested grades changed in 2006 after their win. In 2004 and 2005, the elementary level tests were administered in grades 3 and 5, middle level tests in grade 8, and high school tests in grades 9, 10, 11, and 12. High school test administration did not change in 2006 and 2007, but the other tested grades changed from 3, 5, and 8 to all grades 3–8. This provided additional test data, for a much more robust analysis.[5] Although the data charts in this book were created across the years, the reader should view 2003–2005 and 2005–2006 separately for an accurate comparison.

NPS's performance in reading and math at the elementary level was just a few percentage points below the state's scores in both subjects, with the district's lag narrowing considerably by 2007. In figures 6.1 and 6.2, the district remains about five points below the state in proficiency rates until 2007, when the performance gap narrows to about two points lower in both subjects, showing very similar performance between the two subjects.

Middle school performance in reading was not as strong as at the elementary level, but remained consistent with the state and improved over time. However, figure 6.3 shows a significant drop in middle school math proficiencies (approximately 30 percentage points for each) both for the

FIGURE 6.1
District and state elementary school reading proficiencies: All students

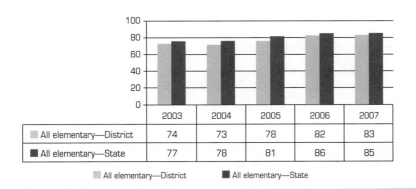

	2003	2004	2005	2006	2007
All elementary—District	74	73	78	82	83
All elementary—State	77	78	81	86	85

FIGURE 6.2

District and state elementary school math proficiencies: All students

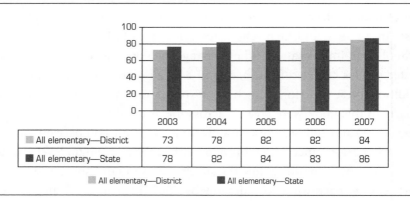

	2003	2004	2005	2006	2007
All elementary—District	73	78	82	82	84
All elementary—State	78	82	84	83	86

■ All elementary—District   ■ All elementary—State

FIGURE 6.3

District and state middle school math proficiencies: All students

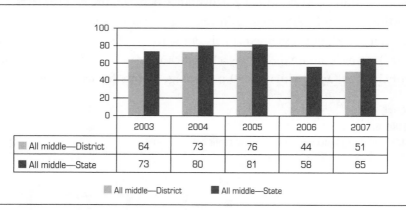

	2003	2004	2005	2006	2007
All middle—District	64	73	76	44	51
All middle—State	73	80	81	58	65

■ All middle—District   ■ All middle—State

district and state, perhaps attributable to the addition of two more grade levels to the middle school Prize analysis.

For high school, NPS's performance looks very positive in reading, with the district staying within a few percentage points of the state each year. Ironically, both the district and state started with the percentage of students scoring at or above proficiency in the low 90s in 2003, then decreased in percentage points in 2004 and 2005, and moved back in 2007 exactly to where they both started in 2003 (figure 6.4).

Because the only large ethnicity groups in NPS are African American and white, those groups provide the most relevant comparisons for examining gap performance. Figures 6.5 and 6.6 illustrate that the district narrowed the gap between African American and white students' elementary reading

FIGURE 6.4
District and high elementary school reading proficiencies: All students

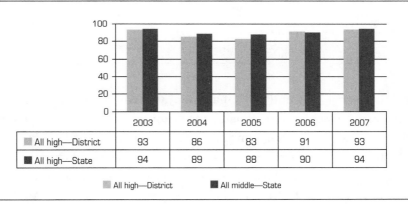

	2003	2004	2005	2006	2007
All high—District	93	86	83	91	93
All high—State	94	89	88	90	94

All high—District   All middle—State

FIGURE 6.5
District elementary school reading achievement gap between African American and white students

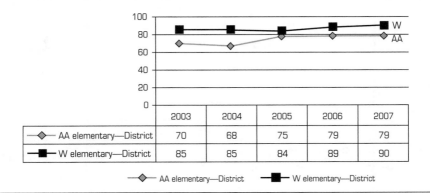

	2003	2004	2005	2006	2007
AA elementary—District	70	68	75	79	79
W elementary—District	85	85	84	89	90

AA elementary—District   W elementary—District

FIGURE 6.6

State elementary school reading achievement gap between African American and white students

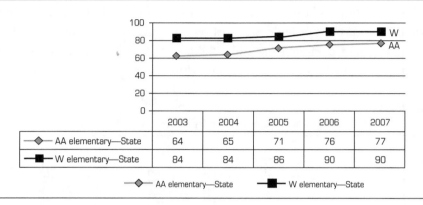

	2003	2004	2005	2006	2007
◆ AA elementary—State	64	65	71	76	77
■ W elementary—State	84	84	86	90	90

scores between 2005 and 2007 at a faster rate than the state. The district's gaps are narrower because it maintained similar performance to the state's white students while maintaining a higher percentage of African American students at or above proficiency compared to the state over time.

Figures 6.7 and 6.8 illustrate similar performance in elementary math in a comparison of the district and state's gap between African American

FIGURE 6.7

District elementary school math achievement gap between African American and white students

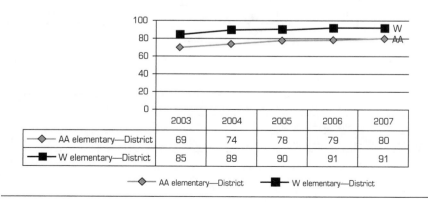

	2003	2004	2005	2006	2007
◆ AA elementary—District	69	74	78	79	80
■ W elementary—District	85	89	90	91	91

FIGURE 6.8

State elementary school math achievement gap between African American and white students

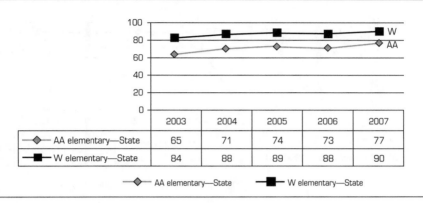

	2003	2004	2005	2006	2007
AA elementary—State	65	71	74	73	77
W elementary—State	84	88	89	88	90

and white students. Again the district outperformed the state with both ethnicity groups, and in narrowing the gap between African American and white students.

NPS also narrowed the gap between low-income and non-low-income students in elementary reading at a faster rate than the state. Figures 6.9 and 6.10 illustrate that the district's gap between income groups remained

FIGURE 6.9

District elementary school math achievement gap between low- and non-low-income students

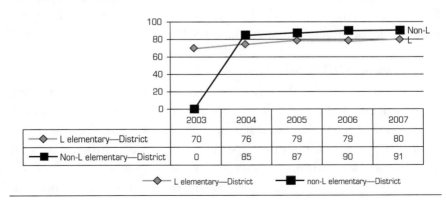

	2003	2004	2005	2006	2007
L elementary—District	70	76	79	79	80
Non-L elementary—District	0	85	87	90	91

FIGURE 6.10

State elementary school math achievement gap between low- and non-low-income students

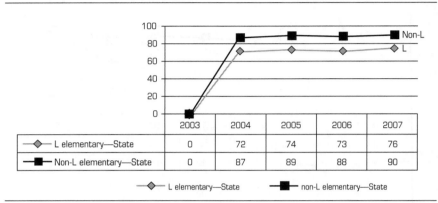

	2003	2004	2005	2006	2007
L elementary—State	0	72	74	73	76
Non-L elementary—State	0	87	89	88	90

L elementary—State   non-L elementary—State

smaller over each year between 2004 and 2007, while maintaining a higher percentage of low-income students at or above proficiency when compared with the state.

When compared with similar districts in the state in the residual analysis, NPS had all positive residuals, meaning it performed higher than expected when compared with similar districts in the state in all subjects and grade levels in 2004 and 2005. As illustrated in figure 6.11, there was no residual data reported for any school levels in 2003 and for high school in 2005. The residuals look different in 2006 and 2007, perhaps because of the addition of the additional grade levels in the Prize methodology during those years. Between 2004 and 2007, residuals for elementary reading remain high, and are positive for middle and high school reading.

High School Graduation Rates

Graduation rates under the three formulas used in the Prize report cards all appear below the national average of approximately 73.2 percent in 2003-2005.[6] Using the averaged freshman graduation rate, the district had estimated graduation rates of 52 percent. Since its performance in other academic areas was strong, we asked the superintendent of that time, Dr. John Simpson, if he could speak about why their rate was not higher. His

FIGURE 6.11
District reading residual analysis: All levels

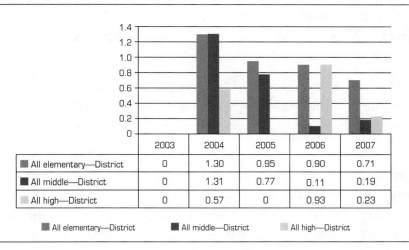

	2003	2004	2005	2006	2007
■ All elementary—District	0	1.30	0.95	0.90	0.71
■ All middle—District	0	1.31	0.77	0.11	0.19
▨ All high—District	0	0.57	0	0.93	0.23

■ All elementary—District   ■ All middle—District   ▨ All high—District

response was that the reforms made in the district would take about four to five years to reach the high school level. In his words, "We started in elementary schools, and now we've moved into middle schools and we're seeing improvements there. All five of our high schools are accredited now." He also mentioned how complex graduation rates are, with the many calculations that are used.

DISTRICT PRACTICES BY THEME

There is a particular feeling when you visit NPS Public Schools. Educators at all levels speak enthusiastically about their students, seem driven and committed to providing a "world-class education," and display a remarkable hospitality that makes visitors feel very much at home. When discussing their challenges, they are very upfront and honest and often use "we" when they talk about improving student achievement, providing supports, or solving problems. A typical conversation might sound like, "Well, we did not do well in middle school math, so we met, reviewed the data, and came up with a plan. We also asked the teachers, 'What do you think happened? What do you need?'" We felt we were in a very well-connected, trusting, and thriving system when visiting NPS. The accomplishments of this diverse district with highly mobile Navy families are impressive. Illustrating the positive changes made in the district, one NPS principal said,

> There is a big excitement in our district now; everyone is seeing success. Realtors weren't taking people to NPS—they were going to the neighboring bigger city. That's not happening anymore; everyone sees we are really shining.

In NPS, the state standards are "the floor, not the ceiling," and its districtwide mantra of "All means all" is known by every stakeholder in the district and community.

NPS's commitment to higher standards required a change in the mindset of everyone in the school system, and a change in the way students were taught. Prior to the arrival of now-retired superintendent John Simpson in 1998, the district made excuses for poor performance, citing the high rates of poverty and the presence of challenging student populations. Dr. Simpson instilled a "no excuses" mentality in the district by developing a districtwide philosophy of teaching and learning, establishing a culture of trust, providing better supports to schools, basing decisions on data, and establishing shared accountability throughout the district. The end result was a well-aligned system created through construction of a common curriculum requiring higher academic expectations for all students, bolstered by "instructional non-negotiables" and a collaborative culture connected by a well-articulated common goal.

Describing that process in NPS through the five separate themes of NCEA's Framework is particularly difficult, as many of the district's practices span the themes. Although the reform process in NPS began with setting clear and specific goals, the type of instruction the district selected to realize those goals was very specific in both content and implementation. Therefore, this chapter discusses Instructional Programs, Practices, and Arrangements before Staff Selection, Leadership, and Capacity Building to illustrate how the instructional program drove NPS's reform process.

Curriculum and Academic Goals

When John Simpson came to NPS in 1998, he thought its student performance was "abysmal." Just 38 percent of third-graders passed the state's Standards of Learning, or SOL, test in English; only 26 percent of eighth-graders were proficient in mathematics; and only 18 percent of high school students passed Virginia history and U.S. history. Believing that the few pockets of high-performing schools could be replicated, Dr. Simpson strove to duplicate their successes by working with his team to adopt their practices. They began by recentralizing curriculum and instruction, starting with reducing twenty-four different reading programs down to one used by the successful schools. The district wanted its instructional program, which will be further detailed under the next theme, to address higher levels of thinking and help create a structured system that would ensure alignment, faithful implementation, and tools and supports for schools and teachers.

NPS used the Virginia standards as the foundation, or the "floor," for the district curriculum and as a guide for instruction. The standards were considered to be only a minimum threshold and not adequate to meet the district's goal of having their students compete nationally. To ensure that everyone clearly understood the state standards, the district broke them down into specific skills in literacy, math, and other core-content areas. This process was completed through collaboration between teachers, central office, parents, and higher education partners. When the process was complete, teachers were given specific learning objectives, curriculum maps, quarterly pacing calendars, monitoring rubrics, and multitask performance assessments to support the curriculum.

During the site team's second Broad Prize visit to NPS in 2005, the team found that the already-comprehensive curriculum maps had several useful enhancements, including "essential questions" that help clarify the purpose of each lesson, a one-page view of the objectives aligned to the quarterly tests, and support resources for teachers. Additionally, pacing guides had been burned to CDs that provided hyperlinks to specific activities and common technical vocabulary to align content across the district.

NPS's curriculum is developed and revised by teams of teachers who use notes of suggested changes that all teachers write in their curriculum guides throughout the year. During the revision process, vertical teams of teachers work together to wrestle with a specific task, such as introducing algebra at lower grade levels to ensure that instruction is aligned appropriately from higher to lower grades. To expand that example—vertical teams of teachers met to discuss what skills students "came in with" and needed for algebra. They wanted to focus on threading through the concepts and building on them, rather than teaching the same superficial skills, such as prime and composite numbers, repeatedly. The end result was a well-articulated strand from pre-K to grade 7 that prepared students on an in-depth level for algebra.

Specific objectives are grouped into six-week increments, giving teachers flexibility to decide how to cover a given topic, with remediation and acceleration built into daily lessons as needed. Quarterly benchmark assessments are given at the end of each six-week period to monitor progress on the objectives. The districtwide quarterly assessments (and in some schools monthly assessments) are administered, and extensive walk-through observations are provided to struggling schools to ensure that the curriculum is being consistently implemented. The district's quarterly assessments are also used to determine regrouping of students according to their learning needs.

Having students study the same material within a quarter is important in a district with such high levels of student mobility. One elementary teacher talked about the shift to more instructional uniformity:

> It was a good thing for kids who are moving from school to school. It's nice to know every school is teaching the same thing in the same general amount of time. Kids would move to another school and might miss something because everyone was teaching the same year, but the sequences are all different. Now NPS is trying to get us all within the same information within a quarter.

However, the same teacher pointed out that when problems arose, the district afforded teachers the necessary flexibility to handle them. She explained that a number of her students from out of state were behind in Virginia history, so the pacing guide was adjusted to accommodate the gap.

District core-content teachers, department chairs, and grade-level leaders are responsible for helping teachers learn about and fully align the curriculum. District instructional support specialists spend 70 percent of their time in classrooms helping teachers appropriately implement the curriculum. Their approach is one of support rather than a "gotcha." Support for curriculum implementation occurs on an ongoing basis during the entire school year.

In an early interview in 2003, Dr. Simpson mentioned that a certain number of NPS teachers were uncomfortable with the shift in focus to more standardized curriculum and instructional practices, and many of those teachers ultimately left the district. A central office leader in a 2006 interview agreed, noting that it took about three years to get a "critical mass" of teachers on board with the district's new curriculum and standards. However, she said Dr. Simpson was the right person to lead the charge because:

> You could feel a change in the seriousness of purpose with the work, and you could feel a change in strength of leadership. You could really feel it as clearly as you could feel the wind blow. This was a new day, a consistent message that was committed and passionate, highlighting what was possible.

In focus groups during the site visits, principals and teachers primarily spoke favorably about the curriculum, stating that it was clear, and that the pacing guides were particularly useful. Principals and teachers felt that the district communicated the curriculum throughout the system and gave appropriate support for implementation.

Instructional Programs, Practices, and Arrangements

To meet the district's goal of building a "world-class" system, NPS needed to find instructional programs that focused on higher-order thinking skills. Believing that literacy should be the foundation, the district adopted Patrick Finn's Powerful Literacy and Powerful Math models for its instructional program. Powerful Literacy, a fourteen-character skill set, is built on the premise of moving beyond functional literacy (e.g., memorization of facts) to activities that develop higher-order thinking skills. Thus, teachers design and teach lessons in which students analyze and synthesize data, ask questions, solve problems, and make connections to other knowledge. The same concept applies to Powerful Math. Instead of focusing on simply "finding the correct answer" to a given math problem, students often work in groups to make presentations about their solutions, or write individually to explain how they arrived at a given answer.

The district's central office introduced the new instructional design gradually through frequent training sessions addressing several Powerful Literacy strands at a time, tying the strands to the district curriculum guides, textbooks, and other materials. "The key," said one central office administrator, "is getting teachers comfortable with it. If the teachers are comfortable, the students will be comfortable."

As with all of its initiatives and processes, the district was vigilant about communicating the same clear message to all stakeholders. Whenever any outside consultant came to work with the district on the new program, key central office staff members were always present to ensure that the same message was delivered consistently.

Implementation of the instructional program was strengthened by the district's "instructional non-negotiables." Put into place shortly after the Powerful Literacy and Powerful Math strands were adopted, the instructional non-negotiables outlined how the district as a whole should function as a learning community:

(1) Teachers and administrators shall focus on high-quality instruction; (2) schools shall be communities of learners who engage in collegial planning, sharing, collaboration, and weekly professional development; (3) teachers and principals shall engage in data-driven decision making to ensure a laser-like focus on teaching and learning; and (4) teachers shall maximize the use and integration of technology.

While the collaborative concepts in the instructional non-negotiables might help align and support the new instructional program, it was difficult to get teachers comfortable with such a demanding program and ensure that it was being implemented correctly and consistently across the district. About a year after NPS rewrote its curriculum and adopted an instructional focus based on higher standards for all students, the district decided to merge the Curriculum and Instruction and Professional Development departments into the Leadership and Capacity Development (LCD) department, whose purpose was to build the capacity of staff to deliver the instructional program. To support that effort, LCD instructional specialists were required to spend 70 percent of their time each week on campuses working directly in classrooms with teachers, providing guidance on planning and instruction, giving feedback, and even co-teaching. Very serious about that commitment to schools, the leader of the LCD department said that she frequently checked the logs of the instructional specialists to ensure that they had spent the full 70 percent of their time in this capacity.

To target school support, LCD specialists often review data and work with principals to identify areas of focus and develop goals for the year. School visits are typically arranged with the principal and sometimes involve observing every classroom on a specific grade level, working with teachers during grade-level planning, or working with principals to analyze school data. One school department chair said of her LCD specialist, "I can talk to her about things that are bothering me, and we observe teachers together to determine what my department should be focusing on." The director of the LCD department voiced her belief in the importance of "empowering people that are the closest to the work." An important element of building empowerment is allowing the work to "flow both ways" by creating an environment where there is no fear in asking for help. Teachers in the district agree that support from LCD is useful and that "it's nice knowing we have someone to call for help."

NPS's instructional program, instructional non-negotiables, and curriculum are all district-driven and -supported. After recentralizing its instructional programs, the district mandated 2.5 hours of daily language arts instruction and one hour of mathematics instruction at all elementary schools, as well as a yearlong reading class in addition to English for all sixth-grade students. The district also mandates that major components are followed within a block, so that in an elementary classroom you will first see shared reading, then a reading basal lesson, then small-group instruction. The tight structure and uniformity has worked well for creating consistency across schools. The consistent schedules are well suited for addressing large-scale remediation when the need arises; for example, when the district implemented daily science warm-ups after data revealed what appeared to be a memory retention issue in science.

District and school personnel agree that there is a balance between structure and flexibility, since schools are encouraged to offer unique instructional arrangements to meet the needs of all students in learning the objectives. In fact, supported by a special grant, late buses are available for students who need additional instructional time after school. Additionally, students travel from classroom to classroom through flexible grouping that looks very similar to Aldine's grouping practices.

Staff Selection, Leadership, and Capacity Building

During the two site visits to NPS, the site team found that the district does not appear to have problems finding candidates to fill leadership or teacher positions. According to Dr. Simpson, a large number of the district's school leaders were eligible for retirement when he first came on as superintendent. Since that time, the district has invested heavily in building strong leadership development programs, and Dr. Simpson reported in 2005 that the district has been able to draw from its own ranks to fill principal and assistant principal positions. District leaders asserted in interviews that internal leaders were more desirable than external candidates, as they help them maintain the district's culture and provide program consistency. An academy coordinated with a local business consortium has helped the district develop principals before they are active in leadership positions. In 2005, central office leadership asserted that around 95 percent of Norfolk's principals came from within the system. New principals attend the Center for Creative Leadership's training in Greensboro, North Carolina, three days before school opening and then monthly during their first year. Additionally, new principals are supported by mentors, through cluster meetings, and with a district-developed "Principals' Guide."

The district has been focusing on recruiting minority teachers to reflect its student demographics. A citywide job fair allows the district to recruit and prescreen hundreds of potential certified teacher applicants. To add another level of screening to their hiring process, the district uses the Gallup Teacher Perceiver, a structured interview that consists of a set of open-ended items based on Gallup's research on what are believed to be the characteristics that make the best teachers. The interviews may be conducted face to face or by telephone. The district also increases its candidate pool by maintaining contact with teachers on career breaks and promoting job-sharing opportunities.

NPS's comprehensive induction program, along with other district supports for teachers, has helped the district maintain a low rate of teacher turnover. A three-tiered induction program supports teachers during their first three years and includes numerous pre-school-year and monthly activities for teachers and a strong mentoring program. Numerous testimonials from new teachers described the high level of support and confidence they had gained from the induction program.

The merging of the professional development and curriculum and instructional departments into the LCD department helped improve alignment of and access to professional development for teachers. In addition to the time LCD staff spent with teachers, professional development provided teachers numerous opportunities to learn how to interpret, analyze, and react to data. Teachers found the training to be helpful and reported feeling more at ease using data as they gained more training and experience with the district's data systems.

To help build collegiality and add to alignment across the district, common planning time is mandated at all school levels so that teachers can meet frequently. The local chapter of the American Federation of Teachers and the superintendent worked together in 2004 to make common planning time available at the elementary level, and it is also available, but more sporadically, on the secondary level. At least twice weekly, one day is set aside for professional development and another for collegial planning. At least twice weekly, meeting time is set aside, with one session for professional development and the other for collegial planning.

The site team observed several teacher team meetings. In one, teachers were working in a group reviewing item analysis results for a mathematics exam. The department chairs leading the meeting were surprised that so many teachers had problems with one particular objective. They decided that they would review their lesson plans for that objective and work with one teacher who appeared to have done a much better job getting her students to master it. The teachers seemed very comfortable and open talking about data and instruction. Their attitude matched conversations the site team heard throughout the central office and from school administers and teachers. Those conversations illustrated a collective sense of accountability, including comments like, "We saw the data and realized that lesson really bombed, so we got together to figure out how we could do it better." This district exemplified the popular expression "using data as a flashlight instead of as a hammer."

Collaboration had not always been present in NPS. One district administrator said that over the past few years, teachers had become more excited about sharing and working together. She described the change as

> making teaching much more public and more of a science. The days are gone when you shut your door and things were fine as long as it was quiet. Now there is teaching and learning going on. What we want to see is an engaged class.

Focus groups with principals and teachers confirmed that all stakeholders felt well supported and connected to the district central office and to each other. New principals and teachers in particular felt that the district responded immediately and effectively to their requests and concerns and provided useful training. Teachers and principals also cited other colleagues and the opportunity for collaboration as being an important and useful form of support.

Monitoring, Analysis, and Use of Data

Interviewees at all organizational levels at NPS frequently refer to data; it seems to be a regular part of their daily lives. NPS uses numerous types of data to continuously measure student progress. Many teachers, principals, and administrators mentioned the "cultural shift" the district experienced in using data as an informative rather than punitive tool. One administrator explained,

> We set benchmarks to tackle our achievement gaps in math and reading, and those are the drivers for a lot of the work we are doing. We don't wait once a year for the state assessments; we assess throughout the year to figure out where children are. We believe in assessment for immediate intervention.

Although the district had focused somewhat on data before Dr. Simpson's arrival, they have strengthened their accountability practices with the help of Douglas Reeves's Center for Performance Assessment. Reeves helped the district refine its accountability system through training and tools that enabled it to use data as a part of its daily culture. Data not only served as a mechanism for driving decisions, but also created common dialogue and set processes for the district, schools, and classrooms. One principal described how Reeves helped him organize his school in vertical data teams. While the public review of data at first was unnerving to his teachers, in the end he said they voiced appreciation for the process. "Doug always said the data will provide the buy-in!" said the principal. Several central office administrators agreed that Reeves was a key element in building their accountability system because he "presents a very logical, easy-to-understand, research-based message."

The district manages its data through two Web-based data systems; one is a data warehouse that allows queries to be run on longitudinal data, and the other, called Assessor, houses the district's quarterly benchmark assessments. Giving teachers almost immediate results, the quarterly assessments are in the same format as the state assessments and are scanned into Assessor immediately. District leaders feel the quarterly assessments have been crucial for improving instruction in the district. As one administrator described it,

> There's immediate feedback for the teachers and for the students. As for the item analysis, it has been very powerful because there's lots of discussion going on in classrooms about the thinking behind it. Students can reason through the answers they chose, whether or not they were correct or incorrect answers. This is a huge change.

Both data systems give district leaders, principals, and teachers immediate reports displayed graphically. The system's goal is to provide 24/7 access to teachers, with results available within one to three days of testing.

The quarterly benchmark assessments are given at all grade levels. In addition to those assessments, most of the schools have developed common assessments, given at least every month. The teachers explained that the monthly assessments are very useful for catching instructional problems early so that remediation remains minimal. On a regular basis, teachers meet in "data teams" to review the data, make common plans, and adjust instruction. Illustrating the supportiveness of those meetings, one elementary teacher described how her principal meets with data teams on vertical and horizontal levels, often asking questions like, "Your class scored a 90 on this objective, but Miss X's scored a 70. What can you tell her about your lessons on that?"

Dr. Simpson believed that it was important to hold everyone involved with the district accountable, from teachers to board members. One important tool for communicating data across the system is the district's three-tiered Comprehensive Accountability System (CAS). The CAS is used to hold all levels accountable, from the district to feeder patterns to schools. Data is compared longitudinally over five years to monitor improvement. Tier I indicators include state- and district-level data, Tier II focuses on school-level data—primarily the quarterly assessments—and Tier III provides a narrative of qualitative data that describes the context of each school's accountability results. The entire accountability cycle begins with a review of past performance, is then used to build school and department accountability plans, and ends with departmental, school, and division performance reports to summarize the year's progress.

School performance is also monitored by executive directors and content specialists who review the same campus reports, looking at targets and benchmarks for gap closures. After the review, these administrators meet with principals on a regular basis to look at their data and discuss adjustments. The executive directors spend a great deal of time having ongoing discussions about assessment data. Paying particular attention to literacy, the executive directors make sure that any students with a low third-grade reading score have the appropriate intervention and resources. One executive director explained that multiple meetings occur on a monthly basis to review data at central office and with school leaders. When asked what a school visit for data review might look like he described it as:

> You will see data notebooks and access to data on computers. Some schools have data walls to show off their successes as well as their weakness. Everyone bought in to the importance of the data. Some schools moved from central data notebooks to providing them for teachers and sometimes students, who keep journals and graphs of their own progress.

Illustrating the sensitivity shown toward creating an environment that is open and trusting about data, the same executive director mentioned, "It's a tough navigation as we talk about quarterly assessments. It's a difficult balancing act to make sure schools don't think we are evaluating them; it's an instructional tool."

The first year of CAS implementation in 1999 was eye-opening for the district, particularly for principals. At that time, over half the district's school leaders received warnings that their schools needed to improve or that their jobs would be in jeopardy.[7] Principals were required to develop strategic plans to improve their school performance, and the board backed Dr. Simpson's accountability efforts amid the buzz this initial reform created. At the end of 1999, the scores showed significant gains, and Simpson slowly gained more support and acceptance as the right leader for the district.

Interviewees throughout the system made positive comments about the district being very data-driven. Illustrating his attitude change over time, one principal stated,

I have been debating the use of data for the last six years. I have changed in the last nine months with the reading assessments because we are better measuring comprehension than we ever have been. Now we are really working on comprehension, and teachers are seeing that it is making a difference with all the programs and data we are using.

We heard frequent references to data use in our visits to NPS schools. One elementary school principal mentioned that data is used to identify teachers who have particular instructional strengths to share with their other teachers. To obtain more frequent feedback on student performance, teachers at that school developed three-week common assessments by looking at their quarterly data results. The principal described the process and her role in one interview as follows:

The teachers create common assessments from looking at their quarterly data. They sit down during their planning time and decide what tasks they're going to give every student on their grade level. They look carefully at the content and the design and they administer those assessments. After the teachers do those assessments, they turn in the results to me because I want to be made aware of which children did not reach the 85 percent mastery level. That way, we can intervene. Even on those three-week assessments, we want the names of those students.

The same school also uses portfolios to keep a record of student work products such as writing pieces. Teachers mentioned that the practice was implemented districtwide, and "worth the work" to monitor progress and provide information to other teachers whenever students moved to another school or classroom.

When we asked teachers at a different elementary school how they used data, one group of teachers was particularly enthusiastic about the utility of their quarterly assessments. Once teachers receive the results (which happens in thirty minutes, because a Scantron machine is used) the teachers work together in grade-level groups and review each test by item analysis. In these meetings, which are a standard practice districtwide, teachers ask questions like, "Half the class missed number 3, why? Let's look at choice A and why they picked it." These drill-down sessions help teachers formulate next steps for re-teaching what was missed and helps them analyze how to improve future lessons.

When we visited Norview high school in 2004, the teachers described the school as being very "data-driven." One team of teachers at Norview mentioned that they review data frequently and talk about how to reduce achievement gaps between student groups. Data has also influenced the professional development program at Norview. Through data review, teachers identified "questioning strategies" as an area that needed improvement. After attending training on the topic, one teacher said that it had improved her teaching to the extent that she had been requested to become a trainer on questioning strategies herself.

Teachers also reiterated that the data was not only useful, but it was administered in a trusting climate of support rather than punishment. They appreciated being able to adjust classroom instruction for their students on an ongoing basis, and many felt that they were well supported when they needed anything. One teacher in a focus group interview stated, "I used to think we just put Band-Aids on things, but I don't think that way anymore." In an interview with new teachers, one mentioned that she received data that was "presented in a way that is easy to read." She said she would receive a packet with all the data "broken down into manageable chunks," and she was allowed to pull whatever data she needed. In our site visits, we found many teachers voicing enthusiasm about using data to monitor student progress. Whenever teachers were asked their opinion about their district and school successes, they pointed to data-driven decision making and accountability. One said, "There *is* a magic bullet: data-driven decision making!"

Recognition, Intervention, and Adjustment

NPS's vigilance in constantly monitoring student performance helps the district provide immediate interventions to schools, teachers, and students. Struggling schools are identified through the Virginia system that lists schools as being either accredited, with several gradations of great to average, or not accredited—all tied to the state assessment test. Schools that are not accredited in NPS become "focus schools." Wanting to try something innovative in 2005, the district paired its focus schools with demographically similar "demonstration schools," which were high performing. The partner schools worked together with the help of Doug Reeves in a process during which they visited each other and did walk-throughs. Principals worked together through highly structured sessions, focusing on reviewing data and discussing performance concerns and solutions. Principals from both types of schools asserted that they learned a lot from each other through the process. In addition to the focus schools, schools that do not meet benchmark requirements receive immediate attention. The district provides financial and staff support, as well as help from Reeves to interpret their data and make instructional decisions.

In addition to the support teachers receive from curriculum guides, principals, and instructional specialists, the district has a professional review board of central office staff poised to assist teachers who need additional help. The board has assisted teachers with behavioral management, organization skills, and classroom delivery, and has helped reduce the number of teachers leaving the system. According to both teachers and principals, the support teachers receive from the LCD department is invaluable as well.

Interventions for struggling students are applied more as an ongoing process rather than as a type of program that occurs outside of the regular instructional day. Ongoing adjustment of instruction based on continuous student performance data is one of the main techniques used by teachers and principals to ensure students are learning their instructional goals for each quarter and subsequently for the year. When students show signs of trouble, one of the first interventions applied by teachers is to use flexible grouping based on data. If a student is having trouble with one particular skill in math, like estimation, he may move to another classroom to work with a teacher who is particularly good at teaching that skill for a short period of time. The concept of collective accountability for all students within a given school makes the flow of students in and out of different classrooms possible. A student with more significant problems might receive more targeted instruction during resource time in elementary school to avoid missing regular classroom instruction.

One creative intervention used in a middle school we visited was to reserve a block of time in the schedule for "double dose" instruction. The school determined which subject would be taught during the "double dose" hour by reviewing assessment data. If a majority of students were struggling with writing, then the double dose block would be used for writing instruction, and students who needed more writing instruction would be scheduled for that class. When a semester was over, the school reviews the data to determine which subject would be addressed for the following semester.

Several of the high schools mentioned that they reviewed the reading assessment results for each incoming student to identify students in need of additional reading intervention. Those who need it are enrolled in a remedial reading course. Additionally, the high school offers the typical interventions, such as before- and after-school tutoring and Saturday school, which helps students make up absences. One teacher mentioned that the Saturday school had high attendance; sometimes well above one hundred students on a given day.

A focus on early grades marks another of the district's efforts to intervene early. The district is focusing on preschool education and has piloted eighteen Title I Jump Start programs. Additionally, all K–2 students are assessed three times a year through an electronic assessment system that provides immediate feedback to teachers on how students are doing in reading comprehension, fluency, word recognition, and phonemic awareness. For older students, the district mandates an in-school remediation program for students who do not meet the state standards. Schools start the program at the beginning of the school year rather than wait until the end of the school year. Additionally, programs are available both before and after school.

More as a form of prevention than intervention, the district emphasizes early childhood education by offering 106 pre-K classes and two early childhood centers. During our 2005 visit, the district was also planning a summer preschool program for three-year-olds based on student needs. Principals and teachers felt that the district does a good job focusing on prevention rather than extensive intervention. One teacher described the process as "putting in safety nets so that no one falls through the cracks."

INFLUENCING FACTORS

The relationships between the board, labor associations, and the superintendent are very positive, unified by a focus on student achievement. Regardless of their affiliation, most stakeholders were well informed about the district's focus and goals and referred to the mantras that formulate the district's work, such as "All means all" and the idea that the district was creating a "world-class system."

School Board

NPS is led by a seven-member board appointed by the city council for two-year terms for a maximum of twelve years. The board is charged with setting policy that will ensure proper implementation of educational programs in the district.[8] The board also approves staff hirings to assist with overseeing the instructional program in the district. According to interviews conducted in 2003, board members liked the fact that members were appointed, as they felt they were better able to attract people who were committed to education rather than those interested in politics.[9]

School board members interviewed in several site visits characterized their relationship with the superintendent and district leadership as "harmonious." Citing Dr. Simpson's practice of keeping board members well informed, one long-standing member admitted that in previous years, the board had engaged in more micromanagement. However, after attending a leadership institute for urban districts, they learned that their job was to set policy and to let the superintendent lead. The member attested that the board had no qualms about stepping back and letting Dr. Simpson and his successors take the reins, as each leader had proven to be trustworthy and skilled.

School board leaders Dr. Teresa Whibley and Dr. Anna Dodson, no matter when they were interviewed, seemed to always have their fingers on the pulse of the district. When asked about the district's successes, they cited the importance of keeping consistent goals and focus over time, actualizing their mantra for students—"All means all"—and focusing on relationships with parents and the community. Although it was not directly referenced in interviews, an article found on the Center for Public Education Web site described an initiative spearheaded by Dr. Dodson in 2002 to increase parental involvement within the district.[10] The program involved inviting ten parents from different schools to attend monthly board meetings, which included a dinner with board members prior to the meeting. Parents responded positively to the program, so much so for one parent that she showed interest in becoming a future board member herself. NPS's board has won several awards for performance as a model urban school board, including the National School Boards Association CUBE (Council of Urban Boards of Education) award for excellence in 2006.[11]

Union/Association

NPS's teachers are represented by the National Education Association (NEA), which is affiliated with the Virginia Education Association and the Norfolk Federation of Teachers (NFT). Although Virginia is a nonbargaining state, the teacher associations in NPS operate under a memorandum of understanding with the district. An association president who had served with her association for twenty-four years attested to the benefit of bringing the association and community together to exchange ideas about reaching the district's goals.

The district's relationships with the teacher associations have also benefited from frequent communication. When asked to describe the association's role with the district, another association leader responded that it was to support teachers to help them "turn around performance." She felt it was important to help make things better rather than "just stirring the pot." Both associations worked with principals and teachers and even provided outreach to parents as part of their support role.

Although one interview during the first Prize visit alluded to past discord between the district and the association, we heard only positive comments about and from the union regarding the district and particularly its leadership. One union leader spoke quite favorably of Dr. Simpson, mentioning that "he hasn't forgotten what it meant to be a teacher." She stated that she appreciated that he often called to inform them about "what was coming down the pipe," and that he treated the board respectfully and visited them frequently.

The same leader also mentioned that the district and union worked well together for the same goal—to improve student achievement. She felt it was important to ensure that students had the best teachers in their classrooms, and that principals were often encouraged to "do their job" to ensure that students did not have subpar teachers. This was important she asserted because, "we are not there to just protect teachers, but also to help them improve and in some circumstances we will counsel them out of the profession."

Community

Community engagement has long been an important activity for NPS, to the extent that it appears as a performance indicator on the district and schools' accountability systems. NPS's level of support from the community has grown enough that it hired a Community Engagement Coordinator in 2005. Responding to Dr. Simpson's message years ago that the district was an important community asset, the district has benefited from community partnerships that are too numerous to detail. The most noteworthy partnerships include the Greater Norfolk Corporation, which provides funds to support a large leadership training program; the Norfolk Foundation, which funded an early childhood education initiative; and the military, which has always been a strong, silent supporter of the district. In turn, the district works closely with the Norfolk Workforce Board to ensure workforce skills are being addressed in the district curriculum.

The Greater Norfolk Corporation and the Panasonic Foundation were both mentioned frequently in interviews with various stakeholders. The Greater Norfolk Corporation consists of a group of citizens interested in helping the district replenish its large supply of retiring principals. The Corporation works with the district on leadership training and engages in discussions on how to become a "purpose-driven organization." The Panasonic Foundation was a key partner in helping the district build accountability systems. This work resulted in the Panasonic-sponsored Leadership Learning team that convened for several hours a month to engage in professional development activities to help build cohesiveness in the district's central office administrative team.

I witnessed firsthand the level of community commitment to the district when I attended a black-tie dinner honoring NPS's Broad Prize win. The crowded room was full of community and district members who were recognized with numerous accolades from civic leaders, including members of the City Council, Governor Mark Warner, Mayor Paul Fraim, and Senator George Allen. The city continued the celebration by holding a special recognition dinner for teachers and providing free admission at the local zoo for students.

Parents

Parent involvement has always been a high priority in NPS. Every year, the district administers a survey to students, teachers, and parents about their perceptions of the school and district. Survey results help the district assess how well it is serving and supporting various stakeholders who are crucial to student success. One strong indicator of NPS's success with parent engagement is the fact that many parents are bringing their children back from neighboring districts (sometimes much wealthier districts) to attend school in NPS. One parent we interviewed stated that she moved her daughter to NPS because she heard that teachers in NPS went the extra mile to help students. She said that her daughter was receiving much more individualized attention in her NPS school, and that the teacher also addressed her daughter's issues with skill and sensitivity. Several other parents mentioned that their children's teachers often stayed after school to tutor their children when they were struggling, and some even met students at school on Saturdays. Another stated, "They take the time out and they treat them [students] as if they were their own. Teachers all go beyond the call of duty."

Many parents described their schools as having "an open door policy," a different practice than they experienced in other districts. Parents also appreciated that the district often asked their opinion about school matters, and attempted to find meaningful ways to involve parents beyond chaperoning and cupcakes. Programs and activities referenced frequently by the parents were the invitations to attend school board meetings and the Parent University created by Dr. Simpson. Several praised the Parent University for providing valuable curriculum to parents that helped them understand the different developmental and learning stages to expect from their children.

Principals at all levels worked hard on involving parents in their schools. Several elementary school principals mentioned that they were required to log a certain number of parent-involvement hours, and that their logs were monitored closely to see if they met their goals. Several schools had parent liaisons who focused their entire day on working and communicating with parents. At the middle school level, parent involvement was slightly more challenging, but principals and teachers still were able to keep in close contact with many parents. One principal interviewed at a high school in 2005 explained his viewpoint about parents as:

> The parent I like is an angry parent. If you address it, you have a parent that will support you forever. It's all in the neighborhood. I tell my secretary, "I don't care who it is, you bring them to me." Everyone wants to go to the top; I sit and listen. I say "How would you solve it? What would you do?"

The same principal mentioned that the school communicated with parents through newsletters and had coaches and guidance counselors make home visits, and he himself went to the housing projects to visit parents. He felt he would always have the support of the board, and he also networked through local churches. In return, the principal said that his students' parents were very loyal to him, helping encourage other parents and looking out for him. One parent would frequently say to him, "I'm not going to let them dog your school."

In 2004 when we interviewed Dr. Simpson, he seemed particularly proud of the Parent University, which sounded like a unique program. He mentioned that its last meeting was widely attended and standing room only. That meeting focused on the middle school and featured an author of children's books whose target audience was middle school children. Simpson also mentioned working closely with the Norfolk Development and Housing Authority (NRHA), a highly recognized organization formed in 2003 to build new housing and rebuild and manage existing housing to create homes and neighborhoods that "everyone will want to live in."[12] Through the NRHA, the district is keeping track of one neighborhood that is "up and coming" to ensure that the many NPS students in that neighborhood are doing well. Dr. Simpson believed all NPS's outreach activities were effective, as its latest school data showed an increase in parent involvement over the previous year.

Governance, Organization, and Decision Making

NPS is a midsized district that served 57 schools in 2005, the year it won The Broad Prize, including five high schools. The board is appointed rather than elected. Dr. Simpson said that the board and district leaders have a working relationship with the city, and that they meet regularly with the mayor, vice mayor, and financial executives within the mayor's office. The NPS school board is a sole agenda item at Council meetings several times a year, and works to partner with city council members as much as possible.

When we visited NPS in 2005, Dr. Simpson had retired and his second-in-command, Dr. Denise Schnitzer, was serving as interim superintendent. Despite feeling it had lost a great and dynamic leader, the district seemed to move along with its plans without missing a beat, and continued to drill down deeper to make improvements and narrow achievement gaps. The district's leaders believed that the leadership change did not disrupt the work in NPS because Dr. Simpson had worked hard on "distributing leadership" throughout the district. When asked a question about the district, Dr. Simpson never used the word "I," only "we." Many central office leaders and principals appeared to have strong connections and to be capable of executing the district and school plans. This was prompted by Dr. Simpson's practice of involving multiple key stakeholders in every district practice and providing numerous leadership opportunities at all levels of the district.

When asked about the distribution of authority and decision making, many stakeholders asserted that they had a high level of decision-making authority to meet the needs of the district or their school communities. Central office leaders, principals, teachers, and other internal and external stakeholders often used the same vocabulary and comments when describing their work, suggesting a great deal of coherence through the district's practices. Board members and union leaders mentioned that the district had become more centralized in certain areas, such as instruction, but that ultimately principals were given primary authority to serve their students, while the district served to support the schools with a high level of customer service.

School principals reported feeling very connected to the district and well supported. They met monthly in "cluster meetings" (by feeder pattern), with each cluster being led by a central office executive director. When we asked them how authority was distributed between the district and schools, most school leaders felt very involved in decision-making processes. One asserted that the district was not "top down," but rather a two-way street: some reforms started from the schools and traveled up, and others from the district and moved down to schools. Another principal felt the district had a "chain of command" that aided in effective communication flow. At the schools, the chain moved from faculty input to site administration, then to the district. Another chain moved from Dr. Simpson, through the ranks of central office, and then to school administration, department chairs, and teachers.

In addition to cluster meetings, each school had a school-level teacher of the year serve as a member of the "professional senate." Senate members had the opportunity to meet monthly with the superintendent to discuss teacher-level concerns. Several other specialized groups also met, such as an achievement gap committee. The meetings allowed various stakeholders to provide feedback to the district, and to serve in leadership roles.

Principals in a focus group mentioned that the district had recently hired evaluators to assess the level of service provided by central office to schools. They reported that the results were favorable, and that many of them believed they were much better supported than in previous years. Several principals stated that they could make a call to central office at any time of the day, and they would receive an answer often "within ten minutes." Describing a time predating Simpson's superintendence, one principal stated:

> The lines of communication are open. In our district, it is "What can we do for you?" We had no electricity yesterday so I got [something like] ten calls to see if I needed anything. Years ago, you were afraid to call, but now I would say it is just wonderful and everything is a pleasure. It was a brick wall years ago, but now we know that if we put things on the table, we can move from there to get things done.

The support provided by the Leadership and Capacity Development department also provided a strong connection to and support for schools. Teachers and principals felt the amount of time spent in schools by LCD leaders was extremely helpful and valuable to them.

When we asked Dr. Simpson how the district gained input from the district and schools, he mentioned the senate, cluster meetings, annual climate survey, and ongoing formal and informal meetings between different stakeholders. He believed a high level of frequent, open, honest communication was important for "immediate impact." The purpose of the numerous communication opportunities was "to work on curriculum, assessment, and best practices, discuss what's working, and to tell us how the pace is." To monitor and support instruction, central office leaders "were in schools day in and out, coaching and working shoulder to shoulder with people." This frequent contact and input was a high priority to everyone in the district.

Resource Allocation

Stakeholder input was also a key element in the district's fiscal practices. When we visited the district in 2004, Dr. Simpson told us that NPS was in its third year of planning with an ongoing budget committee. The time frame was generous to allow time to evaluate various instructional programs and identify where resources should be continued and where they should be pulled. When the district found no positive effects from year-round schools, it cut the program. The district also cut a program called Light Span (a Web-based reading program) even though staff members liked it, because the data did not support its value. When we asked Dr. Simpson how much fiscal authority schools had, he stated that they had very little, because their literacy focus reduced discretionary spending. According to Simpson, the schools spent 80 percent of their funding on instructional staff, leaving few leftover discretionary funds for any individual programs they might want to support.

Regarding budgeting priorities, central office leaders asserted that they invested most of their funds on hiring strong teachers and on professional development to provide a high-quality, challenging instructional program. While district leaders felt their approach to resource allocation was well structured, they were continuously mindful of finding ways to cut down on "frivolous expenses" and felt it was important to be accountable to the city's taxpayers for resource use. In 2005, Denise Schnitzer told us that the district was fiscally dependent on the city and state for the majority of their funding, and that thus far, "did well" with what it had.

We did not hear about any major budget concerns at the schools; most principals and teachers asserted that they received what they needed, and most seemed to have a well-structured budget process that always began with examining their student achievement data to identify resource needs. One elementary principal described her philosophy toward budget development as:

> Using it [funding] effectively and tying it to your objectives and what you want to accomplish, not just spending it on the latest thing that comes down the pipe. I need to know it's going to work, that my people are asking for it and have seen it working. You can work with less funding if you work effectively.

When schools did desire to fund additional programs not supported by their budget, they often found creative ways to find partners or raise funds. Several high schools worked hard to raise money to fund students' AP exam fees. Few teachers or principals mentioned any marked concerns or issues with the availability of funding.

Climate/Culture

In 2004, John Simpson described the district's climate as "pretty good." He said that it took a lot of work to get it there, and a lot to maintain it. Climate became an important first area of focus for Simpson when he found out through long discussions with principals when he first came on board that they wanted to "do the work" but did not feel as if they were operating in a safe, trusting environment. One of the first opportunities to establish trust was through the new district walkthrough protocols. To ensure everyone was comfortable with the new open-door data collection practice, Dr. Simpson agreed, "almost signing in blood," that the results would not be shared with principals' supervisors. Taking a year to get everyone comfortable with the walkthroughs, the district saw teachers and principals gradually opening up and desiring to share and discuss their walkthrough results, even with their supervisors. Dr. Simpson believed that "success breeds success." Finding the initial climate of the district to be "cold," Dr. Simpson invested a lot of time in recognizing schools for their accomplishments. He also asked many of the stakeholder groups he met with what "hot buttons" he should avoid at first in his initial first months of leading the district.

Dr. Simpson also created a cultural focus of high standards and accountability through holding several book-talks with district leaders. Several central office administrators and principals mentioned the lessons they learned from reading and discussing books collaboratively such as *Who Moved My Cheese?* and *Good to Great*.[13]

When asked to describe NPS's climate, district leaders pointed to improved relationships. Through their annual stakeholder survey, parent responses illustrated increased trust in and satisfaction with the district, and teacher responses indicated that they felt well supported by the district, each other, and their principals. One district leader felt the positive principal comments resulted from the district's focus on training principals with better leadership skills. Several principals and teachers described the district climate as being "exciting" due to the steady increase in student achievement. One teacher mentioned that parents were choosing to move from the once more-desirable Virginia Beach area to NPS because of the district's increasingly positive reputation. In interviews, parents described the district and teachers as "caring" and cited several examples where they felt teachers had made a measurable impact on their child's achievement or overall confidence and attitude toward school.

From my outsider's perspective, I found the district to be warm and inviting; staff members at all organizational levels were overwhelmingly positive and friendly. The attitude was exemplified by numerous discussions that highlighted the importance they placed on supporting and providing a high level of "customer service" to each other, and particularly to teachers. There seemed to be a great deal of trust and openness about the district and excitement about their success in helping students meet raised expectations and demonstrate increases in achievement.

REFORM AND STUDENT ACHIEVEMENT—BRINGING IT TO SCALE

In 1998, Dr. Simpson took the helm of a district he felt to be in need of radical improvement. According to a case study written about NPS reform, educators in the district and the community also believed the district needed a drastic change as well.[14] Dr. Simpson began his work in NPS by investing time in listening to various stakeholders and recognizing any achievement possible to encourage educators in the district. With the help of various district and school personnel, as well as several organizations and consultants like the Panasonic Foundation and Douglas Reeves, the district worked together to build a roadmap to raised achievement for all students. Although the district had engaged in similar reform work using concepts from the Total Quality Management philosophy, Dr. Simpson refined the process to ensure that each identified goal and strategy had an assigned name and a deadline to add more accountability and ensure execution. The next steps in the reform work entailed communicating a clear message with common vocabulary to all stakeholders; creating mechanisms for systemwide communication and input; creating leaders at all levels of the district; ramping up the educational program; creating an open and trusting culture; and—overarching the whole—providing a strong data management and accountability system. The ensuing system was so seamless and well coordinated, you could hear the same mantras and citations from parents, teachers, board members, principals, and central office leaders: "All means all," the need to look at the "brutal facts," the importance of narrowing achievement gaps, the creation of a "world-class system," and the importance of a customer-service attitude.

When asked what districtwide reform had the greatest effect on student achievement, district leaders referred to the presence of a lot of data and their monitoring processes. One leader felt particularly strongly about the walkthroughs, which he believed helped talented teachers share their skills with other teachers. During the 2005 interviews, district leaders had been implementing walkthroughs for over three years and had seen a shift from "competition" to a demand for more walkthroughs. School leaders pointed to "data-driven decision making." One elementary teacher said that quarterly assessments helped teachers intervene as soon as students began to struggle, as those assessments provided nearly real-time data. A high school principal mentioned that "holding students and parents accountable" sparked collaborative dialogue about "how can we do this [improve achievement] together?" Also referring to data, middle school teachers stated that their formative assessments helped them better meet the needs of individual students.

While we heard about significant improvement in student achievement and other success stories, the district still has challenge areas. District leaders cited graduation, the dropout rate, and high school as their biggest challenges during the 2005 interviews.

To boost high school achievement, district leaders mentioned focusing on "freshmen success"—ensuring freshmen had organizational skills and tools to help them keep up with the faster pace of high school. Other leaders pointed out that high school improvement was a K–12 effort, and that while they were proud that all their high schools were fully accredited, there were still pockets within those schools of "kids that may not be getting it." Agreeing, one high school principal voiced the same concern—helping students and parents obtain the right support so that students could graduate within four years. A middle school principal said her school's challenge was maintaining its high level of success and reaching the final small group of students who were still struggling. Teachers in that middle school mentioned that the increased accountability in the district had posed a challenge several years ago, but that now the principal believes "that challenge kicked us into shape and was a gift." In the elementary school, staff noted issues they were facing with transient children and voiced concerns that they were going to have to meet that challenge with less money. They were particularly concerned about their ability to meet the needs of a growing population of English language learners.

Current Performance and Practices

Since NPS won The Broad Prize in 2005, it will not be eligible to participate again until 2009. The last data available through The Broad Prize analysis and report cards shows increased performance in most grade levels in reading in 2007. However, math performance decreased considerably both for the district and state. Figure 6.12 illustrates that African American and low-income students outperformed the state in all but the middle school level. The percentage of students at or above proficiency in high school reading was in the 90s for African American, white, and low-income student groups.

Figure 6.13 compares the district and state math proficiency rates for 2007 at all three grade levels. The chart illustrates stronger performance from the district than the state in elementary mathematics for African American, white, and low-income students. The district also performs similarly, although slightly lower in proficiency rates, at the high school

FIGURE 6.12
District and state 2007 reading proficiencies: All levels

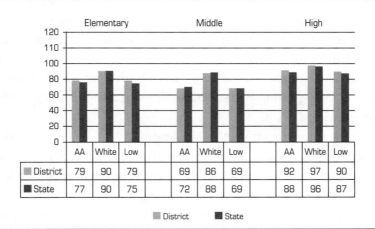

	Elementary			Middle			High		
	AA	White	Low	AA	White	Low	AA	White	Low
District	79	90	79	69	86	69	92	97	90
State	77	90	75	72	88	69	88	96	87

FIGURE 6.13

District and state 2007 math proficiencies: All levels

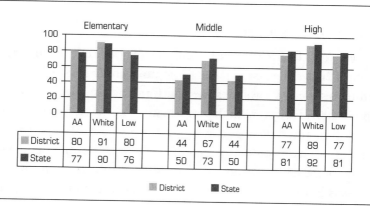

	Elementary			Middle			High		
	AA	White	Low	AA	White	Low	AA	White	Low
District	80	91	80	44	67	44	77	89	77
State	77	90	76	50	73	50	81	92	81

District ▪ State

level. What is interesting is that 2007 shows a significant drop in middle school math proficiency rates for both the district and state in comparison with the other grade levels, which represents an approximately thirty-point decrease in the number of students at or above proficiency from 2005 in each student group by the district and about a fifteen- to twenty-point decrease in performance from 2005 for the state.

Interviews with two key central office administrators in 2006 found the district continuing to forge ahead with the same accountability and instructional plan since it won the Prize. A new superintendent, Dr. Stephen Jones, came into the district just a few months prior to the Prize announcement in July of 2005. One of his first remarks upon receiving the big Prize check from Mr. Broad was, "I must be the luckiest superintendent in history," joking that he had served as NPS's leader for only three months before receiving a prize.

Another change mentioned by the interviewees was the experience of hosting numerous visitors from other districts who wanted to learn about their practices. When asked about their focus for the near future in 2006, they mentioned working on better defining and serving students in the gifted program, focusing on consistency and rigor in high school, and creating equal access to Advanced Placement programs.

In reviewing the Superintendent's Proposed Educational Plan and budget for fiscal year 2009–2010, I could not find much information about specific programmatic and policy changes being made in the district.[15] The plan does contain a letter from Dr. Jones explaining the impact of the ongoing recession experienced by the country and thus the state, with a primary focus on dealing with a $5.2 million cut from funding by the city. The key strategies cited by Dr. Jones in addressing those cuts were to maintain class size and the educational programs, preserve special programs, maintain recruitment and retention initiatives, and provide support to teachers. To address the cuts, the letter stated that the district was proposing cutting 230 positions, many through natural attrition due to declining enrollment. Although Dr. Jones anticipated receiving funds from the President's stimulus package to schools, he was unsure at the time of writing how those funds would be distributed to the district and used.

CONCLUSION

NPS's reform efforts almost naturally fall into an organized story format, as they were easily captured across the district's system of consistent messaging and were played out with extreme focus and intentionality. NPS represents a strong well-integrated system that has affected student achievement for all student groups. Two important practices affecting achievement were moving beyond the minimal state standards and making school support a priority from the central office. Curriculum is well aligned and communicated throughout the system through very detailed pacing guides for teachers and the "instructional non-negotiables." A focus on pushing math skills, particularly algebra, down to earlier grades has also been instrumental in raising achievement.

This system has successfully selected appropriate areas of focus and interventions by frequently studying and analyzing data. Students are assessed frequently through quarterly benchmark assessments, and principals and teachers clearly use data on a daily basis to plan, monitor, and adjust instruction.

John Simpson believed the changes made within the district resulted in real shifts in culture and attitude about students and learning. He felt that the work "energized people" and changed their beliefs that things could change for the better. Denise Schnitzer, his interim successor, felt that Dr. Simpson's commitment to a "no excuses" mentality was a huge contributing factor to the district's success. She stated, "This belief was so deeply ingrained in him, it permeated the system."

7

Scaling Up Beyond Schools and Districts

Discussion and Recommendations

This study utilized years of interview data and other supporting research to describe the reform stories of five award-winning, nationally recognized urban districts. They provide compelling examples of powerful, organized systems that have increased student performance and narrowed ethnic and income achievement gaps. The districts intentionally built integrated systems that coordinated practices, resources, and supports between the district central office, school administration, and teachers. The end result was large-scale improvement in teaching and learning that provided a strong educational program to all students, regardless of their color or zip code.

With the data results from The Broad Prize process and the voices of stakeholders on every level, from the districts and their surrounding communities, these cases illustrate how these districts took reform to scale. Their stories cover multiple years, show sustainability backed by data, and describe the actions and principles that the districts believe really mattered as they worked on improving their students' achievement. The specific details of each case are useful to understand how the practices came about, but are not necessarily generalizeable. Although the five districts share similar demographic characteristics, they operate within very different organizational and community contexts. However, the management principles

255

that affect the instructional core and alignment of the system levels share similarities that are applicable in diverse settings.

Though there are many common practices across these districts, each also took a slightly different route on their reform journey. This chapter uses the NCEA Best Practice Framework themes along with other stakeholder engagement and organizational practices to identify similar methods the districts used to improve their student achievement and then draws out the key lessons we can take from those methods.

SYSTEM SIMILARITIES

There are many great examples of schools or even districts that are improving student achievement. However, many of those examples fail to provide an organizational framework to analyze and understand the practices that can be generalized, and the pieces that are crucial for the coherence necessary for long-term reform to scale. The similarities found across these five cases point to practices that can positively impact the instructional core and are appropriate to apply within various contexts. These practices are detailed below in a similar fashion to the cases using the themes in the NCEA Best Practice Framework and then describing similar aspects of the influencing factors. However, it is important to acknowledge that attention to all the theme areas is necessary for scaling up reform. Having the right staff in place is important, but may be less successful without a curriculum that clearly outlines a seamless preK–12 educational program with post–high school outcomes in mind. Providing teachers with excellent data is not helpful if there are no interventions in place to respond to instructional gaps uncovered by the data. The pieces must all be in place and coordinated holistically in order to build coherence and effectiveness.

Curriculum and Academic Goals

Curriculum is a term that has expanded over time to describe all of the teaching, learning, and assessment materials available for a given course of study. The five districts featured in this book began their improvement strategies with a focus on their curriculum. Although each district had a set of state standards to follow, each underwent an intense curriculum development process to better define those state standards, align the standards across grade levels, apply more rigor to what they felt were minimal state standards, move particular subjects down to lower grades (such as algebra), or increase focus in some areas (as Norfolk did with literacy).

In each case, the curriculum development process was facilitated through central office curriculum directors and instructional experts, who convened teams of school instructional leaders and teachers from all grade levels to engage in a collaborative curriculum overhaul. Following a structured approach, the teams used data and teacher input to identify instructional gaps and problems to create a more seamless and aligned preK–12 instructional sequence in each subject. The process was often approached by backward mapping from the system's end-point—what a graduate from the system should know and be able to do—to lower grades.

The curriculum in each district was broken down into smaller, more manageable units—often called benchmarks—that were articulated across each district's annual instructional calendars in the form of curriculum or pacing guides. The benchmark units typically lasted six weeks and had accompanying benchmark or quarterly assessments to make sure students mastered the content for each unit. Additional tools provided to teachers included model lessons and uniform instructional pieces such as warm-ups or homework assignments to ensure instructional continuity regardless of student mobility.

Although there were some exceptions, most teachers interviewed saw the curriculum guides and tools as sources of support rather than as constraints on their professional judgment. This was particularly true for new teachers, who found the clarity of the standards and their pacing to be extremely helpful. Other teachers asserted that the curriculum guides put the issue of pacing, or *what* to teach, on central office but left the decision of *how* to teach to teachers. The districts seemed dedicated to helping teachers adjust to the new curriculum and new expectations: in the instances when teachers thought that the pacing guides put unreasonable expectations or inappropriate constraints on classroom instruction, those teachers were provided flexibility and support by central office staff, who helped them adjust the pace to fit their needs.

Each district also had an annual curriculum revision process that included teachers, central office curriculum specialists, and district leaders. The inclusive process added a crucial element of vertical and horizontal alignment of district standards, sparking ongoing dialogue between district, school, and classroom staff about what students needed to know in every grade and subject. The districts believed that their curricula gained better clarity and refinement each year. While developing and maintaining a detailed and aligned curriculum might be considered a basic and straightforward process, many systems fail to create a seamless preK–12 curriculum containing no skips or unnecessary repetitions in content. Teacher comments from all five districts indicated that the districts had been successful in developing such seamless curricula; teachers believed that students were coming to their classrooms better prepared for their appropriate grade or subject. Additionally, teachers appreciated being involved in the curriculum-development process as an acknowledgement of their professional knowledge and as an opportunity for them to take on leadership roles.

Faithful implementation of the curriculum was crucial in all five districts and was handled through multiple communications, monitoring, and support processes. The districts communicated curriculum contents to school leaders and teachers through numerous trainings, curriculum guides, and vertical and horizontal team meetings, and by allowing teachers to observe in each other's classrooms. Additionally, in most cases, the curricula and accompanying tools were easily accessed online.

Benchmark or quarterly assessments and walkthroughs by instructional specialists or school leaders were the main mechanisms used by the districts to monitor curriculum implementation. When issues arose, teachers had many sources of support, such as instructional coaches, principals, or other teachers. Curriculum interventions were frequently described by teachers as a welcome provision of support rather than an opportunity for administrators to criticize.

In addition to pacing guides and formative assessments, instructional coaches or specialists, and principals, other teachers supplied immediate classroom-based support for curriculum implementation. Boston's Collaborative Coaching and Learning model is an example of a successful structured coaching model in which teachers work with each other.

Curriculum directors provided another strong source of support from each district's central office. Multiple site visits and interviews at the districts pointed to very strong, extremely knowledgeable curriculum directors who facilitated the curriculum-development process. In addition to their knowledge base, part of the strength of the curriculum directors lay in their ability to create and manage participative curriculum processes that mined district expertise and subsequently generated stakeholder support.

The district and school goals were also an important driver of the districts' curriculum development process. Often goals began with a simple mission or vision, like "Ensure academic achievement for all students" or "Build a world-class education system." From there, the necessary components of the vision/mission were defined and became the goals. The most important and common elements of the districts' goal planning processes were that goals be clear, measurable, and few in number. Additionally, the goal-planning processes had to balance alignment between district and school goals with affording some level of customization to meet the unique needs of schools. Districts accomplished this balance by providing a basic framework or focus areas for goals—such as the two specific goals in Garden Grove related to academic and ELL achievement—and then having schools work in committees to review data and add sub-goals that provided appropriate benchmarks on the way to those goals.

Staff Selection, Leadership, and Capacity Building

Leadership is a commonly cited driver of reform.[1] One reason districts struggle with creating stability and lasting reform systems is that superintendent tenure in most districts lasts four years or less, while many reform efforts take a minimum of five years.[2] The superintendents in the five districts served beyond the typical term, ranging from six years (Long Beach) to eleven years (Boston). Leadership stability was cited by all five districts as being crucial to their success. To ensure that success did not cease when one strong leader moved on, each of the superintendents cultivated other capable leaders in their systems. Dr. Chris Steinhauser in Long Beach and Dr. John Simpson in Norfolk referred several times to this process as "distributive leadership." Similarly, Dr. Laura Schwalm (Garden Grove) created a strong, very small central office staff of seven key leaders who could easily step into each other's roles at any time.

The leadership development programs in all five districts provided another source of stability. Targeting internal candidates, these programs produced new principals from within their systems, resulting in leaders who immediately brought district knowledge and experience to their new roles. The programs also provided uniform training and support, both of which are key to ensuring that all leaders have the same skills and information. This proactive practice of building leaders from within the system afforded these districts the flexibility of choosing who would lead their schools, as they were able to replace weaker principals with those better suited for the job. This was particularly important in Boston, where the district moved over 70 percent of their principals out of their schools and replaced them with stronger leaders.

None of the districts reported having sizeable problems filling leadership or teacher positions, although a few districts did face difficulties finding adequate principals at the high school level and teachers in hard-to-fill areas (special education and bilingual education, for example). To address these difficulties, the districts typically developed specialized "grow-your-own" programs to target areas like bilingual education or offered annual stipends ranging from $1,000 to $5,000 for teachers in particular subject areas, like math and science. Streamlining hiring processes by simplifying application processes, better defining desirable qualities for future candidates, moving hiring timelines earlier in the year, and adding additional screening tools—such as the Gallup Teacher Perceiver—were extremely effective for increasing and strengthening the hiring pool. Principals in particular mentioned that they were able to "get a jump on the hiring frenzy" by "snatching up" the best teachers early. They also explained how much easier it was to search through electronic teacher applications in the comfort of their own schools rather than "going downtown and wading through huge stacks of paper applications."

Additionally, improved interview processes appeared to yield stronger, more suitable candidates by adding performance-based components such as teaching model lessons, providing sample lesson plans, or responding to various instructional scenarios. Some interviewees mentioned that the districts' improved school and district performance, coupled with their association with the highly publicized Broad Prize, also helped attract candidates.

Once the districts found the right people to move their vision forward, they worked hard to provide whatever was necessary to succeed. All districts were successful in retaining a fair number of their new hires by providing mentors, professional development, time for collaboration, and other supports. All districts had particularly strong induction programs for teachers that covered their first three years rather than just the first year. New and experienced principals and teachers in the majority of the focus group interviews provided comments and anecdotes illustrating the immediate support they received from the districts. Districts provided such assistance by placing supports directly in the schools. For example, central office leaders in Boston who traditionally had spent most of their time in the main district office shifted their focus to spending time in schools. Similarly, instructional specialists like those in Norfolk spent 70 percent of each week working with teachers. Principals also began spending more time in classrooms providing feedback to teachers, and instructional coaches were housed primarily at schools, where they could work with teachers on a daily basis.

The difference in how professional development is implemented in these five districts compared with how it is implemented in other districts is noteworthy. Typically, professional development in other districts occurs in a vacuum and is separated from district/school goals and teacher/student needs. Many professional development leaders have pointed me to a thick book full of trainings for teachers to self-select from a wide array of core-subject offerings. Teachers in those districts often complain that the trainings they attend are irrelevant to what they do in the classroom and are often random repeats from previous years. The five districts featured in this book connect professional development to what teachers do in the classroom by using data to target training offerings. They have also shifted to more school-based training to meet school needs, and they provide training follow-up through classroom visits by trainers, principals, or other teachers, as in Boston's Collaborative Coaching and Learning model. Norfolk took the concept one step further by merging its Curriculum and Instruction and Professional Development departments into the Leadership and Capacity Development department. Teachers in these five districts cite professional development as a crucial source of support, and they appear to enjoy talking about the things they are learning and how they use their new skills in their instruction.

Another common source of support cited by teachers was other teachers. Teachers highly valued the ability to meet with other teachers to share ideas and materials, review data, and discuss instructional solutions, and to observe other teachers to see how they handle classroom management or unique instructional techniques. The key to making that actually happen and be useful was to schedule regular meeting times, ideally twice a week, and have some type of structure like an agenda and a skilled facilitator. The time was most easily carved out when common planning time was possible. If that was not possible, teachers met before or after school; in some cases, districts worked with their unions to make common planning time a regular part of the school schedule.

Teams of teachers met by grade level or subject, or in vertical teams. After seeing numerous collaborative teacher meetings (even in high schools!), we asked a high school principal how and when collaboration became such a common and comfortable practice. She cited the No Child Left Behind Act as the catalyst, as it "created a common language for teachers about teaching and learning for the first time." Not only was collaboration a supportive and efficient way for teachers to share their workload, but it also created uniformity across grades and subjects, greatly helping with instructional alignment.

Instructional Programs, Practices, and Arrangements

Program selection in all five districts was a very structured process that included using data to identify programmatic needs, using committees made up of teachers and district leaders for selection, piloting larger programs, and evaluating programs after they were put into place. Although program selection was mostly a district-driven process in four of the districts, Aldine allowed schools to select their own programs, as long as they yielded appropriate student achievement.

Finding graduation to be an inadequate end-goal for preparing students for college or skilled careers, all five districts attempted to ratchet up instruction to higher cognitive levels. Norfolk, Long Beach, and Boston approached this goal by mandating particular instructional strategies, and Aldine required that teachers focus on Bloom's Taxonomy. Garden Grove eliminated most remedial classes and focused on providing innovative instructional supports to students within their appropriate grade levels. Though it was not mentioned in the case studies, post–Broad Prize site visits to Garden Grove and Long Beach found both districts engaged in a partnership to increase success in Advanced Placement classes. The partnership provided AP training and certification for teachers and developed "bridge builder" classes to help students master AP content and pass their AP exams. Additionally, all the districts were working to move instruction down to lower grades, particularly algebra. Laura Schwalm noted that she and others are continually impressed with the skills they see in classrooms even down to the kindergarten level, although she cautioned about the importance of "not getting too carried away." However, she said that more of her district's sixth-graders are "proficient" or "advanced" on the state assessment, which she found to be an important predictor of success in high school.

Not only did all districts aim to increase instructional rigor, but their overall approach to instruction was holistic and tied to what they wanted graduates to know and be able to do, rather than just preparing them to pass tests or follow textbooks from start to finish. Interviewees commonly made statements like, "If we provide a good instructional program, the test will take of itself" or "The curriculum must include skills beyond the test, like listening and speaking."

Classroom instruction was frequently monitored by principals and other district leaders as a means of ensuring that instructional programs and practices were being implemented correctly and were yielding adequate results. When data or walkthroughs pointed to problems, leaders were quick to identify the source of the problem and either provided additional instructional supports to teachers or changed instructional programs if the program was the problem.

Monitoring, Analysis, and Use of Data

Data is clearly an important driver for improving district and school practices and processes in the five districts. Among the core philosophies in all of the districts is a commitment to collecting and using data to inform individual, classroom, school, and district instructional decisions—not simply to test whether student performance on exams had risen overall. To this end, these districts have four crucial elements in place: (1) powerful data management systems; (2) various data collection tools; (3) an accountability tool to manage all the data pieces; and (4) a culture of trust that values data.

The districts play a large role in collecting data and providing it to all district stakeholders to help them make informed decisions. Whether in one large data system as in Aldine, Boston, Garden Grove, and Long Beach or in two as in Norfolk, the districts provided an easily accessible Web-based data system to central office leaders, administrators, and teachers. The best systems provided users with multiple data points on student achievement, student demographics, and other record data (attendance, discipline referrals, etc.) through multiple years. The systems found in these districts allowed their users to build their own queries with tools like easy-to-use drop-down boxes and printable charts and graphs that are informative and easy to interpret. Aldine, Boston, and Norfolk also used these systems to provide additional resources to teachers, such as model lessons, item analysis graphs, and resource materials.

In addition to having powerful data management systems, the districts also developed data collection tools to provide ongoing systemic feedback on student progress. One of the main tools used to inform classroom instruction in the five districts was formative or benchmark assessments. Many of these assessments were easily loaded into the data management systems with the use of scanners that provided almost immediate assessment feedback to teachers. The formative assessments provided useful data to teachers to help them catch instructional problems early so that intervention could be minimal and immediate. Teachers also used formative assessment data to group students for short-term interventions or to pair students with teachers based on particular instructional strengths.

In addition to assessment data, all five districts used walkthroughs to collect observation data on classroom instruction. Different from typical classroom observations used primarily for teacher evaluations, all five districts followed a structured walkthrough process to monitor and support classroom instruction. Members of the walkthrough teams underwent training to use a rubric to document specific target practices or activities, such as using appropriate questioning techniques with students. In Norfolk and Aldine, district leaders took particular care in building a trusting environment prior to implementing the walkthrough process to make sure teachers felt comfortable with it. The leaders assured schools and teachers that walkthrough data would not be used for formal evaluations and would not go directly to central office. This initial approach helped teachers view the walkthroughs as opportunities to ask for support, share practices, and align activities across classrooms. Once teachers and principals found that the process was used solely to improve instruction, they felt comfortable and open about having outsiders visit their classrooms. Norfolk's superintendent John Simpson mentioned that the teachers eventually were requesting to share their own walkthrough observation results with area superintendents.

In addition to comprehensive student data management systems, the five districts pulled all the data and monitoring pieces together with an over-arching tool for monitoring district and school performance. These tools were implemented and reviewed several times a year, and they include both summative and formative assessment data, walkthrough observations, and in some cases qualitative data about school performance. Each of the tools has different features and formats to manage goal-planning processes and strategies. Aldine uses a Baldrige-based scorecard that includes formative, summative, and walkthrough results that directly feed into action plans. Scorecards have been implemented at the classroom, grade, feeder-pattern, and district levels. Boston's Whole School Improvement Plan includes for-mative and summative assessment data tied to school goals that feed into the district's goals. Garden Grove monitors school performance through the Single School Plan, which utilizes formative and summative data along with data from Action Walks to measure progress toward school and dis-trict goals. Norfolk's Comprehensive Accountability Plan includes three tiers that contain summative and formative performance data as well as a narrative that analyzes the different data points within the schools' context. Long Beach indicated in its 2005 retro study interviews that it was begin-ning to develop a scorecard process similar to Aldine's.

All of these monitoring systems are public within the district through a local intranet or through a district Web site to connect different system levels and create an open accountability environment. Teachers, principals, and district staff say that their use of data has identified areas where indi-vidual students or groups of students are struggling and has led to frank, honest conversations about "the brutal facts," as Dr. Simpson said. When it became clear to educators in the five districts that data was collected not to evaluate or judge them, but rather to help them become better teachers and leaders, many become more willing—even eager—to dig into the data.

In some cases, the results even helped teachers inspire students and parents to use the data themselves.

Creating an atmosphere that is comfortable with frequent, if not daily, scrutiny of student, teacher, and administrator performance requires care and consideration. Multiple interviews conducted in the five districts supported the belief that data was truly used "as a flashlight rather than a hammer" for improving student achievement. Statements like "We looked at the data and just didn't get it right, so we worked together to find a better way" were frequent, and we heard such statements at all levels of these five districts. Administrators in particular showed great care and thoughtfulness when implementing new data systems, like the walkthrough process in Norfolk, or when starting benchmark testing, as in Garden Grove. These leaders understood that establishing trust was a first important step prior to the rich conversations they were able to have about data results.

Clearly, the leaders' efforts in establishing trust were helpful. In several interviews, teachers mentioned their initial concerns when first implementing benchmark tests. Some teachers candidly described their shock at seeing holes in their instruction, and others revealed that they had held initial skepticism about students' ability to meet the benchmarks. These teachers said that eventually the data showed student successes and encouraged them to continue to raise expectations for their students. Concerned that maybe the number of tests would be burdensome for teachers, one site visit team member asked teachers at each district the same question: "What do you think of all this testing? Is it one of those necessary evils that you just get through, or do you find it useful?" The majority of the teachers in the five districts responded that the testing was considered a normal part of instruction, diagnosing exactly what students understood. The formative tests in particular gave them immediate feedback on their classroom instruction.

Recognition, Intervention, and Adjustment

Once issues and concerns were uncovered through the districts' data monitoring processes, all five districts had structured interventions available to meet the needs of struggling schools, teachers, and particularly students. Regardless of the level, many interventions were developed or identified collaboratively within a group, and several districts like Aldine followed a structured problem-solving method like root cause analysis. Struggling schools were provided with ample support and attention from central office leaders with occasional assistance from outside experts. Schools demonstrating significant problems were often designated as "focus schools" and had a range of interventions available to them. Interventions for focus schools were quite varied, ranging from the simple addition of instructional coaches, targeted professional development for staff, or additional funds or materials, to the option of a soft or hard reconstitution—replacing either a portion of or all of a school's staff members.

As a highly valued resource, teachers in the five districts had many supports and interventions available to help them in time of need. In addition to the basic instructional supports such as curriculum pacing guides and instructional coaches, teachers could request targeted professional development or receive assistance from specific district-level committees. Training and support from the district committees addressed core instructional skills, including behavior management, organizational strategies, or classroom delivery models. Principals were groomed to readily assist teachers by receiving training in the same instructional strategies used by teachers and in how to conduct effective observations and consultations. As a result, many teachers named their school principal or assistant principal as a valued source of support for classroom instruction.

Interventions for students in all five districts began with a long-term focus on prevention and early intervention informed by the availability of almost real-time student performance data. All the districts had extensive preschool programs, and several were working to further expand those programs. Early intervention also meant assessing students frequently, with an emphasis on closely monitoring specific target reading skills (such as phonemic awareness, comprehension, etc.) three times a year in the early grades.

Some particular instructional techniques were considered to be helpful for reducing the need to intervene and were considered a part of everyday instruction. Those methods included using differentiated instruction to meet individual student needs and creating flexible grouping within and across classrooms to provide short-term remediation in certain skill areas. Additionally, some districts, like Garden Grove and Long Beach, focused closely on appropriate classroom placement as a crucial prevention measure. Students displaying more pervasive instructional issues were provided a number of options, with the focus on keeping remediation efforts within the instructional day rather than before or after school. Individual intervention plans for students were mentioned in several of the districts, and all districts discussed addressing student intervention in a collaborative team approach. For students not passing benchmarks or state assessments, before- and-after school programs and tutoring were available, and some students were retained in particular grades to master content before transitioning to the next grade.

Several types of intervention programs or arrangements were implemented to target the needs of specific student populations. Long Beach developed an International Student Registration Assessment Center to assess and properly place ELL students on the correct English performance level. For middle and high school students, several districts had eighth- or ninth-grade academies to ensure that students were mastering the appropriate prerequisite skills before moving to the next grade level. Some, like Garden Grove, provided double blocks of instruction in a particular core subject to help students "keep moving forward" and receive remediation at the same time. Boston focused on improving student performance in high school through building small learning communities called high school academies.

Teachers implementing any intervention were well supported by intervention teams and through targeted professional development. Interviews with teachers confirmed that they saw a reduction in the need for intensive interventions outside of school as a result of students coming to them better prepared than in previous years, when their systems were not as well defined or aligned.

INFLUENCING FACTORS

Even with the right pieces pulled together within a school system, issues can arise if the right relationships are not maintained to help hold those pieces in place. The five districts share some commonalities in how they cultivated stakeholder relationships by outlining their roles within the district and engaging in thoughtful, strategic communication and collaboration.

School Board

Each superintendent had a strong and positive relationship with the school board. The superintendents all invested time in communicating frequently with their boards and making sure the boards were informed of any issues as soon as possible. Superintendents made sure that their own communications about the boards were continually positive, and they made efforts "to always make [the board] look good." For their part, board members appreciated being kept informed and appeared to trust and admire the skills of the superintendent leading their districts. When asked their role within the district, board members were quick to point out that it was to set policy, not micromanage the work. Each board also seemed to have little dissension within their membership, and appeared to know the district's goals, concerns, and practices well.

While most districts had elected boards, Boston and Norfolk had appointed boards. Boston superintendent Tom Payzant mentioned his appreciation for the stability created for his district and him by working with an appointed board "with the right people on it." It helped BPS stay focused on their steady reform plan for over ten years. Norfolk board members believed that appointments helped the district find members more interested in supporting the district than in politics.

Union/Association

Another key relationship that was skillfully maintained in all five districts was with each district's teachers union or association. While the associations in right-to-work states did not have the same bargaining power as the unions in Boston, Garden Grove, and Long Beach, all the districts made it a point to involve association or union leaders in key decision-making processes that affected teachers. In some districts, that relationship was strained at times; overall, it worked best when everyone agreed that the association/union's role was to support teachers and, by extension, the district and school goals.

It seemed that the more a union with bargaining power got involved in educational issues beyond teacher support, such as scheduling, the more time district leaders had to invest in managing the relationship with the union, as Tom Payzant did. Although Garden Grove and Long Beach had unions with bargaining power, Garden Grove experienced little to no conflict with its union, which seemed to consistently see its role as supporting not only teachers but also the entire educational program for the sake of students. The relationship in Long Beach was positive until changing union leadership took more interest in educational programming issues, occasionally creating obstacles.

Community

Each of the five districts had a wide range of partnerships with the local business community. These relationships not only supplied program funding like the Boston Teacher Residency, but also served as a reciprocal relationship for the community's greater good. The districts made community groups aware of their goals, needs, and concerns (such as an unsafe neighborhood through which students walked home), and the community partners provided input on the skills they desired in future graduates from the district. In Aldine, the district and community worked together to rebuild a dilapidated apartment complex into a new elementary school. Similarly, Dr. Simpson in Norfolk developed a close relationship with the local housing authority to track conditions for students who lived in low-income housing areas. In Boston, Dr. Payzant was a well-recognized attendee at many community meetings, and was seen as a leader who wanted to keep abreast of community issues and concerns. Lastly, several districts had major partnerships with businesses or foundations that funded major leadership development or teacher training programs. One of the most unique partnerships with higher education existed between Long Beach and California State University.

The close connections with community members were evidenced by community members' knowledge of the districts' goals and by their belief that the district and school doors were open to them. In return, these partners contributed valuable resources such as money, time, and leadership to the districts.

Parents

Frequent communication and open doors were also important elements in the districts' relationships with parents. District leaders and teachers worked hard to connect with parents as often as possible and seemed in tune with parents' needs and challenges. Parents in focus groups appeared to be genuinely happy with their children's schools and described their relationships within the district as "teamlike" and "open." The five districts employed different modes of communication in different languages with parents, using letters, radio, homework hotlines, Web-based parent portals, and home visits to connect with parents in any way possible. Several districts had specific staff, like parent liaisons, to help them with this time-consuming work, but two had to cut those positions due to budget constraints. One important element in each of the districts' work with parents was the focus on moving beyond traditional superficial methods of parent involvement to more meaningful activities that affected both parents and children.

While most districts felt they were making progress in increasing parental involvement, they all voiced concerns about parental involvement at the high school level. Superintendent Laura Schwalm in Garden Grove mentioned that her district finally saw some success with high school parent involvement once the district made more efforts "to go into the community" rather than have parents wait to be invited into the schools.

Governance, Organization, and Decision Making

Although governance is somewhat covered in the section on school boards, the bigger picture of where lines of authority are drawn and who is at the decision-making table were detailed further in each case beyond school board functions. The issue of an elected versus an appointed board was mentioned earlier but is worth repeating. Tom Payzant did not believe Boston Public Schools could have achieved as much as they did without the predictability and stability of an appointed board. Norfolk also believed its appointed board ensured the quality of candidates it sought for board service while eliminating potential political interests. Another governing arrangement that seemed to be crucial for Boston was its close connection with the mayor and the city. As a formal part of the city's structure, the district was seen as a community priority and they could easily access crucial city services. Additionally, the typical organizations necessary to support students in urban schools were right at Dr. Payzant's fingertips. He could speak with the chief of police, juvenile justice, and the fire department in monthly meetings at city hall.

Although we did not focus particularly on departmental organization within the central office and between schools, we found that most of the districts were organized in several "feeder patterns" of mixed grades led by an associate superintendent. One district was organized in grade-levels (elementary, middle, and high school); however, that district meet in vertical teams frequently to stay connected and aligned. The central offices each had at least one position serving as a liaison between central office and schools. The people in these positions often operated with an understanding that the majority of their time would be spent working directly in schools and/ or classrooms. Most of the departments within the central office covered a specialized area such as human resources or instruction, but each district also made sure the departments stayed connected to each other and to the district's goals. When an internal audit at Boston Public Schools revealed that some departments felt they were functioning in a silo, district leadership reorganized their central office to remedy the problem.

Each of the districts featured in this book was led by dynamic, powerful leaders who focused their work systemically and understood which activities were best centralized at the district level and which were best left up to schools. There seemed to be no definitive answer to which activities should be centralized, although most of the districts felt that it was important to have some measure of uniformity and structure in the curriculum and instruction areas. A relatively uniform instructional program seemed to be key for ensuring that students experienced a seamless educational program that contained no skips or repeats, creating continuity for mobile students and aligning program evaluation and professional development activities across schools and within the overall instructional program. In many cases, that meant having the central office work with school leaders and teachers on developing a curriculum that everyone was mandated to use. In a few districts, some instructional strategies were mandated, like the Workshop model in Boston and the instructional non-negotiables in Norfolk. While program selection was often centralized, several districts allowed schools to select their own programs, as long as they received appropriate results. The main criteria used to decide what practices needed to be centralized at the district level or decentralized to schools was the ability to ensure that students received a well-aligned, seamless, and rigorous instructional program, regardless of mobility. Even though many practices were centralized at the district level, principals still were given the authority to run their campuses "as they saw fit." The district leaders trusted their principals, and felt they were best positioned to make decisions and identify necessary resources for their unique school settings.

In addition to having the vision and ability to carve out and communicate a clear road map for the district, the superintendents all worked to create distributed leadership across their systems. In interviews, the superintendents often described their district's work with words like "we" instead of "I," and it was obvious that the other central office and school leaders they had in place carried the same message and ability to implement the road map. Additionally, these superintendents felt it was important to mentor and support leaders within their system, and to provide multiple leadership opportunities at all district levels, particularly to teachers. This concept of distributed leadership seemed to be particularly important for creating a stable, consistent culture that helped the work continue past one person. When Dr. Simpson retired and left Norfolk, the district continued with its road map, and as with the other districts, continued to show successes.

The schools often were organized for decision making in a similar fashion as described above. Elementary schools seemed to be small enough for teachers to stay connected to each other and to school leadership; in secondary schools, department chairs or teacher leaders served as liaisons between school leadership and teachers. Teachers were often provided a mechanism to voice their opinions to central office and school leaders, and they had opportunities to serve on various committees to engage in work products, practices, or policies that would directly impact them. In many schools, we found teachers who sat on leadership teams, helped develop the district curriculum and curriculum guides, led professional development trainings, and presented at national and state conferences. One of the most important mechanisms for connecting decision makers to each other and to district and school goals was scheduled time to meet with educators at various levels within the district. Some crucial factors in making sure that teachers in different grade levels and schools in general stayed connected was common planning time, scheduled time for vertical team meetings, and the creation of different decision-making bodies that involved multiple levels of stakeholders. In the midst of all this cross-fertilization was a superintendent who was an instructional leader and who was accessible, highly visible, and in tune with the farthest-reaching corners of the system.

Resource Allocation

The most common themes found in interviews addressing resource allocation was the alignment of resources with district and school goals, the importance of responsible fiscal management, and the need to ensure that budget shortfalls would affect classroom instruction minimally or not at all. Additionally, most resource decisions were informed by data and made by teams of multiple stakeholders.

The practice of tying purchases to specific district and school goals is not commonly seen in districts. In early 2000, I worked with a team of researchers on a resource allocation study in twenty-one Texas districts of varying achievement levels. What we found was: (1) there was no structured method for allocating resources; budgets were often patched together randomly from different funding pots or done by pure formula; (2) fiscal decisions were often made by gut feeling or by using what everyone else used; and (3) there were few clear mechanisms for crafting budgets or evaluating fiscal decisions.[3] The districts featured in this book did not operate with the above practices. In each of these five exemplary districts, we were told that for the most part, school personnel had what they needed, as long as they could demonstrate how their purchase requests tied to district and school goals. This philosophy also held true when it came to the pursuit or acceptance of grant or donated funds as well. For example, if a foundation offered Garden Grove $2 million for something that did not align with its goals and plans, the district would reject the funds. Additional funds taken simply because they were easy to obtain were seen by the districts as more of a distraction than an asset.

Unlike what we found in the Texas resource allocation study, the exemplary districts in this book looked at resource allocation in a holistic manner: Purchasing decisions were made within the districts' overall plans, and there were clear practices and policies for making budgets and spending funds. When a decision needed to be made on whether to fund or cut a program, districts reviewed data to ensure the program was yielding expected results; if it wasn't, it was cut. In the same vein, programs were often piloted first within one classroom or school before large-scale investments were made. Each of the districts also seemed to highly value the importance of fiscal responsibility, to ensure their funds were well invested to make the most out of what dollars they had, and out of respect to taxpayers, grant funders, and their own reputation.

The districts experiencing difficult budget shortfalls cut at the central office first, as they were highly committed to leaving their instructional programs as untouched as possible. These districts and schools were particularly creative in finding ways to save and raise extra funds, and schools were quite savvy in obtaining grant funds and community support. When the cuts became deep enough to necessitate more drastic measures, districts had to face difficult decisions like cutting positions, as often personnel expenses were their largest budget item.

Budgets were developed at the district and school levels through a collaborative process with numerous stakeholders at the table. Several of the districts were quite transparent about their budgets, and a few even had them posted on their district Web sites. At the schools, principals felt they had an acceptable amount of authority over their budgets. We heard in several districts that there was little room for discretion, since some line items, such as personnel, were already budgeted by the district and took up as much as 65 percent to 80 percent of their allocations. However, principals still believed they were able to fund what they needed to run their schools and fulfill student needs. When principals in Boston wanted to house instructional coaches directly at their schools rather than at the district, the district leadership listened and made the change, even though it caused some reluctance from the coaches at first.

Schools that felt they were experiencing budget constraints mentioned the lack of funds for items like computer- and technology-related purchases and additional support programs for students such as summer programs. We did notice that many districts seemed to successfully shield their schools from budget shortfalls, as teachers in these districts did not seem to believe they had any less to work with during tight times. Another interesting finding across schools was the opinion of many principals that the best investment of funds, particularly additional funds, was in "human capital." This often meant investing in additional instructional coaches who would work directly in the classroom supporting teachers and students. The investment in high-quality human capital was a theme frequently heard in interviews, as districts asserted that it was much more cost-effective to get the right people in place and keep them rather than spend money on recruiting and training new personnel.

Climate/Culture

Climate is one of those fuzzy factors that is difficult to capture and assess but seems to have a powerful influence on every member of an organization. The first impression one gets when walking into a district central office, school, or classroom is visual. Regardless of the age of any school building the team visited in the five districts (there were some *very* old school buildings in Boston), we were greeted by shiny hallways, walls displaying student work and recognitions, and overall clean facilities. Several school leaders talked about the importance of providing staff and students with a building that showed pride in the school.

When we asked district leaders about the district climate, many of them mentioned trust, mutual respect, teamwork, stability, excitement, and a strong commitment to the students. District leaders frequently talked about the importance of relationships at all levels within the district and described working hard to make close connections with each other and with the schools. The districts created several mechanisms by which school staff members could provide input and engage in the work of the district. When describing the district's work, district leaders used the word "we" instead of "I" and emphasized the importance of building leaders within all levels of the district. They often discussed the importance of taking time to build trust and comfort and solicit feedback before embarking on significant changes. When implementing new processes like walkthroughs, district and school leaders clearly understood what it meant for teachers to suddenly host a team of visitors in their classrooms. Conversations around data were always posed from a customer-service view, with questions like, "What do you think happened?" and "How can we help you with that?"

At the schools, principals and teachers used the same words district leaders used—*trust, collaboration, excitement*—when discussing their schools' climate. Principals and teachers felt well supported and connected to the central office. They believed their students' accomplishments and the momentum achieved within the district over the past few years marked an exciting time to be in their schools. Teachers often talked about the significance of having other teachers with whom to work and share ideas and materials. Many teachers said they met with each other so often that they felt like a big family.

When we asked how school staff members were able to connect with their students and help them grow and succeed, we heard countless poignant stories about school teams pitching in to buy prom dresses and saw tears of pride for students who were turning their lives around. The parents who sat in on school and focus group interviews agreed that their school principals and teachers were dedicated and helpful to their children. They felt the schools made a point of keeping in close contact with them and treated them as equal partners in their children's education. Even the students we talked to voiced appreciation for all the support they received at school and felt that their teachers and principals personally cared about them.

While *climate* describes the results of how different levels of a district "feel" to individuals and groups, *culture* seems to reflect an actual shift in thinking that becomes ingrained in the system. Several common themes that could be defined as "cultural shifts" found in the five exemplary districts show evidence of a change in beliefs about teaching and learning, and about creating and sustaining long-term changes or reform to scale. At the school level, we heard numerous teachers and principals refer to "the open door" as a symbol of teachers becoming more comfortable with hosting visitors in their classrooms and sharing their techniques and tools. This was a big change in some of the districts from past times where teachers "closed their doors" and focused on their favorite topics or lessons. To open the doors, district and school leaders worked hard on creating trust, openness, and a feeling of collective accountability for all the students in a school. Data helped connect people to each other in problem-solving activities and added another level of transparency. Many district interviewees made statements like, "You cannot hide from the data."

At the district level, the cultural shifts appeared to be an understanding that improving achievement for all students meant looking at the entire system holistically. It meant redefining the concept of "reform"—from layering the latest and greatest practice on top of last month's or year's practice to building a cohesive plan, and "staying the course," making changes and adjustments as needed to improve the work. Central office leaders also shifted their thinking about providing easily accessible supports to schools and applying a customer-service attitude that lent itself well to creating trust and mutual respect. Across the systems, many educators mentioned changing their beliefs about the level of rigor their students could handle, and that their focus and goals should move beyond graduation to preparing students for college and/or skilled careers.

REFORM AND STUDENT ACHIEVEMENT—BRINGING IT TO SCALE

Although district members cited some specifics (like moving to high school academy formats), when asked about which reforms had the greatest effect on student achievement, the majority of the responses referred to curriculum alignment, data and monitoring, and shifts in philosophical beliefs about teaching and learning. When they mentioned data and monitoring, interviewees most frequently referenced data from formative assessments and classroom walkthroughs as the linchpins of their improved instructional practices. Both pieces were believed to provide continuous feedback on student progress and classroom instruction and to spark important conversations about teaching and learning. Overall, however, when speaking about reforms, district personnel referenced "reforms" as practices within an overall cohesive plan that clearly outlined goals for teaching and learning rather than discrete events. Thus, while interviewees often showed an appreciation for having more data through benchmark assessments, for example, they described the data as an additional tool that helped them reach academic goals for their students.

The philosophical shifts were more idealistic and hard to capture, yet were confirmed through multiple references across the systems. Such shifts were defined as changes in fundamental beliefs about whether students could reach higher academic levels or about whether poor performance was something the district could realistically influence. Teachers admitted that they did not believe at first that all their students could reach higher instructional targets, but when benchmark assessments started to prove them wrong, they found themselves changing their beliefs. Central office leaders confirmed that they began to see teachers' attitudes change about benchmark assessments, resulting in fewer defensive comments about assessment results and more questions about how their instruction affected student learning.

As expected in urban districts, these five exemplary districts faced numerous challenges. As challenges are relatively context-dependent, the obstacles mentioned by the districts were predictably varied but held a few common threads. The most frequently referenced challenges had to do with the districts' ability to sustain and improve upon their hard-won successes within their complex and difficult circumstances. Typical responses to questions about challenges referenced concerns about student mobility, attrition and dropout rates; student and parent engagement; and the needs of specific populations, like English language learners. While some districts were worried about future funding, others were more preoccupied with maintaining the crucial relationships that could either help or hinder their ability to stay on what they felt was the correct course.

SIMILAR SYSTEMS—DIFFERENT PATHWAYS

The five districts selected for this research all engaged in a process that started with the acknowledgment of unacceptable student performance. Now they are receiving recognition for raising and improving student achievement and closing ethnic and income achievement gaps. Key practices shared in their reform processes included the development of clear and specific curriculum and academic goals; the setting of high instructional targets to prepare students for college or skilled careers; the ability and attract, retain, and support the right talent to implement the curriculum; creation of alignment through consistent messaging and employment of collaborative processes; the presence of strong data systems that constantly measure progress; and the ability to quickly intervene when problems arose.

Although the end results are similar, each district's approach to creating systemic alignment was somewhat different. For example, while all districts began working on their curriculum by clarifying, aligning, and filling in gaps within their state standards (interestingly, all five also began this work prior to NCLB), Aldine, Long Beach, and Garden Grove began their reform focus largely with curriculum refinement and alignment. Norfolk also aligned its curriculum, but took a very different approach by adopting a specific curriculum—Powerful Literacy and Powerful Math. Boston's curriculum alignment was a slower process, and its initial focus was a five-year plan and their powerful data management system.

Analyzing the districts' different approaches to improving the instructional core is also interesting. While the previously mentioned elements all supported the instructional changes, the actual methods used to meet higher learning standards for students were different in each district. Aldine set about instructional improvement largely through pedagogical techniques such as Bloom's Taxonomy. Boston used an inquiry-based workshop model. Garden Grove focused on eliminating its non-college-track and courses and on providing interventions during the instructional day to support students struggling with grade-level work. Similar to Norfolk, Long Beach applied a mandated set of instructional practices, the Essential Elements of Effective Instruction, which utilized common pedagogical techniques, Bloom's Taxonomy, and elements of the traditional lesson plan cycle, including using data to guide instruction. Additionally, Long Beach's partnership with CSU helped it better align instruction to prepare students for college. Norfolk used the "Power" curriculum strands in combination with instructional non-negotiables to raise its instructional rigor. These various instructional techniques, along with organizational alignment and supports, helped each of the five districts make marked improvements in student achievement.

A WORD ABOUT STANDARDS AND TESTING

Each of the districts in this book was successful because it was able to clearly define what should be taught and learned, and able to monitor the progress of schools, principals, teachers, and students through various monitoring and assessment systems. There is much controversy around the standards movement. Many believe that standards dictate what students will learn and stifle the craft of teaching, and that testing narrows the curriculum and encourages educators to cheat. I could list a thousand references in my endnotes; we have all heard these arguments, and I certainly can see where these beliefs originate. I have spoken to parents who removed their children from public schools because those schools were doing test-prep worksheets all year long and ignoring writing until the Spring writing exam. I have interviewed teachers who learned great instructional skills in teacher preparation programs only to be limited to similar drilling techniques in their schools. However, the five districts in this book, and many other districts I have visited through years of research and the Prize process, have produced impressive results for students who previously may have been ignored. In these districts, instruction is related to an overall seamless educational plan, teachers work together and pore over data, and the system uses data and assessments simply to target specific needs of various stakeholders in the system. The conversations around data are open and respectful, and at times painful as they uncover what John Simpson has called "the brutal facts." However, the conversations are out on the table, and they are causing educators to solve problems together.

As many of these district leaders point out, it is up to the adults in the system to create the right conditions for standards to raise rigor and instruction beyond the cloak of aggregate scores, and for assessment results to be used as a flashlight rather than a hammer. As they formulated their reform paths, the five districts took care to attend to fears and concerns and built trust and support at each system level.

During the 81st legislative session, which just ended in Texas, I grew concerned at the number of policy makers who lamented the evils of tests. Several proposed bills that would limit the number of assessments a school would be allowed to implement, likely through a narrow interpretation of what testing is and can be. The districts in this book each gave some form of formative assessment to students on a quarterly, monthly, and even weekly basis. Assessment data was used to adjust instruction along the way in whatever specific area was needed. Without the ability to assess mastery of instructional content frequently, these systems likely would not be as successful. To use a colorful phrase from Dr. Schwalm, it would be "like waiting for the autopsy rather than using diagnostics."

LESSONS FOR DISTRICTS

While there is some variation in how the districts approached their reform efforts, their similarities in addressing the instructional core across all levels of the organization provide useful lessons about systemic reform. The details can be found earlier in this chapter, but below is a distilled summary by theme and category:

Curriculum and Academic Goals

- Create a clear and specific curriculum that communicates exactly what students should know and be able to do. The process should seamlessly map backward from the end-product of the system—a graduate prepared for college or skilled careers—down to preschool. There should be no unnecessary repeats or gaps between the instructional objectives.
- Communicate the curriculum across the entire system and support fidelity of implementation through curriculum documents, training, support, and monitoring.
- Create benchmark or quarterly assessments to monitor student performance and curriculum implementation as frequently as possible. Provide results to teachers and principals as soon as possible.
- Align district and school academic goals and keep them few in number. All goal-development processes should involve multiple stakeholders and should be informed by data.

Staff Selection, Leadership, and Capacity Building

- Hire and retain the right people to deliver the curriculum by streamlining hiring processes and implementing screening and interview practices that move beyond a paper job application.

- Provide staff with multiple supports that are easily accessed and are delivered directly in classrooms as much as possible.
- Align professional development with curriculum and academic goals. Inform professional development planning by reviewing data and providing follow-up to training when possible.
- Train district and school leaders on the district curriculum and instructional strategies. Create new leadership avenues for all staff members to distribute strong leadership throughout the system.

Instructional Programs, Practices, and Arrangements

- Use a structured process informed by data to select, pilot, and monitor programs. Eliminate programs that do not yield appropriate results.
- Provide programs that can address diverse student needs, including remediation and acceleration.
- Implement instructional strategies that encourage higher-order thinking skills and increase academic rigor.

Monitoring, Analysis, and Data Use

- Consider investing in a student performance–management system that can collect formative and summative assessment data and student record data together. Maximize accessibility through a secure Web-based platform that allows users to develop various queries and produce charts that are visually easy to interpret.
- Provide adequate training on data use and encourage collaborative data review processes.
- Consider adopting a structured walkthrough process to monitor curriculum implementation, provide immediate support, and demonstrate strong teaching strategies.
- Provide a tool or process for collecting various data pieces on all system levels to build a clear picture of performance and spark conversations on where to focus resources and attention.
- Build a culture of trust that embraces the use of data to inform decisions and instruction rather than as a tool for blame or punishment.

Recognition, Intervention, and Adjustment

- Provide a wide array of supports and interventions for struggling schools, teachers, and students. Interventions should be selected through a collaborative process involving key stakeholders and should be informed by multiple data sources.
- Focus interventions with prevention in mind by concentrating on the early grades and by performing frequent and early assessments.
- Provide as many in-school interventions as possible, such as using differentiated instruction and flexible student grouping, examining multiple data points to place students in the correct courses, and double-blocking certain courses.
- Align intensive out-of-school interventions (tutoring, summer school, etc.) with the regular instructional program.

Other lessons to be learned through these five cases extend beyond the Framework and address issues of systemic and sustainable reform. The retro study of past winners (Garden Grove, Long Beach, and Norfolk) provided additional information regarding what changes were made by these districts over time and whether they were able to successfully sustain or improve upon their performance. Those systemic reform lessons include:

- Adopt a long-term focus that includes high standards. Leaders in all five districts emphasized that reform takes time and that districts must balance the tension between demands for short-term quick fixes and the goal of sustainable long-term change.
- Focus on doing a few things well. The five districts focused on a very limited number of academic goals and embarked on a reform path that did not shift or change. Relating decisions back to their goals helped them avoid the common churning and layering resulting from having too many goals or implementing too many reforms. In other words, refine rather than reform.
- Monitor constantly to assess progress toward goals. Monitoring systems in the five districts helped schools and teachers make adjustments and provide supports early to reduce the need for more drastic interventions.

- Build supports for sustainability. Supports in the five districts came in the form of building relationships with and between all stakeholders, involving stakeholders at all levels in decision making, and building leaders within all levels of the system to implement the district and school plans.
- Use a customer-service approach. Putting students at the front of their focus, the five districts placed a high priority on providing members at every system level with the right tools and support to ensure student success. Problems were addressed through a lens of collective accountability and were addressed collaboratively and collegially.
- Use a model or conceptual framework to organize thinking around systemic reform. The model should capture the necessary system elements and be simple enough to easily communicate and capture the necessary information.

LESSONS FOR POLICY MAKERS

The Framework illustrates how work can be distributed across the levels of a district system to coordinate alignment and resources and utilize time and talent more effectively. In a similar vein, there are areas in which state education departments and legislators can support that work to alleviate some of the burden on districts. Below are suggestions for consideration:

- Provide districts with fully aligned state standards that will prepare students for college and the workforce. Such a process would require ample time, a commitment to rigor, involvement with educators across the preK–16 continuum, and a shift away from interest-group politics such as those that commonly occur in social studies and science.
- Before making policies about testing, learn more about how your local districts are using formative assessments. Do not assume that all tests are created and implemented equally and encourage cheating and narrowing of curriculum.
- Provide districts with the means to attract and retain talented teachers and principals. Supporting incentive-pay programs that allow districts

to reward educators for extraordinary work or provide additional hiring stipends or retention bonuses has shown some positive results based on early studies.[4] Additionally, one useful tool for districts has been the ability to provide certification to principals or teachers through their own training programs.

- Provide districts with adequate data systems so they do not have to create them on their own. The data systems should provide longitudinal data and the ability to link teachers to students. A district's ability to connect to data in higher education systems would also be very useful in following graduates who leave their system. If states supplied districts with these data elements, the districts could concentrate less time on developing the systems themselves and spend more resources on analyzing and responding to data.

CONCLUSION

After years of studying and implementing reforms in districts and schools, educators and researchers seem to agree that reform needs to look different, and that there are some important areas of focus, such as clearly defining what should be taught and learned; getting the right people to deliver the instructional program; ensuring that the curriculum is delivered through research-based practices and programs; using data to drive decision-making and monitor ongoing progress; and having an array of interventions for the entire system. Additionally, there is an emerging belief that reform needs to have a preK–12 or even preK–16 focus that cuts across all organizational levels of a district in order to affect student achievement to scale. The strongest systems map backwards from the skills higher education institutions and businesses need from high school graduates. The biggest challenge in all of this work is to engage in a sustainable reform path that changes instruction in a meaningful way in an entire system: reform to scale.

The detailed analysis and comparison of five nationally recognized urban districts through the NCEA Best Practice Framework captures the process each district used to pull the pieces together and create reform to scale beyond one great teacher or school. Each began with unacceptable student performance and ended up with a well-aligned system showing significant gains across all student groups. According to these districts, tight coordination between the district, schools, and classrooms is important for providing an equal education across all schools within a district—a constant challenge for urban systems. Although direct causality cannot be established between practices and performance with five cases or with this type of methodology, many district and school personnel attributed their successes to the practices illustrated here.

The overarching message coming from these districts is echoed through their leaders, who stress that there is no silver bullet or fast path to school reform. They describe the work as being hard and time-consuming and say that it requires a concise, uniform message and practices that are supported by a committed community. The case studies suggest that systemic reform must work in two ways: (1) alignment of the system's parts—the district central office, school leadership, and classroom teachers, and (2) alignment of the system's practices across schools and throughout all grades. The end result should be marked improvements in the instructional core—an impact on teaching and learning.

Although the cases identified many similarities in the five districts' approach to aligning instructional and organizational practices, the details of implementation and the path they followed to improve student achievement differ. Districtwide systems must be built according to each district's context and needs. As it has become clear that focusing on one piece of a system or one practice will not create enduring change, it is also becoming clear that systemic change cannot simply be replicated district by district. It must be designed and implemented by district and school staff with a clear focus, goals, and messaging and be bound by various forms of accountability.

NOTES

Introduction

1. The $2 million Broad Prize for Urban Education, established in 2002, is the largest education award in the United States given to school districts. The Prize is awarded each year to honor urban school districts that demonstrate the greatest overall performance and improvement in student achievement while reducing achievement gaps among low-income and minority students.

The Broad Prize for Urban Education has four goals:

- Reward districts that improve achievement levels of disadvantaged students.
- Restore the public's confidence in our nation's public schools by highlighting successful urban districts.
- Create competition and provide incentives for districts to improve.
- Showcase the best practices of successful districts.

Each year, Broad Prize scholarships are awarded to graduating high school seniors from the finalist and winning districts who demonstrate a record of academic improvement during their high school careers and have a financial need. Seniors from the winning and finalist districts are eligible for two- or four-year scholarships of up to $20,000, depending on the type of higher education institution they choose to attend. For more information see http://www.broadprize.org/about/overview.html.

2. Richard F. Elmore, *School Reform from the Inside Out: Policy, Practice, and Performance* (Cambridge, MA: Harvard Education Press, 2004); Frederick M. Hess, *Spinning Wheels: The Politics of Urban School Reform* (Washington, DC: Brookings Institution Press, 1999).

3. Elmore, *School Reform from the Inside Out*, 14.

4. Ibid., 12.

5. Heather Zavadsky, "How NCLB Drives Success in Urban Schools," *Educational Leadership* 64 (2006): 70, 71.

6. Heather Zavadsky, "Building Effective Practices Through a Systems Approach: Elementary Schools," http://www.just4kids.org/en/files/Publication-Building_Effective_Practices_Through_a_Systems_Approach_Elementary_Schools-04-01-04.pdf/.

7. Stacey Childress et al., eds., *Managing School Districts for High Performance: Cases in Public Education Leadership* (Cambridge, MA: Harvard Education Press, 2007).

8. Amanda Datnow, Vicki Park, and Priscilla Wohlstetter, *Achieving with Data: How High-Performing School Systems Use Data to Improve Instruction for Elementary Students* (Los Angeles: University of Southern California, 2007); Jeffrey C. Wayman, Vincent Cho, and Mary T. Johnston, *The Data-Informed District: A District-Wide Evaluation of Data Use in the Natrona County School District* (Austin, TX: University of Texas, 2007); Heather Zavadsky and Amy Dolejs, "Data: Not Just Another Four-Letter Word," *Principal Leadership* 7 (2006): 32–36.

Chapter 1

1. Frederick M. Hess, *Spinning Wheels: The Politics of Urban School Reform* (Washington, DC: Brookings Institution Press, 1999).

2. James S. Coleman, *Equality of Educational Opportunity* (Washington, DC: U.S. Department of Health, Education, and Welfare, 1966).

3. National Commission on Excellence in Education, "A Nation at Risk: The Imperative for Educational Reform," http://www.ed.gov/pubs/NatAtRisk/index.html/.

4. Richard F. Elmore, *School Reform from the Inside Out: Policy, Practice, and Performance* (Cambridge, MA: Harvard Education Press, 2004); Hess, *Spinning Wheels*.

5. Sally Kilgore, "Comprehensive Solutions for Urban Reform," *Educational Leadership* 62, no. 6 (2005): 44–47.

6. Mike Kennedy, "The Reformers," http://asumag.com/Maintenance/business/university_reformers/index.html/.

7. Hess, *Spinning Wheels*.

8. Stacey Childress et al., eds., *Managing School Districts for High Performance: Cases in Public Education Leadership* (Cambridge, MA: Harvard Education Press, 2007), 1.

9. Georges Vernez et al., *Evaluating Comprehensive School Reform Models at Scale: Focus on Implementation* (Santa Monica, CA: RAND Corporation, 2006).

10. Geoffrey D. Borman, Shelly Brown, and Gina M. Hewes, *Early Learning and the Social Composition of Schools: A Multilevel Analysis* (paper presented at the annual meeting of the American Educational Research Association, New Orleans, LA, April 2000).

11. Kati Haycock, Craig Jerald, and Sandra Huang, "Closing the Gap: Done in a Decade," *Thinking K–16* 5, no. 2 (2001): 3–22.

12. Joy Frechtling, "Evaluating Systemic Educational Reform: Facing the Methodological, Practical, and Political Challenges," *Arts Education Policy Review* 101, no. 4 (2000): 26.

13. Reginald Leon Green and Carol Plata Etheridge, "Collaborating to Establish Standards and Accountability: Lessons Learned About Systemic Change," *Education* 121, no. 4 (2001): 821–829.

14. Elmore, *School Reform from the Inside Out.*

15. Robert D. Muller, "The Role of the District in Driving School Reform: A Review for the Denver Commission on Secondary School Reform," http://www.dpsk12.org/pdf/district_role.pdf/.

16. Wendy Togneri and Stephen E. Anderson, "Beyond Islands of Excellence: What Districts Can Do to Improve Instruction and Achievement in All Schools," http://www.learningfirst.org/publications/districts/, 11.

17. Robert D. Muller, "The Role of the District in Driving School Reform: A Review for the Denver Commission on Secondary School Reform," http://www.dpsk12.org/pdf/district_role.pdf/.

18. Karin Chenoweth, *"It's Being Done": Academic Success in Unexpected Schools* (Cambridge, MA: Harvard Education Press, 2007).

19. Hess, *Spinning Wheels*; Elmore, *School Reform from the Inside Out.*

20. Planning and Evaluation Resource Center, "Step 2: Theory of Change and Logic Models," http://www.evaluationtools.org/plan_theory.asp/.

21. Elmore, *School Reform from the Inside Out*, 223.

22. National Center for Educational Achievement, "Best Practice Framework." For a graphic of this framework, see http://www.just4kids.org/en/research_policy/best_practices/framework.cfm/. The NCEA Best Practice Framework, developed by Dr. Jean Rutherford, features three primary components: organizing themes, organizational levels, and school system practices. The organizing themes represent the broad topics that connect the identified practices across the three different organizational levels—district, school, and classroom—which provide a second organizational dimension to the Framework. Within each of the five themes, each organizational level plays a particular role in consistently higher-performing school systems. Different levels of the school system must be involved, to differing degrees, in order to reach maximum effectiveness in the specific theme area. The assignment of practices to a specific school level may be as important as the practices themselves; in other words, "who" is as important as "what."

23. NCEA, "Best Practice Framework."

Chapter 2

1. National Center for Education Statistics, *Common Core of Data: Public Education Agency Universe* (Washington, DC: U.S. Department of Education, 2004).

2. American FactFinder, U.S. Census Bureau, http://factfinder.census.gov.

3. State demographics from Texas Education Agency, 2004 Academic Excellence Indicator System (AEIS), http://ritter.tea.state.tx.us/perfreport/account/2004/state.html.

4. *Low-income* is defined as students on the free and reduced-price lunch program.

5. As explained on the 2008 Broad Prize report cards (page 28), an ordinary least squares regression (OLS) analysis was conducted to determine the extent to which each Broad Prize–eligible district performed better or worse than other districts in its state given the district's percentage of low-income students. Specifically, the dependent variable in the regression analysis was the percentage of test takers in a district in each of the three education-level groupings (elementary, middle, and high school) who were proficient or above on the state test. The independent variable was the percentage of test takers at each level in the district who were low income. The difference between the district's actual percentage of students who scored at or above proficiency and the predicted or expected value is the residual. A positive residual indicates that the district is performing better than expected on the state test given the percentage of low-income students taking the test, while a negative residual indicates lower-than-expected performance. To review report

cards and their explanations, see http://broadprize.org/resources/reports2008. html.

6. National Graduation Rate: National Center for Education Statistics, Averaged Freshman Graduation Rates for Public School Students, 2003–04. http://nces. ed.gov/pubs2007/dropout05/AveragedFreshmanGraduation.asp

7. National Center for Education Statistics, *Common Core of Data: Public Education Agency Universe* (Washington, DC: U.S. Department of Education, 2004).

8. The *Averaged Freshman Graduation Rate* (AFGR) divides the number of students graduating in year Y by an average of the grade 8 enrollment in year $Y-4$, grade 9 enrollment in year $Y-3$, and grade 10 enrollment in year $Y-2$.

The *Urban Institute Cumulative Promotion Index* (CPI) assumes that graduation is a process composed of three grade-to-grade promotion transitions (9 to 10, 10 to 11, and 11 to 12), in addition to the graduation event (grade 12 to receipt of a diploma). Each of the transitions is calculated as a probability, based on current-year statistics, by dividing the enrollment of the current year by the enrollment of the previous year for the grade in question. These separate probabilities are then multiplied to produce the probability that a student in that school system will graduate.

The *Manhattan Institute Graduation Rate* divides the number of students who receive a diploma in year Y by an estimate of the number of students in the ninth-grade cohort three years earlier. The estimate of the ninth-grade cohort size is a smoothed estimator that takes into account population changes and student mobility among districts and states rather than dropping out.

9. The cognitive domain of Bloom's Taxonomy involves knowledge and the development of intellectual skills. This includes the recall or recognition of specific facts, procedural patterns, and concepts that serve in the development of intellectual abilities and skills. The Taxonomy has six major categories, starting from the simplest behavior to the most complex: knowledge, comprehension, application, analysis, synthesis, and evaluation. The categories can be thought of as degrees of difficulty. That is, the first one must be mastered before the next one can take place.

10. The Accountability Rating System for Texas Public Schools and School Districts uses a subset of the performance measures computed for the Academic Excellent Indicator System (AEIS) to assign a rating to each public school and district. Schools and districts have been rated since 1994 using this system. The levels move from lowest to highest: Academically Unacceptable, Academically

Acceptable, Recognized, and Exemplary. More information is available at www. tea.state.tx.us/perfreport/account.

11. The common assessments were required across almost all grade levels in 2004. In a discussion with a district leader in 2008, I discovered that the common assessments had become optional due to a state-level policy limiting the number of days students can be tested. However, the district leader indicated that some teachers still choose to implement the common assessments and that the quarterly assessments are still required.

12. See http://my.triand.com/.

13. The Baldrige Criteria for Performance Excellence use a systems perspective to help organizations with performance management. The criteria are divided into seven key categories: Leadership, Strategic Planning, Customer and Market Focus, Information and Analysis, Human Resource Focus, Process Management, and Business Results.

14. Texas Association of School Boards [TASB], *A Guide to Texas School Finance*, 2008.

15. Ibid.

16. This figure was pulled for the 2004 school year. In 2008, it rose to $364,500 per WADA. WADA, or weighted average daily attendance, is a formula used in Texas to account for additional needs for certain types of students. Weighted programs include special education, vocational, bilingual, gifted and talented, and compensatory education. A weighted student count is used to distribute guaranteed yield funding.

17. "SchoolWorks," Aldine Independent School District Fact Sheet, 2008, http:// www.broadprize.org/asset/1177-tbp2008aldinefactsheet.pdf.

18. See www.desktopanalyst.net.

Chapter 3

1. National Center for Education Statistics, *Common Core of Data: Public Education Agency Universe* (Washington, DC: U.S. Department of Education, 2004).

2. "Strong Foundation, Evolving Challenges: A Case Study to Support Leadership Transition in the Boston Public Schools," Aspen Institute Education and Society Program and Annenberg Institute for School Reform at Brown University, http:// www.annenberginstitute.org/pdf/BostonCaseStudy.pdf.

3. For more information about pilot schools and a list of these schools, see http://www.bostonpublicschools.org/node/20.

4. John Portz, "External Actors and the Boston Public Schools: The Courts, the Business Community, and the Mayor," http://www.wilsoncenter.org/topics/pubs/ACF19F.pdf.

5. "Strong Foundation, Evolving Challenges."

6. Portz, "External Actors and the Boston Public Schools."

7. National Center for Education Statistics, "Common Core of Data: Public Education Agency Universe" (Washington, DC: U.S. Department of Education, 2006).

8. Paul Peterson and Fredrick Hess, "Check the Facts: Few States Set World Class Standards," *Education Next* 8, no. 3 (2008): 71–73.

9. *Trial Urban District Assessment:* NAEP began the urban school district assessment on a trial basis in 2002, in a few large urban districts in participating states. The purpose of the TUDA is to allow reporting of NAEP results for large urban school districts and to allow the NAEP program to evaluate the usefulness of NAEP data to cities of different sizes and demographic compositions.

10. "Strong Foundation, Evolving Challenges."

11. Paul E. Barton, "Chasing the High School Graduation Rate: Getting the Data We Need and Using It Right," Educational Testing Service, February 2009, http://www.ets.org/Media/Research/pdf/PICCHASING.pdf on May 28, 2009.

Averaged freshman graduation rate percentage estimates by racial/ethnic group in 2004–05 were: white—80.4%; black non-Hispanic—60.3; Hispanic—64.2; Asian/Pacific Islander—90.5; Native American—67.2. from www.nces.ed/gov/ccd/tables/freshman_03.asp, downloaded 6/12/2008.

12. National Center for Educational Achievement, "Best Practice Framework," http://www.just4kids.org/en/research_policy/best_practices/framework.cfm/.

13. National Center for Educational Achievement, "The 2003 Broad Prize for Urban Education: Boston Public Schools Case Study," http://www.just4kids.org/en/files/Presentation-Zap_the_Gap_The_District_Frontier_-_Boston-11-07-03.pps.

14. Barnett Berry, Diana Montgomery, and John Snyder, "Urban Teacher Residency Models and Institutes of Higher Education: Implications for Teacher Preparation," survey, Center for Teaching Quality in Partnership with the Aspen Institute, 2008, ED503644.

15. The Boston Plan for Excellence (BPE) was established in 1984 to support city schools. In 1995, as part of the Whole School Improvement Plan, BPE began to partner with the district to refine professional development. BPE is funded through BPS, the Annenberg Foundation, the Carnegie Corporation, and other state and federal grants.

16. http://www.bostonpublicschools.org/node/285/.

17. Dr. Reilinger still served as a board member as of publication of this book in 2009. She served as the Committee Chair from 1998 to 2008, and was first appointed in 1994. For more information see http://www.bostonpublicschools.org/node/278.

18. According to Chris Horan, BPS Chief Communications Officer, BTU represents support personnel such as nurses and counselors, but secretaries, custodians, and bus drivers have membership under separate labor unions.

19. "Strong Foundation, Evolving Challenges."

20. National Center for Educational Achievement, "The 2003 Broad Prize": Boston Public Schools Case Study.

21. S. Paul Reville and Celine Coggins, eds., *A Decade of Urban School Reform: Persistence and Progress in the Boston Public Schools* (Cambridge, MA: Harvard Education Press, 2007), 265–267.

22. Ibid., 266.

23. Ibid., 266.

24. Ibid., 267

25. John Portz, "External Actors and the Boston Public Schools."

26. National Center for Educational Achievement, "The 2003 Broad Prize": Boston Public Schools Case Study.

27. http://www.bostonpublicschools.org/assignment/.

28. Student Assignment Task Force, "Recommendations of Boston Public Schools" (report, Boston School Committee, September 22, 2004).

29. Monique Ouimette and Rosann Tung, "Family and Student Choices in Boston Public Schools," http://www.ccebos.org/Choice_in_Boston_Public_Schools.pdf/.

30. Ted Landsmark, "It's Time to End Busing in Boston," *Boston Globe*, January 31, 2009, http://www.boston.com/bostonglobe/editorial_opinion/oped/articles/2009/01/31/its_time_to_end_busing_in_boston/.

31. Reville and Coggins, *A Decade of Urban School Reform*, 243–270.

32. Ibid., 248

33. Ibid., 249

34. An instructional approach used to make academic instruction in English understandable to ELL students. In the sheltered classroom, teachers use physical activities, visual aids, and the environment to teach vocabulary for concept development in mathematics, science, social studies, and other subjects.

35. "Strong Foundation, Evolving Challenges."

36. Boston Public Schools, http://www.bostonpublicschools.org/node/285/.

37. Ibid.

Chapter 4
1. Garden Grove Unified School District, "GGUSD Profile," http://www.ggusd.k12.ca.us/profile.asp.

2. American FactFinder, U.S. Census Bureau, http://factfinder.census.gov.

3. National Center for Education Statistics, "Common Core of Data: Public Education Agency Universe" (Washington, DC: U.S. Department of Education, 2004).

4. Garden Grove Unified School District, "GGUSD Honored with New Award from Education Trust for Improving Student Achievement," http://www.ggusd.k12.ca.us/departments/pubinfo/03-04/Ed percent20Trust percent20Award percent2011-03.html.

5. The 2008 Broad Prize for Urban Education Report Card-Garden Grove USD, http://www.broadprize.org/asset/1216-gardengrove_ca.pdf.

6. Scores range from 1 to 5. Individual colleges have their own rules as to scores that qualify for course credit. These are recommendations from the College Board:

   5: Highest qualifications to receive credit for a college class

   4: Very highly qualified

   3. Qualified

   2: May qualify

   1: Probably not qualified

7. The 2008 Broad Prize for Urban Education Report Card-Garden Grove USD, http://www.broadprize.org/asset/1216-gardengrove_ca.pdf.

8. College Board, *5th Annual AP Report to the Nation: California Supplement*, http://www.collegeboard.com/html/aprtn/pdf/state_reports/09_0467_St_Report_CALIFORNIA_X1a_081223.pdf, p. 5.

9. Chrys Dougherty and Heather Zavadsky, "Giving All Students the Keys to College and Skilled Careers: One District's Approach," *Phi Delta Kappan* 89 no. 3 (2007): 194–199.

10. There are five performance levels or "bands" in the California Academic Performance Index: Far Below Basic; Below Basic; Basic; Proficient; and Advanced. For more information see the 2008–09 Accountability Progress Reporting System at the California department of Education Web site at http://www.cde.ca.gov/ta/ac/ap/documents/infoguide09.pdf/ .

11. The district stopped using the same curriculum guides around 2005 because it found that teachers were torn between following the guides and trying to follow guidelines in their textbooks. To eliminate the confusion, the district focused more on instructional strategies; the guides are available for reference for pacing.

12. Reciprocal teaching involves a dialogue between teachers and students, in which teachers and students take turns leading. The dialogue includes summarizing, question generating, clarifying, and predicting.

13. See "Guide to 'A-G' Requirements," University of California Web site, http://www.ucop.edu/a-gGuide/ag/a-g/welcome.html.

> The intent of the 'A-G' subject requirement is to ensure that students can participate fully in the first-year program at the University in a wide variety of fields of study. The requirements are written deliberately for the benefit of all students expecting to enter the University, and not for preparation for specific majors. UC faculty consider the Subject Requirement to be effective preparation, on many levels, for undergraduate work at the University. This pattern of study assures the faculty that the student has attained a body of general knowledge that will provide breadth and perspective to new, more advanced study. Fulfillment of the 'a-g' pattern also demonstrates that the student has attained essential critical thinking and study skills.

14. AVID (Advancement Via Individual Determination) is designed to increase schoolwide learning and performance. It is a fourth- through twelfth-grade system to prepare students in the academic middle for four-year college eligibility. The mis-

sion of AVID is to ensure that all students will succeed in a rigorous curriculum, enter mainstream activities of the school, increase their enrollment in four-year colleges, and become educated and responsible participants and leaders in a democratic society. See http://www.avidonline.org/info/ for more information.

15. National Center for Educational Achievement, "The 2003 Broad Prize for Urban Education: Garden Grove USD Case Study," http://www.just4kids.org/en/files/Presentation-Closing_the_Gap_No_Small_Roles_in_Big_Change_-_Garden_Grove-11-12-04.

16. The Academic Performance Index (API) measures the performance and growth of schools and districts based on the test scores of students in grades 2 through 12. The API is a single number on a scale of 200 to 1,000 that indicates how well students in a school or district performed on the previous spring's tests. An API is calculated for the whole school plus its "numerically significant subgroups," including socioeconomically disadvantaged students, English learners, and students with disabilities.

17. The system is on a two-year cycle that gives a "base" score for the first year and a "growth" score in the second year. The Base API, which is usually released in March (for example, 2008), comes from the previous spring's test scores (2007). The Growth API, released in late summer (2008), comes from 2008 spring test scores. The system was originally developed for and applied to individual school sites only. School districts received their first API scores in 2003 to meet the requirements of the federal No Child Left Behind (NCLB) Act. Individual schools have growth targets, but districts do not.

18. Education Data Partnership, http://www.ed-data.k12.ca.us.

Chapter 5
1. National Center for Education Statistics, *Common Core of Data: Public Education Agency Universe* (Washington, DC: U.S. Department of Education, 2004).

2. Lynn Olsen, "Inside the 'Long Beach Way,'" *Education Week*, September 4, 2007, http://www.edweek.org/ew/articles/2007/09/05/02longbeach.h27.html.

3. University of California Web site at http://www.ucop.edu/a-gGuide/ag/a-g/welcome.html.

4. "Zap the Gap: The District Frontier, Long Beach Unified School District," presentation at the Fourteenth Education Trust National Conference, Washington,

D.C. November 7, 2003. www.just4kids.org/en/files/Presentation-Zap_the_Gap_
The_District_Frontier_-_Long_Beach-11-07-03.pps.

5. A Guide to California's School Finance System, Ed-Data Education Data Partnership, February 2007, http://www.ed-data.k12.ca.us/articles/article.asp?title=
Guide percent20to percent20California percent20School percent20Finance
percent20System.

6. National Center for Educational Achievement, "The 2003 Broad Prize for Urban Education: Long Beach Unified School District Case Study," 5.

7. Long Beach homes and prices, May 9, 2009, http://www.zillow.com/local-info/
CA-Long-Beach-home-value.

Chapter 6
1. National Center for Education Statistics, *Common Core of Data: Public Education Agency Universe* (Washington, DC: U.S. Department of Education, 2004).

2. Norfolk Public Schools, "NPS Fast Facts," http://www.nps.k12.va.us/index.
php?option=com_content&view=article&id=673/.

3. American Community Survey (ACS). The American Community Survey
(ACS), a nationwide survey, is a critical element in the Census Bureau's reengineered decennial census program. The ACS collects and produces population and
housing information every year instead of every ten years. See http://www.census.
gov/acs/www/SBasics/.

4. Virginia Department of Education, "School Division and State Report Card,"
https://p1pe.doe.virginia.gov/reportcard/.

5. "The Broad Prize for Urban Education, 2008: NPS Public Schools Report
Card," May 19, 2009, http://broadprize.org/asset/1216-norfolkcity_va.pdf.

6. National Center for Education Statistics, "Public School Number of Graduates:
School Year 2005–06," http://nces.ed.gov/CCD/tables/2008353_01.asp/.

7. Megan Gillespie, Dorothy C. Kelly, and Tierney Fairchild, "All Means ALL:
Maintaining Success in NPS Public Schools," http://harvardbusinessonline.hbsp.
harvard.edu/b02/en/common/viewFileNavBean.jhtml?_requestid=60172/.

8. Norfolk Public Schools, *School Board* newsletter, http://www.nps.k12.va.us/
index.php?option=com_content&view=article&id=465&Itemid=382/.

9. National Center for Educational Achievement, "The 2003 Broad Prize for Urban Education: Norfolk Public Schools Case Study," http://www.just4kids.org/en/files/Presentation-Zap_the_Gap_The_District_Frontier_-_NPS-11-07-03.pps/.

10. Center for Public Education, "Rolling Out the Red Carpet in Norfolk, VA." http://www.centerforpubliceducation.org/site/c.kjJXJ5MPIwE/b.1504577/k.B4E/Rolling_out_the_red_carpet_in_Norfolk_VA.htm/.

11. National School Boards Association, "CUBE Award Goes to Norfolk Public Schools," http://www.nsba.org/HPC/Features/AboutSBN/SbnArchive/2006/October2006/CUBEAwardgoestoNorfolkPublicSchools.aspx/.

12. Norfolk Redevelopment and Housing Authority, "Vision and Mission," http://www.nrha.norfolk.va.us/about/.

13. Spencer Johnson, *Who Moved My Cheese? An Amazing Way To Deal With Change In Your Work And In Your Life* (New York: Putnam, 1998); and Jim Collins, *Good To Great: Why Some Companies Make The Leap—and Others Don't*, 1st ed. (New York: HarperBusiness, 2001).

14. Gillespie, Kelly, and Fairchild, "All Means ALL."

15. Norfolk Public Schools, "Superintendent's Proposed Educational Plan & Budget: Fiscal Year 2009-2010," http://www.nps.k12.va.us/images/pdf/fy09-10_supts_proposed_budget.pdf.

Chapter 7

1. Michael Fullan, *Turnaround Leadership* (San Francisco: Jossey-Bass, 2006).

2. Ibid.; and Frederick M. Hess, *Spinning Wheels: The Politics of Urban School Reform* (Washington, DC: Brookings Institution Press, 1999).

3. Celeste Alexander et al., *Resource Allocation Practices and Student Achievement: An Examination of District Expenditures by Performance Level with Interviews from Twenty-One Districts* (Austin, TX: Charles A. Dana Center and Southwest Educational Development Laboratory, 2000).

4. National Center for Performance Incentives, "Teacher Educator Excellence Grant (TEEG) One-Year Report," http://www.tea.state.tx.us/ed_init/teeg/exeval.htm/.

ABOUT THE AUTHOR

Heather Zavadsky is the director of policy and communication at the University of Texas System Institute for Public School Initiatives (IPSI). She has a PhD in educational policy and planning from the University of Texas at Austin, an MEd in education administration, an MEd in special education from Southwest Texas University, and a BA in elementary education from Washburn University. She also holds principal and superintendence certifications from the University of Texas at Austin. Prior to starting at IPSI, she managed The Broad Prize for Urban Education for the National Center for Education Accountability from 2003 to 2007. Her research interests and experiences include school resource allocation, urban school reform, accountability, data-driven decision-making in schools, program evaluation, and the impact of autism on families and educational systems.

INDEX